The Lost World of Mitchell and Kenyon

ONE WEEK LOAN

D0767669

The Lost World of Mitchell and Kenyon

Edwardian Britain on Film

Edited by
Vanessa Toulmin, Patrick Russell and Simon Popple

This edition first published in 2004 by the
British Film Institute
21 Stephen Street
London W1T 1LN

The British Film Institute promotes greater understanding and appreciation of, and access to, film and moving image culture in the UK.

Cover artwork adapted by ketchup from design by Eureka! Design Consultants Ltd
Cover Image: M&K 205 – *Blackpool North Pier* (1903)

Set by D R Bungay Associates, Burghfield, Berkshire
Printed by Cromwell Press, Trowbridge, Wiltshire

British Library Cataloguing-in-Publication Data

A catalogue record for this book is available from the British Library
ISBN 1-84457-046-0 (pb)
ISBN 1-84457-047-9 (hb)

Contents

III The Films as Historical Evidence

    Andrew Prescott   125

13 Mitchell and Kenyon: Ceremonial Processions and Folk Traditions
    John Widdowson   137

14 'Startling, realistic, pathetic': The Mitchell and Kenyon 'Boer War' Films
    Simon Popple   150

15 The Seaside and the Holiday Crowd *John K. Walton*   158

16 The Football Films *David Russell*   169

17 On the Move in the Streets: Transport Films and the Mitchell and
    Kenyon Collection *Ian Yearsley*   181

18 Tram Rides and Other Virtual Landscapes *Patrick Keiller*   191

    Notes on Contributors   201

    Index   203

I
Overviews

Introduction to the Mitchell and Kenyon Collection

Vanessa Toulmin, Patrick Russell and Simon Popple

The primary inspiration for this book is the Peter Worden Collection of Films. This collection, subsequently referred to throughout the text as the 'Mitchell and Kenyon Collection', or simply the 'Collection', was donated to the *bfi* National Film and Television Archive at the British Film Institute by Peter Worden. The discovery of the Collection is one of the most important finds in the field of early British film studies and its prior history is best summarised by the donor himself:

> Assisted by his son John, Sagar Mitchell had continued to run [his] shop at 40 Northgate, Blackburn well into his old age. I can remember, as a boy, going into the shop … and being confronted by this well-dressed, but – as he seemed to me – rather severe old man with the waxed pencil-tapered moustache. He died, aged 85, in 1952 when I was fourteen years … Throughout the 1970s, 80s, and into the 90s I had monitored the probability that … some film material … was probably still stored in the 40 Northgate property … Then [in November 1995] … the appearance at auction of SOME of these films occurred … when 70 small boxes, mainly of enacted material (dramas and comedies) were bought by The Cinema Museum. [In] June 1994 … [I received a message from someone that several] specimen rolls of 35mm had been brought in to him, which he wanted me to look at. On examination, these were all stylus-inscribed at the 'head', were typically 50' to 100' in length, and clearly M&K because they had been found in the cellar of 40 Northgate. This building had been unoccupied for about eighteen months … and contractors employed to strip it out totally … In the cellar had been found three metal drums … crammed solid with film, and if I didn't 'rate' them they were going into the skip! … curbing my excitement, [I] arranged for the three drums to be delivered to me. My main concern was that they should be stored in as stable and secure an environment as I could – in the short term – provide; so I went out and bought a chest freezer – which was never switched on!
>
> Slowly, over the next couple of months, I removed each film and noted all idents … The films were … invariably very dusty and filthy to handle … in one [metal drum] was found a ripped piece of newspaper: page 13, with that day's runners at Newmarket. I was subsequently told by a Mrs Morris at the racecourse that the newspaper related to activity in 1922 – which, interestingly, is the same year as the dissolution of the M&K partnership! I surmise that a 'junior' employee had been told to store away the films, rather than destroy them, and had removed them from shelves where they had lain … gathering dust … As the years went by, I spent what was, for a private individual, a ridiculous amount of money having 35mm conservation positive prints made from this material, all of which turned out to be camera original negative. Clearly this was an impossible project for me to adequately fulfil, both financially and in terms of physical resources. Logic intervened … having regard to the unique nature of the Collection, which rewrites early British cinema history, agreement was reached for the entire 1994 'find' to be taken over by the *bfi* on behalf of the nation. This took place in July 2000 … [1]

The Collection thus joined other surviving materials associated with the Mitchell and Kenyon firm, including the small number already archivally preserved, and the fiction films alluded to by Worden and since lovingly restored by the Cinema Museum. The Peter Worden Collection, consisting almost exclusively of local actuality films – became the subject of a four-year collaborative partnership between the *bfi* and the National Fairground Archive at the University of Sheffield, culminating in the present volume and the accompanying DVD release. This project involved the preservation and restoration of the entire Collection, and extensive research, generously funded by the Arts and Humanities Research Board, into the context of each film and of the Collection as a whole. This enables us for the first time to properly examine a series of neglected relationships between early films and producers, exhibitors and audiences, within a multi-regional rather than national metropolitan framework. These films were the product of a highly developed system of commissioning by itinerant regional showmen and were intended to be an evolving, contemporaneous source of entertainment and news. The research project has so far been able to begin the process of uncovering details of the commissioning, the key showmen involved in exhibiting these films and the network of venues in which they were exhibited. It has examined contemporary advertising, reviews, and other sources, and the insights yielded add to the already considerable richness of the strikingly restored films. The present volume represents the first step on a long road to fully exploring the consequences of the discovery of this national treasure. The writers who have contributed to it offer their initial reflections – from the fields of film history, archiving, local history and a variety of subject specialisms – on the potential of Mitchell and

M&K 59: Alfred Butterworth & Sons, Glebe Mills (1901) capturing the impact the movie camera continues to hold on children then and now.

Kenyon to rewrite our understandings of the history of early film-making and many aspects of British social and cultural life.[2] The deliberate inclusion of voices from a variety of scholarly disciplines is a part of wider current efforts by the moving image archive community to encourage the use of film and television archives as unique resources for, and inspirations to, those working outside of, as well as within, the confines of film and television studies. This book also marks the conclusion of a project which is groundbreaking for having so systematically brought together in the form of its lead partners the mutually enriching, but sometimes mutually misunderstood, trajectories of film archiving and academic research. As such, it is intended as something of a blueprint for future collaborations between moving image archives and academic institutions. Certainly, if these future collaborations prove as rewarding for the archivist, the academic and the layperson as this one has done, then the immediate future for British film heritage could prove exciting indeed.

NOTES

1. Edited from correspondence between Peter Worden and Patrick Russell, on the latter's request for an account of the donor's involvement with the Collection, so that its full history could be placed on file at the *bfi*.

2. The opinions expressed in all of the following essays are, of course, those of the authors, and not necessarily those of the editors.

1 Mitchell and Kenyon: A Successful, Pioneering and 'Travelled' Partnership of Production

Timothy Neal, Vanessa Toulmin and Rebecca Vick

Until the discovery of the Peter Worden Collection, the firm of Mitchell and Kenyon were little more than an interesting regional film company operating in the north of England in the first decade of the twentieth century. Known largely for their surviving Boer War reconstructions, very little has been written about the company's contribution to film history. The restoration and subsequent research initiatives by the University of Sheffield and the *bfi* have revealed a partnership of commissioning, production and exhibition of unparalleled significance in early British film history. It is now important that the story of the company itself is significantly re-evaluated.

Memo from Mitchell and Kenyon to Sidney Carter, 17 February 1902 (Sydney Carter Collection, West Yorkshire Archives).

Sagar Mitchell was born on 28 October 1866 in the Lancashire town of Blackburn, where his parents John and Jane Eliza Mitchell owned the Alliance Temperance Hotel on Northgate. In 1887, he founded a photographic business with his father and by 1894, Sagar and John Mitchell, importers and manufacturers of optical and photographic apparatus had moved from 17 to 40 Northgate.[1] James Kenyon was born on 26 May 1850 and in 1880 he and his wife, Elizabeth Fell, inherited her uncle's furniture-dealing and cabinet-making business based at 21 King Street, then further premises at 22 Clayton Street.[2] Kenyon's association with the entertainment industry may have predated that of his partner as he had a successful penny-in-the-slot-machine business from the late 1890s onwards which was incorporated into Mitchell and Kenyon's business activities in 1902.[3]

In 1938 Mitchell recollected the origins of their innovative enterprise in the following fashion:

> I was (with Mr Jas Kenyon as partner) making cinematograph projectors and accessories. I designed the machine and made the pattern and we got our costumes from Mr Page ...[4] The first exhibition of the cinematograph in Blackburn ... was a private show given on my promises at 40 Northgate and the Editor of *The Blackburn Times*, the late Mr Rostron, was present ... A few weeks later Mr Page gave me a contract to show pictures for several weeks and we had a very successful run.[5]

Mitchell and Kenyon first reached national prominence in September 1899 with the release of three Norden film titles:

MESSRS MITCHELL & KENYON'S CINEMATOGRAPH FILMS.
We have the pleasure of illustrating here three portions of three cinematographic films manufactured by Messrs. Mitchell and Kenyon, of 40 Northgate, Blackburn, and 21 King Street, in the same town. This firm ever busy catering to the wants of the photographic dealer's customers have an excellent stock of films, particulars of which may be had on application to either of the above offices. Each film bears the initial, opposite every separate picture, of the firm. Our photos are from the three 'Norden' films, which can be confidently recommended ... Amongst the new subjects portrayed on the 'Norden' films, we may mention *The Tramps Surprise*, a very laughable series, *Kidnapping by Indians*, an exciting incident, and *The Tramps and the Artist*, the latter being a distinctly humorous set.[6]

Family portrait of Sagar Mitchell *c.* 1890.

Fiction films played an important role in Mitchell and Kenyon's development but the numbers of fiction films produced were far less than non-fiction by a ratio of at least 10:1. The non-fiction titles encompass many subjects including: factory gate films, school exits, processions and calendar customs, sporting events, transport films and phantom rides, public entertainment and leisure, plus the appearances and activities of personalities of the day. The income generated must have been considerable because in September 1901, Mitchell and Kenyon, who had until this point continued to occupy their respective premises on Northgate and King Street, moved to premises at the rear of Kenyon's property at 22 Clayton Street, where they installed a laboratory and studio. The Clayton studio and its facilities for fiction films were described by a reporter in 1907:

> I will conduct you to the stage owned by Messrs. Mitchell and Kenyon, makers of films in Blackburn. We step across from their office in Clayton Street, and passing down the side of a small chapel, open a door that leads to a piece of waste ground. On the one side the space is bordered by the roofs of the houses down in the street. There is an ugly wall to the right, while in front we see a high wall, in which are several gratings. There is an outlook of housetops and irregular walls, some broken. And in the corner near to the bethel is the stage. … It swings up and down like a drawbridge, and when it is open a slight interior is seen under a rough shedding. When the stage is up it acts as a wall to the shed, and here the 'properties' are kept. … On this little stage grim tragedies have been enacted … wild burlesques … [r]omance …[7]

Mitchell and Kenyon's operational practices were directly linked to exhibition companies based in the north of England and travelling cinematograph operators from the Midlands upwards. However, on a critical level, an area of production that brought notoriety for Mitchell and Kenyon (and the canon of work with which people might have been more familiar prior to the emergence of this Collection) were their 'fake' Boer War films. The outbreak of the war in October 1899 prompted the pair to recreate or 'fake' (essentially fictionalised) scenes from the battlefields. From 1900 they produced fake war films of events in the Transvaal and the Boxer rebellion in China. These were filmed in the countryside around Blackburn.[8] The titles were available direct from the manufacturers but were also distributed by Gaumont, Walturdaw and Charles Urban. Ten of these reconstructions survive including *The Dispatch Bearers* (1900), *Winning the VC* (1900) and *Attack on a China Mission* (1901), the latter being one of the few films featuring Mitchell himself. These reconstructions were extremely popular and were extensively shown throughout 1901 over the length and breadth of the country. The advert carried in *The Showman* in September 1901 listed a further series of Boer War films but it is not clear when these were filmed.[9]

By 1901, Mitchell and Kenyon were producing three distinct genres of films: actualities, fiction and fake. By December of that year, they had added a new type of filmic representation to their already impressive output, a reconstructed actuality of a crime event, the *Arrest of Goudie* (1901),[10] a type of 'reconstruction' like the 'fakes' listed above but this time depicting the events leading up to the real-life arrest of an embezzler, Goudie. This film is significant because it reflects the pioneering and innovative efforts of the film-makers Mitchell and Kenyon to offer their audiences something different in content and style with groundbreaking use of editing.[11]

The Mitchell and Kenyon research project has demonstrated that the company's relationship with fairground showmen exhibitors was fundamental to its development (and their non-fiction productions) and would last for over ten years. In 1898, George Green commissioned them to film a series of local views for projection on Green's Cinematograph at Blackburn Easter Fair.[12] In 1900, Green advertised further local films of operatives leaving Audley Street Mills, to show at the annual Easter Fair held on Blackburn Market.[13] Mitchell and Kenyon continued to be associated with Green until at least 1907.[14] Twelve fairground showmen commissioned films from Mitchell and Kenyon in the years up to 1908 including such famous names as Captain Thomas Payne, Pat Collins and President Kemp. The number of local films shot for projection at the Bioscope shows is difficult to estimate however, over 100 of those surviving were made for this purpose, and by December 1900 Mitchell and Kenyon were advertising that 'nothing is so great a draw as a local subject' and proposing films of over sixty towns to various showmen.[15]

The relationship that the company established with the showmen, initially on the fairgrounds, developed into a wide network of contacts taking them outside the Lancashire locality. In 1900 their movements were dictated by the requirements of the fairground showmen with filming taking place as far afield as Nottingham. However, by 1901 they became associated with the burgeoning stand-alone exhibitor trade, resulting in them travelling further to Birmingham, Newcastle, Hull, Glasgow and Carlisle with around 150 local films surviving in the Collection made during the course of the year. These journeys would have been made on the existing train network, and as well as transporting film cameras and equipment Mitchell and Kenyon may have brought developing equipment in order to satisfy the showmen's desire to exhibit the films as soon as possible to maintain the immediacy and impact of the local films.

Although the local films produced for the showmen were part of their stock in trade, Mitchell and Kenyon were continuing to advertise titles under the banner of their trade name, Norden Films. In February 1901, Mitchell successfully obtained permission to film the funeral of Queen Victoria in London and Windsor. On that occasion he 'was perched on a site near a lamp-post at Hyde Park Corner from four o'clock in the morning until late in the afternoon in order to secure the necessary pictures'.[16] The films were shown in many parts of the country[17] and over 900 ft of film was available at the price of one shilling per foot. The report in the *Blackburn Times* provides greater detail:

> The cinematograph was much in evidence at Cowes, in London, and at Windsor at the Royal funeral last weekend. A local firm, Messrs Mitchell and Kenyon, of Northgate, were very successful. They had two operators at work, one opposite Apsley House, at Hyde Park Corner, and the other at the turn of the road at Windsor. They used no less than 1,000 feet of film and took no fewer than 16,000 photographs for reproduction by the cinematograph as living pictures. The operator at Windsor took the whole of the procession from start to finish. The pictures give a beautiful view of the blue-jackets hauling along the gun carriage bearing the body of the Queen, after the horses of the Artillery had been unhitched in consequence of proving unmanageable. In London the procession was much longer, but the operator took all the most interesting parts of it. We may mention, by the way, that the firm took photographs for cinematograph purposes of the Royal Proclamation in Blackburn, and in several other Lancashire towns. The appearance of these pictures on the cinematograph screen will be looked forward to with considerable interest.[18]

Royal events would continue to occupy Mitchell and Kenyon the following year. Films from both Southport and Accrington appear in the Collection dated 28 June 1902, the date of the Coronation of King Edward VII. It could appear from this that Mitchell and Kenyon were operating with more than one film crew in Lancashire, but it should be noted that the latter films M&K 301, 303, 795: *Coronation Festivities at Accrington* (1902) were exhibited by Albert Wilkinson who also worked as a camera operator for the in-demand film-makers. Wilkinson may have been one of the showmen who used Mitchell and Kenyon to develop his own material rather than commissioning them to shoot films on his behalf. By 1902, Mitchell and Kenyon was a successful and well-established film company producing hundreds of local films each year for a wide variety of venues from Bristol to Glasgow.

James Kenyon was clearly involved practically in the 'staging' of a number of the films. M&K 772: *Sedgwick's Bioscope Showfront and Stage Show* (1901) and M&K 61: *Pendlebury Spinning Co.* (1901) reveal him at work, controlling the crowds, and clearly at ease with his role. The well-documented incident at Roker in Sunderland, which resulted in hundreds of pounds worth of equipment being lost in the waves demonstrates a more dangerous aspect of his involvement with the camera.[19] Sagar Mitchell's technical knowledge and sense of adventure was without doubt and according to his obituary, 'He was one of Britain's first photographic dealers to go to the Continent for new equipment. More than fifty years ago he was at Leipzig Fair in search of new German apparatus.'[20] Similarly when Mitchell and Kenyon tried to film an aerial view of the coast near Southport (*c.* 1910), a complicated technical feat, Mitchell was present for an event, which was an epic in itself. Mitchell described this adventure in the *Blackburn Times* in 1931:

> The object was to photograph the coastline from Southport to Liverpool – a thing unheard of in those days, and although the results were partially successful they did not come up to expectations. This was because the wind was so strong that the machine could not be prevented from rolling. 'We were perched on a couple of ordinary bicycle seats without any fuselage about us. After a rough trip, during which we found ourselves in danger of being shot-up while flying over a rifle range, we made a rather bumpy landing in the sand.' [21]

Throughout the Edwardian era, the company continued to produce fiction as well as local films. Titles such as *Cool Proceedings* (1902) and *No Bathing Allowed* (1902) were advertised.[22] Further success was gained with the filming of M&K 214–22: *A Trip to North Wales on the St Elvies* (1902), which was widely shown, as was M&K 193: *The King's Ride in the Isle of Man* (1902).[23] They also produced *A Tragic Elopement* (1903), distributed by Charles Urban.[24] At 320 ft and made up of tableaux in six parts, this film marks their transition to more elaborate scenarios. Also in this year, they released *Diving Lucy* (1903), which was billed in the United States in February 1904 as 'The biggest English comedy hit of the year'.[25]

Mitchell and Kenyon continued to release fiction titles alongside their specially commissioned actuality films. *Driven from Home* (1904) and *The Miser and his Daughter* (1904), both serious dramas verging on the maudlin, were also advertised at this time.[26] Sold exclusively by the Charles Urban Trading Company, possibly their most ambitious title was *Black Diamonds* or *The Colliers Daily Life* (1904), which told the story of a miner's life. The film was a mixture of drama and local film, combining actuality shots with dramatic events staged for the camera such as an underground explosion.[27] M&K 92 and M&K 765 are both considered to be fragments from this feature although it is interesting to note that they are not easily distinguishable from other 'factory gate' films.

Despite their innovations in producing fiction titles, with non-fiction locals, Mitchell and Kenyon remained constant to their successful 1900s' formula. They continued to act on commission for the travelling exhibition circuit and travelled to Glasgow in 1906 for New Century Pictures, and in 1907 and 1908 they filmed in locations as far apart as Gainsborough, Llandudno and Halifax.[28] However, around this time there appears to be a gradual drop in activity, reflected in the fact that in 1906 James Kenyon retired from his furnishing business.[29] In 1907 Mitchell resumed possession of his Northgate shop but Mitchell and Kenyon continued to make films together up until 1913, including the Coronation parades for George V in three locations, Chorley, Clitheroe and Great Harwood.[30] Although this pioneering partnership was not dissolved officially until 1922 there is no evidence of any film production after 1913. James Kenyon moved to Southport in 1915, returning to Blackburn *c.* 1921, four years prior to his death in 1925. Sagar Mitchell, who had continued with his Northgate photographic business, died in 1952.

Mitchell and Kenyon took advantage of the latest developments in new technology and built themselves a strong reputation for high quality, competitively priced films, which brought them commissions from fairground exhibitors, and meant they travelled the length and breadth of the country. Clever staging, orchestration, marketing and, most importantly, choice of subject matter brought them much success, as they caught on film people and events that might otherwise have been forgotten with the passage of time. There is a tendency, however, to see the end of the Mitchell and Kenyon partnership as in some way a failure. The question is always asked: Why did they stop making films together after 1913?; the implication being that something went wrong in their relationship. In the trajectory that is the development of early film in Britain however, Mitchell and Kenyon are far from unusual in ending their production around the early 1910s. They were one of the most successful pioneering film companies and have left a volume of work unparalleled in the annals of early British film history. For this alone they should be considered a success without reserve.

NOTES

1. They were advertising the 'Norden' camera in 1891 although this was clearly a stills camera: advert for 'The "Norden" Camera, No 8' as well as 'Cameras, Lenses, Slides, Plates, Paper, Chemicals, Compressed Oxygen, Limelight' in *Tum-O'-Dick-O'-Bobs' Blegburn Dickshonary*, Blackburn, 1891.
2. *The Photogram*, October 1901, p. 319.
3. See advertisements for Kenyon and Co., suppliers of automatic amusement machines in the Showmen's Year Books for 1900–2 (Manchester: Showmen's Guild of Great Britain, 1900, 1901, 1902).
4. E. H. Page was proprietor of the Lyceum Theatre, Blackburn.
5. *Blackburn Times*, 6 May 1938.
6. *The Optician and Photographic Trades Review*, 29 September 1899, p. 46. Sixty-five of these fiction titles can be found at the Cinema Museum in London. A full list of the fiction titles will be published in the *bfi*'s forthcoming Mitchell and Kenyon Filmography.
7. 'The Romance of a Cinematograph Film', *Ideas*, 31 January 1907, pp. 14–15.
8. Peter Worden and Robin Whalley, 'Forgotten Firm: A Short Chronological Account of Mitchell and Kenyon, Cinematographers', *Film History*, vol. 10, no. 1 (1998), pp. 35–51.
9. *The Showman*, 6 September 1901, p. xi.
10. M&K 757–8: *Arrest of Goudie* (1901).
11. For further information see Vanessa Toulmin, 'An Early Crime Film Rediscovered: Mitchell and Kenyon's *Arrest of Goudie* (1901)', *Film History*, vol. 16, no. 1 (2004), pp. 37–53.
12. Letter from Herbert Green to Henry Simpson, 8 January 1945.
13. See *Northern Daily Telegraph*, 1 April 1899, p. 1, for details of the advert for Green's Electric Cinematograph exhibiting 'two splendid living pictures specially taken of the operatives leaving Audley Street Mills, Blackburn, Church Street and Station Road'.
14. See M&K 95: *Blackburn Rovers v. Sheffield United* (1907).
15. *The Showman*, December 1900.
16. *Kinematograph Weekly*, 5 March 1925.
17. *Blackburn Weekly Telegraph*, 9 February 1901, p. 4.
18. *Blackburn Times*, 9 February 1901, p. 5.
19. *Sunderland Echo*, 14 November 1901.
20. *Northern Daily Telegraph*, 2 October 1952 (obituary).
21. *Blackburn Times*, 10 October 1952, p. 5 (obituary for Sagar J. Mitchell).
22. *The Era*, 18 October 1902, p. 32.
23. *The Era*, 8 November 1902, p. 36.
24. *The Era*, 21 November 1902, p. 35.
25. *The Biography Bulletin*, 23 February 1904, p. 111.
26. *The Era*, 13 August 1904, pp. 30–1.
27. *The Era*, 10 December 1904, p. 35.
28. *Urban Catalogue*, June 1905, p. 11.
29. 'Cinematograph Pioneer: Death of Mr James Kenyon' (obituary), *Blackburn Times*, 14 February 1925.
30. *Blackburn Times*, 11 May 1907, p. 8.

2 Truth at 10 Frames per Second? Archiving Mitchell and Kenyon

Patrick Russell

Seventy per cent of the films in the British Film Institute's archives are documentaries. Who really ever wants to blow the dust off any of them?[1]

INTRODUCTION

On a warm afternoon in July 2000, a van pulls into the *bfi*'s J. Paul Getty Conservation Centre in Berkhamsted. Inside are seventeen ice-cream tubs, unlikely receptacles for the *bfi* National Film and Television Archive's most exciting recent acquisition.[2] On arrival, they and their contents – 826 uncored rolls of nitrate film – are transferred to HV2, a 'holding vault' used temporarily to store nitrate material scheduled for imminent work. HV2 is then padlocked shut: inside their new home, the tubs occupy racking totalling 228cm lengthwise and 372cm top to bottom.

Four years later, through screenings, DVDs and a BBC television series, the public is exposed to a 'lost world' revealed in more than twenty-eight hours of moving images largely unseen for a century, interpreted with insight and passion by this volume's contributors.

Of course so mundane a starting point and so spectacular a destination are connected by an intervening journey. This brief account of that journey – Mitchell and Kenyon as an archiving project – provides factual information about the practicalities of such projects, but hints at deeper questions about audiovisual heritage. Technical and logistical tasks, required to conjure a lost world out of seventeen ice-cream tubs, figure in this account, but as a crucial component of what should be understood as fundamentally a cultural, not a solely physical or administrative, process. 'Mitchell and Kenyon', the Collection in seventeen ice-cream tubs, is a tool for understanding aspects of the culture in which it was created; 'Mitchell and Kenyon', the archiving project, reflects aspects of the culture in which those rolls of film were recreated as just such a cultural resource. And since that project causes its own cultural effects, the relationship between these two fields of enquiry is a dynamic one.

Four of the 800 rolls of film in the 'raw' state in which they arrived, prior to active preservation.

1. BEFORE: WHAT? THEREFORE WHY?

Mitchell and Kenyon reminds us (as if this were necessary) that our film heritage relies on a complex interaction of individual and institutional behaviour with sheer luck. The survival of the barrels crammed with nitrate was surprising to the point of miraculous. The importance of Peter Worden's single-handed rescue and stewardship of their contents, and his ultimate decision to transfer them into public ownership, cannot be overstated, and highlights the role private collectors play in shaping future public heritage collections. Much then depends on choices by the institutions caring for such collections, themselves subject to a complex of influences expressed in the contrasting languages of film culture and technology, public policy and management which are all necessarily a part of a modern cultural institution's polyglot discourse. To this extent, a brief examination of the decision to develop Mitchell and Kenyon as a project suggests some of the routine complexities of cultural prioritisation, as well as Mitchell and Kenyon's particular cultural signficance.

The Collection was at the outset more of an 'unknown quantity' than it is today. Salient known facts included: its association with Mitchell and Kenyon, its scale and format (some 800 original negatives), and its vintage (roughly, 1900–13), typology (actuality films and local topicals), general context (commissioning by travelling showmen) and geographical range (every region outside South East England). A few titles were viewable on video copies of relatively inferior quality supplied by Worden (from prints he had paid for). His painstakingly transcribed, numbered list of descriptive inscriptions scratched onto opening frames of 780 of the rolls further suggested the Collection's overall scope. Otherwise, its *contents* were necessarily 'sight-unseen'.

Why was this enough to generate immediate excitement? First, it set off instant reverberations with the existing NFTVA collection. Mitchell and Kenyon themselves were already present in that collection's narrative (hence familiar names to archive staff), though bit-players more than leading characters. Most extant films ascribed to them were fiction, against an even smaller handful of

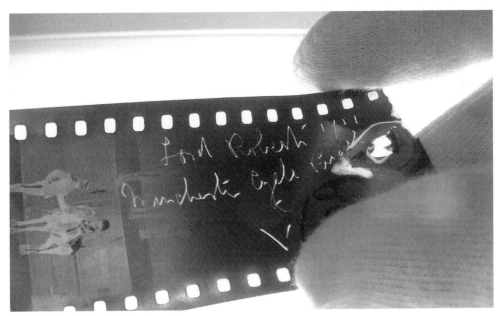

Archaeology and history: an example of the contemporary inscriptions to be found on the opening frames of many items.

actualities deposited by the North West Film Archive. So large, almost exclusively *non*-fictional, an acquisition would transform the profile of film-makers occupying a minor but significant position in what could be termed the NFTVA's 'internal canon'.

Implications for that canon were sure to reach further. The Collection's scale alone justified the publicity claim that it would 'rewrite film history' itself. Adding 800 new titles to the Archive's UK holdings for the period would increase them by perhaps up to twenty per cent, decisively altering the shape and meaning of this portion of the Collection. Their physical characteristics were equally important: virtually all early titles arrived in the form of used prints sometimes generations away from their originals, only now to be supplemented by numerous camera original negatives. As archaeology, these artefacts might yield fresh insight into film technology and manufacture of a formative period; as history, their image content might – subject to good preservation choices being made – allow a clearer view (literally!) of British film-making of that period than ever before. They were categorically different from celebrated nitrate acquisitions such as the Joye Collection (very rich, much larger but consisting of diverse prints having only immediate physical provenance in common), or the Henville Collection (older – including Britain's oldest surviving production, Birt Acre's 1895 Derby – but much smaller and on print stock from which important photographic information was already lost). More suggestive comparisons were international: a later British equivalent to canonical, comprehensive, internally cohesive catalogues of original materials associated with Edison or the Lumières.

However, institutional attempts at 'rewriting' history stand more chance of success when assured of a ready readership in the world outside. Here, the Mitchell and Kenyon Collection raises interesting issues. If film archives have internal canons mapping out particular stretches of cultural territory, it is territory problematically related to that mapped by the canon of a key user constituency: intellectual film culture, centred on academic Film Studies. Collections representing the full range of national production inevitably include more titles made for documentary, informational or other instrumental purposes than ones classifiable primarily as art or entertainment. In the NFTVA's case this means, crudely, that television and non-fiction holdings predominate over feature films and other fiction produced for cinema distribution; yet the latter attract disproportionate intellectual scrutiny.[3] Nonetheless, certain stretches of territory are more equitably 'shared' by archival and scholarly communities. 'Early film' is one such shared canon, partly a legacy of what remains a landmark in archival-academic discourse: the 1978 FIAF Brighton Congress, which brought study of this subset of major international collections into intellectual fashion:[4] study which could never completely ignore non-fiction, though commonly giving it less attention than fictional narrative. A significant minority research community (straddling academic and special interest sectors) developed, its presence exerting some influence on the prevailing film-cultural climate.

In short, Mitchell and Kenyon had an influential readymade 'stakeholder' audience, yet looked likely to assume an intriguing position in its discourse, capable of simultaneously speaking to its interest in early British cinema yet challenging it to stretch its boundaries: chronologically (from Victorian pioneers to their Edwardian successors), geographically (from the South East to the 'regions and nations') and generically (from fiction to non-fiction).[5]

Outside the cinephile community, other archive users' focus was always on moving images carrying documentary content: for example, the broadcasting sector's film researcher community accessing archive content (non-fiction overwhelmingly) for re-use in other media. A new, virtually unseen, collection of early non-fiction would occupy an attractive place in the *bfi*'s portfolio, significantly unencumbered by a traditional barrier to archival access, archives' lack of copyright ownership over most of the content in their care.[6] More importantly, archive-based television reaches a much larger audience than other outlets. The Collection suggested real scope for creative use both of the broadcast medium *and* these more traditional outlets to further the *bfi*'s cultural mission during a period in which increasingly wide access to heritage materials has become central to public cultural policy. For even as non-fiction remains the poor relation in most written film history, it can often touch the layperson most deeply – demonstrated by the regional archives' success in bringing predominantly non-fiction collections to rapturous local audiences. As a multi-regional non-fiction collection of national importance, Mitchell and Kenyon was likely to contain many of the right ingredients for exposing film culture to the most important audience for any cultural body today: the general public, more likely to be engaged by the Collection's window on the 'lost world' of their great grandparents than its implications for media history.

The archival process at its most rewarding should embrace both the intellectual and the physical. As to the former, this project was marked by close collaboration with an expert intellectual external partner, the National Fairground Archive at the University of Sheffield, as well as by the intellectual contributions made by the *bfi*'s archivists. Yet as to the latter it depended crucially on the Archive's proven strength in specialist duplication of technically challenging black and white nitrate at high quality. The parallel running of intellectual and physical processes stood to benefit *all* audiences by offering them a composite cultural 'package'.

Even 'sight-unseen,' the Collection married in-built cultural importance to strategic imperatives and practical feasibility, factors that influenced the next steps.

2. DURING: WHY? THEREFORE HOW?

Preservation planning should reflect cultural judgments.[7] As noted, these included the Collection's carrying both historical value and a more specifically archaeological significance. Paradoxically, preservation designed to maximise one might risk compromising the other. Fragile film can be damaged by duplication, as demonstrated by damage sustained by some of the items previously duplicated elsewhere. Repair was also likely to have long-term effects. Reconciling historical and archaeological value meant retrieving maximum photographic information while minimising use of invasive or irreversible techniques. Dr Joao Oliveira, then Preservation Technical Manager, was responsible for preservation strategy, informed by months of testing. The solution arrived at was to reverse the common practice of modifying damaged, deteriorated material to run safely through printing equipment. Instead, the *equipment* would be modified to accommodate the range of flaws in the negatives without damaging them further.

Some flaws were givens: cellulose nitrate is of course inflammable and inherently unstable,[8] and stock so old

Factory gate: the archive's entry point into the lost world of Mitchell and Kenyon.

would predate standardised manufacturing (rendering it incompatible with modern printers made for maximum precision, for instance in relation to perforation size and shape). But there were further multiple challenges: variable thickness, and many thick stock joins;[9] variable rates of shrinkage between and even within single rolls; discolouration to hues varying from light grey to yellow to deep red-brown; brittleness, buckling, tearing. And yet, the films could still be said to be in amazing condition, for these problems related mainly to their base layer – by contrast, the emulsion layer, holding the photochemical record, evidenced remarkable stability, even as its adherence to the base was at times frighteningly tenuous.

To enlarge shrunken images to original sizes and to standardise frame-line positions, duplication would have to be by optical, not 'contact', printing, ideally employing a liquid gate. Research and Development Special Projects Engineer Phil Read completely re-engineered the gate of an Acme optical printer. The quality of the restoration – therefore the stunning visual quality that we now associate with Mitchell and Kenyon – rested on this modified printer gate. Its many key features included a subtractive light filter system added to neutralise the discolouration, and adjustable transport and registration pins enabling precise image positioning.

A common feature of projects is their need to balance such 'quality assurance' with strict timetables. Mitchell and Kenyon's four-year timetable was ambitious. Acquisitions staff formally identified and accessioned material at the rate of ten to twenty items per week, following the numerical order of Worden's numbered list, and after initial research and development the Research Lab team could often print two or more rolls per day onto composite reels. But projects meet their inevitable complications, necessitating compromise. One entire reel had to be redone due to an unnoticed hair in the gate which would have been visible onscreen. The strict numerical order had to be broken to reduce the number of times printer settings needed altering to match changing frame-line positions. While aiming for high quality, any temptation to spend too long perfecting an individual item's quality to the detriment of overall completion had to be resisted. And any items just too shrunken, buckled or otherwise difficult to print were left to one side: these eventually ran to over 100 too tricky for the Acme to cope with.

This challenge necessitated a second phase of preservation, which took place, under Ben Thompson, in the NFTVA's Main Laboratory, utilising another printer. As a continuous rather than a 'step' printer, the Sigma would be particularly gentle, its sprocket mechanism was also suited for damaged materials, and it could better cope with extreme thickness. It too needed modifying to reduce risk of tearing and to counteract contrast and definition problems. Experiments had to be undertaken to find a film stock fast enough to respond to extremely heavy density of the originals. Pragmatically, repair *would* have to be carefully given to these problematic items to allow duplication – history and archaeology now in tension again, history was the inevitable winner. And a liquid gate was not possible: the Sigma would have to print 'dry'. It seemed likely that even where copies could be made, they would be of reference quality only. Impressively, virtually every remaining item *was* successfully duplicated, and some resulting prints are of very acceptable screening quality. Nonetheless, the characteristics of its source material ensured that overall quality of the Sigma's output was not comparable with the Acme's, many prints having a thinness, heaviness or graininess which could only have been (partially) mitigated by too-expensive intermediate digital solutions.

Innovations in place, Mitchell and Kenyon followed a preservation trajectory normal when working from deteriorated negatives. Initial duplication was to fine grain duplicating positive (ie. a dense intermediate positive), constituting the new master for long-term preservation. From this was produced a duplicate negative, in turn the source for both screening prints and video copies. The decision to invest in both film and video viewing copies again reflected assumptions about the Collection's cultural potential, prints being available for screening but the production of high quality Digital Betacam video anticipating potential footage reuse, and more specifically the possibility of a major broadcast project and likelihood of future DVD release. It also facilitated convenient cataloguing and research use by *bfi* and University of Sheffield staff. The video copies retained the quality of the films from which they were taken, and added important extra elements: considerable care was taken to recreate as accurately as possible the original shooting speeds, which varied across the Collection (the films were shot using hand-cranked cameras) but were often as slow as 10, sometimes 8, frames per second.

Meanwhile, the intellectual process of researching the context for each film title using primary sources, and using the resulting information to enrich the cataloguing of the films' onscreen content proceeded in parallel with the physical processes described in greater detail above. If there is a limitation to such factual accounts of the archiving process, it is that they tend to suggest an entirely linear sequence of events, though in many ways it is a circular process. This can be drawn out by looking at some of the project's potential cultural effects.

3. AFTER: HOW? THEREFORE WHAT?

In terms of the relationship of archaeology to history, staff handling the negatives were struck by quality much higher than that found in the contemporaneous prints they were more used to handling, perhaps implying that negative stock of the period was superior to its print equivalent. Certainly, the relative stability of the nitrate may reflect its having being manufactured in an era of rudimentary manufacturing predating sophistications such as solvent recycling which would have introduced more of the impurities contributing to much more advanced breakdown of many later materials. Often, issues encountered as technical problems requiring practical solutions had broader historical implications. For example, the previously cited need to alter the printer's frame-line settings revealed the likelihood of three different camera gates having been used in the shooting of the Collection.

The first restored film to emerge was M&K 13: *Cresswell and Longworth Miners* (1900), and this marked the point at which staff of the *bfi* and the University of Sheffield fell in love with the films themselves, not just their 'sight-unseen' potential. The high quality of the new copies gave further emotional power to the often strikingly photographed scenes of teeming humanity.

Simultaneously, the research project began accumulating interpretive detail bringing the films and the men behind them further to life. Individual films were transformed by the addition of context – most spectacularly in the case of a film like M&K 757–8: *Arrest of Goudie* (1901), which makes little sense *without* context,[10] more subtly where individual details, such as the appearance of particular showmen, took on new meaning. The starkest illustration of contextual transformation is the very definition of what constitutes a 'film' in Mitchell and Kenyon's output. As 'raw' archive holdings the Collection was accessioned as 826 separate titles. In fact, many are merely parts of the longer film screened, as their inscriptions and contents often suggest but primary research proves. Able to survey the Collection on both levels, as the component artefacts created when shooting, *and* the composite works actually exhibited, our perspective on them is more rounded. What is critical is that such insights are built into the archiving process, rather than seen as confined to a separate realm.[11]

The deeper significance of the research project was its revelation of broader patterns. Though these 826 films were previously lost, it should be emphasised that films *like* this – factory gates, street scenes, phantom rides – are hardly new, indeed are familiar, to the UK's national *and* regional archives' collections. What is new is the coherent model pulling such fragments together, explaining why they existed and challenging any residual preconception of early actualities and local topicals as primitive and unsophisticated, by proving that the patterns behind such fare are complex indeed.

The films themselves evince complexity. As the project progressed, it became increasingly clear that the Collection, easily grouped into a small number of basic categories, did not exhibit great *range*. Instead, its scale gave it *depth*, revealing the complex formal variety possible *within* each category: variety which ninety-nine factory gate films could encompass where isolated examples could not. Meanwhile the sheer volume of human activity depicted enables exhaustive historical interpretation. It has also been observed that the films challenge too rigid a distinction of actuality from narrative, suggesting instead a spectrum along which the proportions of fiction and non-fiction are variably mixed from film to film. The opening of M&K 43: *Workmen Leaving Brooks and Doxey, West Gorton Works* (1901), in which the factory gate workers have evidently missed their cue to start walking and therefore jump into action *after* the camera has started rolling, betrays the degree of construction hidden in what initially appear to be unmediated records of reality.[12]

Contingencies of the Collection's material history, and subsequent application of conscious archival strategy, arguably play a key role in motivating us to pay attention to such visual evidence. Consider this thought experiment. If none of the films had survived well enough to withstand the preferred preservation process, would Mitchell and Kenyon now have quite the same meaning for us? Or consider the real example of M&K 124–8: *Bradford City v Gainsborough Trinity* (1903); 127 was printed on the Acme, the rest on the Sigma and when screened as a composite title the shift from one to the other causes a qualitatively different viewing experience (though one usefully reminding us of the multi-roll construction of the film).

This brings us to a truism of the heritage business, that the qualities intended by heritage materials' original creators and experienced by their contemporary consumers are often supplemented or replaced by qualities for which later generations value them. The research project paints the comprehensive, hitherto repressed, picture of the reality of the actuality film, as a *commodity* in the early film business designed for popular *entertainment,* that Mitchell and Kenyon would themselves recognise. They might be more surprised that in the twenty-first century all their films, including those intended only for local communities, could be consumed both as *documentaries* and as a moving *aesthetic* experience.

Such revaluations are inescapable. Viewing the films today in ninety-minute compilations projected from modern equipment into purpose-built auditoria we cannot but look at them through our own eyes. Hindsight adds emotional depth – the shock of our realisation that the Collection's many camera-friendly young boys will often have died together on the trenches – while, provided no attempt is made actually to falsify history, it is valid to bring out other qualities by subjecting the films to modern creativity.[13]

In this context, an intriguing question posed by the films' restoration is how authentically it recaptures the original spectator experience. Direct comparison is impossible in the absence of surviving corresponding original prints (and would anyway be compromised by their own physical histories), but it is reasonable to assume that the image quality of the new prints is generally higher than those screened a century ago. Though Mitchell and Kenyon produced contact prints direct from then undamaged, non-deteriorated negatives, in other respects those prints must have been compromised by period limitations. They were likely to have been made hurriedly, probably in the camera: hand-cranking it might produce undesirable variations, while image enhancement to mitigate effects of faulty exposure for instance, was quite beyond its scope. And if the negative stock *was* photo-chemically superior, today's modern print stock can reproduce its surviving image record much better. Speculation about such 'inauthenticity' need not end there. While many of the arte-facts reveal no evidence of creative editing of negatives, we can't definitively rule out the possibility that cuts might sometimes have been administered to prints so that we are sometimes seeing a more complete record of the original events. As for the video version recreating the actual speed of the recorded movement, the speeds at which it might have been projected to its original viewers are of course another matter.

How the films are archived therefore shapes what they are: how, as a cultural resource, they are consumed, what, as an evidential resource, they are evidence *of*. At this quality, unedited, and at speeds like 10fps, they may be more photographically 'true' to the lost world they depict than those seen by its original inhabitants, as well as more beautiful. To this extent, the high standard of res-toration enriches audiences' experience precisely by fully actualising the aforementioned documen-tary and aesthetic potential of its source material, even as historical research ensures our correct understanding of its original meaning.

The new restored film elements are today safely stored in controlled vaults at Berkhamsted, while all 826 original negatives – now cored, canned and stabilised – occupy a vault at the *bfi*'s nitrate storage facility in Warwickshire. Other collections now occupy HV2. And the ice-cream tubs? Empty. But this story is less about things than about people. Film-makers and showmen res-cued from cinema history's margins. The dead photo-chemically resurrected, their faces crammed into seemingly every frame. The faces of their descendants delighted and awed at screenings. And the people on whose skills and enthusiasm the project itself depended. Since space does not permit individually acknowledging them all here, this piece ends with heartfelt thanks to just two of them: the late Kevin Patton and the late Phil Read, who, working together over many months, were responsible for technically identifying, preparing and printing most of the Mitchell and Kenyon negatives duplicated in the first phase of preservation; and without whose dedication the journey from ice-cream tub to lost world would have been so much harder.[14]

NOTES

1. Frederic Raphael, 'Biting Back', *Mail On Sunday* (Internet Edition, 22 February 2004).
2. Strictly speaking, food storage boxes bought by Peter Worden specifically to store the films, rather than ice-cream tubs *per se* – but the latter are easier for readers to visualise, and convey the incongruity.
3. The website, www.movinghistory.ac.uk, sketching portraits of UK public sector moving image archives to encourage academic use, illustrates this point. Many people, organisations and genres appearing in these portraits – including that representing the NFTVA's non-fiction collection – occupy familiar places in the archivist's pantheon; yet many remain unknown except to a few academics with specialist interests.
4. Significantly, it was one of the more physically accessible such subsets: a by-product of a historical emphasis on the prioritisation of duplication of unstable nitrate, much, invariably, of early vintage as one of the most urgent tasks of film archives.
5. Sure enough, Mitchell And Kenyon screenings were enthusiastically received at Le Giornate del Cinema Muto and Nottingham Silent Film Weekend – respectively, major international and UK events in this cinematic sub-culture's calendar. National Film Theatre screenings were well attended, but it can be frustrating to see exciting archive programmes covering later developments in non-fiction attract small audiences by comparison.
6. Major collections intellectually owned by the *bfi* include Topical Budget, most British Transport Films and British Coal – most others were deposited with any access beyond private on-premises research reliant on written permission from donors and/or copyright-holders.

7. Since this is a necessarily compressed account, for further information on the preservation process, see: *www.bfi.org.uk/mk/casestudy*.

8. For a dazzling compendium of every possible cultural and technical theme raised by nitrate stock – see Roger Smither (ed.) *This Film Is Dangerous: A Celebration of Nitrate Film* (Brussels: FIAF, 2002).

9. This refers to joins made between original short pieces of stock to make up 100 ft or so of stock prior to shooting; as opposed to subsequent splicing for creative purposes.

10. See Vanessa Toulmin, 'An Early Crime Film Rediscovered: Mitchell and Kenyon's *Arrest of Goudie* (1901)', *Film History*, vol. 16, no. 1 (2004), pp. 37–57. This article illustrates the symbiosis of archaeology and history, whereby examination of the artefacts revealed evidence of editing used to convey narrative.

11. The forthcoming Filmography, grouped by exhibited title, will bring together contextual and content description.

12. My example, but the general point was suggested by Martin Humphries and Simon Brown. Humphries pointed out the converse to this example – the fiction films frequently include 'real-life' elements intruding into the frame outside of the film-makers control.

13. A personalised example: a fun experiment was viewing the films at home with the stereo on – fascinating to see what music fitted, and to speculate whether this 'fit' was caused by formal qualities of music and image or cultural associations. Disappointingly, but hardly surprisingly, Country and Western just doesn't 'go' with Mitchell And Kenyon; but the quintessentially British sounds of The Smiths and Radiohead seemed the perfect complement!

14. I am grateful to my colleagues Rebecca Vick, Ben Thompson, Ruth Kelly, Ros Cranston and Rob White, and to Peter Worden for their comments; to Peter Marshall for taking and supplying photographs; and to Conservation Centre colleagues, especially Ben, the late Phil Read, and earlier Dr Joao Oliveira, for many technical discussions. Any remaining errors are mine!

3 'A real brake on progress'? Moving Image Technology in the Time of Mitchell and Kenyon

Leo Enticknap

INTRODUCTION

1899 saw the emergence of two new production companies in England, one formed by Cecil M. Hepworth, and the other by Mitchell and Kenyon.[1]

The bringing together of these two names illustrates elegantly the nature of the challenge in researching and understanding the relationship between Mitchell and Kenyon and the moving image technologies they used. The latter's evolution during the period covered by the Collection is analogous to that of the Internet in the early 1990s: it was rapid, market-driven, a cottage industry and largely unregulated.[2] By the early 1910s, the rapidly expanding and globalising film industry had caused economies of scale to kick in, prompting the industrialised supply of equipment, film and lab facilities; just as by the late 1990s, major companies and organisations were starting to have websites.

Hepworth was a key player in British film technology's 'cottage industry' phase of the 1890s and 1900s, and the epitome of the Victorian inventor. Although as far as we know he didn't manufacture his own film, Hepworth did, at some point during his career, design and fabricate virtually every other item of hardware needed in the production process, extensive details of which can be found in his various writings.[3] Furthermore, he eventually produced large-scale feature films and was a significant political figure in the industry while at the height of his career, ensuring that his activities received extensive coverage. None of this applies to Mitchell and Kenyon. Like many other early producers in the north of England (e.g. Bamforth and the Sheffield Photo Company), their core business was originally still photography, they only produced films for about a decade and mainly to order, their output was mainly in the form of actuality footage and they purchased their technology 'off the shelf' from a rapidly emerging sector of third-party suppliers who took no direct part in production activity themselves.

Given the relative lack of surviving primary evidence other than the actual films, any attempt to discuss the impact of technology on Mitchell and Kenyon's career and the content of the films themselves must seek to apply contextualising evidence from secondary sources. This is primarily the approach I shall take in this chapter, though there are two important primary sources which will form a key element in this discussion. The first is the films themselves, and the second are surviving models of the camera used to shoot them. This chapter will consider the six areas of technology used to produce, duplicate and exhibit film in the 1900s: film base manufacture, the characteristics of film emulsions, the camera, editing, duplication and projection. By examining these, I hope to illustrate some of the advantages and limitations of these technologies during the period of Mitchell and Kenyon's production, and to show how these impacted on the form and content of the films.

FILM BASES AND EMULSIONS

The chemical composition of the base used for most professional film production remained largely unchanged from the first experimental production by George Eastman in 1889 to the introduction of cellulose triacetate in 1948. In crude terms, it was made by dissolving cellulose in nitric acid, manipulating the resulting compound into a consistent flat surface and then 'drying it on a polished support'.[4] The end product, known as cellulose nitrate, was a flexible, transparent material of extraordinarily high tensile strength. Nitrate had one key drawback: it was highly inflammable. The combustion process also produced highly toxic nitric acid fumes and generated its own oxygen, making a fire impossible to extinguish other than by letting it burn out in controlled conditions.

The earliest recorded film fire in Britain took place at a cinematograph operated by Birt Acres in Piccadilly Circus on 10 March 1896.[5] No one was hurt on that occasion, but the incident which really pushed health and safety irreversibly onto the nascent industry's agenda was a film fire at a fair in Paris the following year, which killed 125 people and seriously injured many others.[6] The volatility of film impacted on its use in a number of ways during the Mitchell and Kenyon period: safety precautions were necessary whenever it was handled or transported, and when projected, reels tended to be kept short. Purpose-built cinemas did not emerge on any significant scale until the late 1900s', and segregated projection boxes were not a legal requirement until the 1909 act. Although the magazine capacity of cameras used by Mitchell and Kenyon gradually increased from seventy feet (1'20" at 16fps) to 500 (8'20") during the course of their career, this was not accompanied by a similar rise in the length of their finished films, largely due to the risks inherent in projecting longer reels using 1900s equipment. Unlike exposure in a camera, projection necessitated bringing the film into contact with a source of intense heat, itself produced by a reaction of volatile chemicals. Given that this typically took place in enclosed and densely populated spaces, exhibition was a lot more dangerous than camera use. The production of film base remained a largely manual process and the volume of stock sold remained relatively low throughout the 1900s. The introduction of band-casting machines enabling the 'industrial scale' manufacture of nitrate in Britain did not take place until 1912.[7]

After its manufacture, film base has the flexible and transparent properties needed to fulfil its mechanical function in a camera, printer or projector. But it cannot in itself record or reproduce a photographic image. That facility is provided by the photosensitive *emulsion*: a chemical compound coated on one side of the base. This undergoes a reaction when exposed to light in a camera or printer, after which it can then be turned into a permanent, visible image for viewing or subsequent duplication. This is done by immersing the exposed film in a series of chemical baths rendering this reaction visible (*developing*) and then desensitising the emulsion to any further exposure (*fixing*). This is known as *processing*. The two key characteristics of the photographic emulsion which could have had a significant impact on Mitchell and Kenyon are its *chromaticity* (which parts of the visible colour spectrum it is sensitised to) and *speed* (relative photosensitivity). As for the former, film emulsions in use during this period either recorded a black-and-white image when exposed to blue light only, or were *orthochromatic*, i.e. sensitised to blue and green light. *Panchromatic* film – which records red as well – did not become widely available until 1926.[8] The effect of this limited exposure range can clearly be seen in one form or another in almost all Mitchell and Kenyon titles. In M&K 291: *Whitsuntide Fair at Preston* (1906), for example, painted detail on the merry-go-round appears to have very little contrast in some places and a lot more in others, according to the extent to which the original colour matches the film's sensitivity. For the same reason, men's suits often appear totally black (i.e. details such as pin stripes are obliterated) and buildings in a street scene a uniform shade of grey.

Surprisingly, speed was not as much of an issue as might be thought. In any case it is impossible to determine with any degree of accuracy the speed of film stocks which were typically used during the 1900s, using today's Exposure Index (EI) scale. As Barry Salt argues:

> The 'speed' of this film in our contemporary sense was largely immaterial, since it was developed by inspection to the correct density under a red safelight, just as is now done in still photography when making positive paper prints. … What *is* important, as far as any possible visible effect in films is concerned, is the lens aperture that was used.[9]

In other words, the characteristics of the emulsion had far less impact on production practices in the Mitchell and Kenyon period than they did even a generation subsequently. The factor which impacted on them most was the camera, its capabilities and limitations.

THE PRESTWICH CAMERAS

As noted above, Mitchell and Kenyon did not follow the lead of Cecil Hepworth, the 'Brighton School' or the other British film pioneers in manufacturing their own equipment. The cameras used by Mitchell and Kenyon were purchased from the London-based firm of Prestwich. John Alfred Prestwich, formerly a stills photographer, made his first appearance in the film industry in 1896, when he was granted a patent with William Friese-Greene for a two-lens projector mechanism intended to minimise flicker.[10] The design was fundamentally flawed and no working model was ever built, but even at that stage Prestwich was gaining a reputation for the quality of his

A trade advertisement for Prestwich hardware that appeared in *The Showman*, 5 January 1901.

engineering. Barnes suggests that, 'the woolly thinking behind the apparatus is obviously Friese-Greene's, whilst the accomplished technical application is due to Prestwich.' He concludes that Prestwich 'was an engineer of outstanding ability who, during the next decade of cinema's history [1896–1906], constructed some of the best cinematographic apparatus of the period.'[11]

Prestwich produced four camera models in total, each of which offered additional functionality and a higher-quality mechanism than its predecessor. The final camera, Model 4, went on the market in 1898 and established itself at the forefront of British film production until the commercial introduction of the Pathé studio camera in 1903 and the Williamson camera in 1904. All consisted of bodies made from oak (as Souto notes, almost all ciné cameras had wooden bodies until the late 1910s),[12] but as the range progressed their film capacities increased, the film transport mechanisms became more accurate and new features were introduced. Prestwich's earliest camera, Model 1, had a seventy-foot film capacity and could only be loaded and unloaded in a darkroom. The position of the shutter blade on its shaft could be altered relative to the aperture, meaning that exposure time was adjustable (though, of course, the speed at which the mechanism was cranked also affected the exposure length). The intermittent mechanism (i.e. the mechanism which, while being continuously turned, enables a film frame to be held stationary during exposure and then advanced) used an epicyclical sprocket wheel, unlike the subsequent Prestwich cameras. The epicyclical intermittent mechanism pulls the entire sprocket drum downwards, thereby advancing the film. The seventy-foot rolls were placed 'raw' inside the body, meaning that the camera could not be loaded or unloaded in daylight.

A subsequent model, known simply as the 'Prestwich Cinecamera', introduced refinements. A much larger body, over twice the size of Model 1, incorporated two independent lightproof wooden containers, or 'magazines', which encased a feed and take-up spool with a film capacity of 300 feet. Not only could almost five minutes now be shot before reloading, but the reloading itself could be done in daylight, simply by replacing the magazine with one containing unexposed film. The epicyclical intermittent was replaced by a 'rack and pinion' claw-type mechanism. This advances the film by means of a claw which is inserted through one perforation on either side of the stock, pushes it downwards by a length equivalent to four perforations (i.e. one frame), retracts, and during exposure returns to its starting position. This does not introduce the extreme mechanical vibrations associated with epicyclical mechanisms, resulting in vastly improved vertical stability in the projected picture. Another advantage is that the perforations are only engaged by the intermittent mechanism when the film is actually in motion (rather than continuously, as in an epicyclical intermittent), thereby causing less wear and damage to perforations.

The Prestwich Cinecamera also featured a 'through the lens' viewfinder, a primitive antecedent to the reflex viewfinders found in cameras today. This was literally a hollow tube running throughout the horizontal length of the case, enabling the operator to see directly through the lens making the exposure. As unexposed film is opaque, it could only be used when the camera was not loaded, and certainly not during shooting. This probably accounts for many of the earlier Mitchell and Kenyon films containing little or no camera movement: the subject was framed using the viewfinder, then the film threaded and the scene shot. It may also explain numerous examples of misframing in the films taken from moving vehicles, e.g. in film M&K 215: *A Trip to North Wales on the St Elvies* (1902), where, despite the use of a short, panning shot on the boat deck, the subject is never satisfactorily framed. Two other additional features in the Cinecamera are worth mentioning: a mounting assembly enabling lenses to be easily interchanged and a footage counter, the Prestwich was 'one of the first [cameras] to be so equipped',[13] showing the operator how much film was left before reloading was necessary.

The final camera produced by Prestwich, and the one probably used to shoot most of the extant films, was Model 4, first marketed in 1898. This featured the magazine system of loading, only this time the magazines were mounted externally, making the camera body itself more compact and enabling it to be operated without a tripod if smaller magazines were used. Model 4 was arguably the earliest camera ever designed which used external magazines: it certainly predated the first mass-manufactured example, the Pathé studio camera, by five years. The maximum magazine size available now held 500 feet, allowing over eight minutes of continuous filming. Barnes notes that 'in camera and projector design there was a move towards larger film capacity' during 1898,[14] but there is little evidence to suggest that this resulted in significantly longer finished films being shown – the lack of a coherent system of continuity editing and the nitrate health and safety issues saw to that.

Apart from generally increased flexibility of use and minor refinements to the film transport and intermittent mechanisms, the main development impacting on Mitchell and Kenyon's production was the addition of a separate 'rangefinder' viewfinder.

In many of the Mitchell and Kenyon films, extended and elaborate camera movements (tracks and pans) can be seen, though slight misframings still sometimes result. These would certainly indicate the use of Model 4 for two reasons. Firstly, the absence of a viewfinder giving at least some indication of the image being exposed through the taking lens would have made such shots virtually impossible. Secondly, slight misframings can sometimes be seen, which become more pronounced

M&K 422: *Lord Robert's Visit to Manchester* (1901), 10 October 1901. The Prestwich 4 in action. In a later sequence from this film, Cecil Hepworth can be seen manoeuvring a camera into position.

the closer the action is to the camera. This is likely to have been caused by the parallax error resulting from the viewfinder's lens being separate to that of the taking lens. A typical example can be
found in film M&K 119: *Sunderland v. Leicester Fosse* (1907). The further away the action on the
football field takes place, the more accurately the camera pans to follow it. But as the game moves
closer to the camera the parallax is magnified, resulting in an increasing degree of misframing. Incidentally, Mitchell and Kenyon possibly owned more than one Model 4. In M&K 422: *Lord Robert's
Visit to Manchester* (1901), a cameraman can be seen positioning a Prestwich Model 4 in the foreground of a shot, preparing to film the unveiling ceremony of a statue.

As Barry Salt has argued, the capabilities and limitations of the lenses available were a major
influence on camera technique in this period. The comparatively large fixed apertures (by today's
standards), typically around f4.5, enabled shooting to take place in both bright and subdued
daylight, though depth of field was limited. The Prestwich Cinecamera and Model 4 were
designed to have easily interchangeable lenses. The lens barrel itself was mounted on a steel plate
which slid into a wooden bracket on the front of the camera. The bracket was mounted on
hinges and could be opened to allow access for cleaning and shutter adjustments. Salt notes that
lenses with a fixed focal distance of 50mm to 75mm were typical around the turn of the century,
though longer 'telephoto' lenses of 100mm to 150mm 'were occasionally used in actuality
filming.'[15] Lenses with a variable focus distance (known now as 'zoom' lenses) were not

M&K 680: *Hollow Drift Children's Procession* (1902). Note the relatively straight angle at which the couple in the
foreground are looking into the camera relative to the point at which the procession disappears into the foreground,
indicating the use of a long prime focal distance lens.

developed until the 1930s. Terming them 'telescopic' lenses, Mitchell and Kenyon appear to have used long lenses as a selling-point, as a surviving advertisement makes clear.

Mitchell and Kenyon used their 'telescopic' lens to greatest effect in crowd and street scenes, probably with the intention of magnifying their subjects to enable easy recognition when the film was projected. One striking example can be found in M&K 680: *Hollow Drift Children's Procession* (1902), in which the angle of the procession disappearing into the foreground shows clearly that a lens of well over 100mm must have been used to take the shot.

EDITING

The technique of cutting and joining individual lengths of film to form a single roll was discovered and perfected almost as soon as film itself was invented. The method which W. K. L. Dickson recalled using during his early film experiments with Thomas Edison involved 'a clamp with steady pins to fit the punch holes, to use in joining the films with a thin paste of the base dissolved in amyl acetate which, I suppose, is still [in 1933] commonly used.'[16] This is now known as cement splicing, and involves the use of a chemical compound which dissolves a thin layer of base on two facing surfaces, which are then pressed together under considerable pressure to form an adhesive seal. It remained the sole method of joining film until the late 1960s. In fact, Dickson's clamp was relatively sophisticated even compared to common practice two decades later: as late as the 1920s, the routine method of producing splices in studios, laboratories and projection rooms was still by hand using a razor blade, without any mechanisation.

Cement joins in the surviving Mitchell and Kenyon elements would suggest that they did it frequently and by hand, though many of these joins were made to form short lengths of unexposed stock into a longer roll for exposure, rather than to edit the processed film for presentation. One case in point is a section of M&K 735: *Congregations Leaving St Hilda's Church* (1902), the first fifty-seven seconds of which consists of a continuous, static shot taken from opposite the church. The second half of the film includes a number of negative joins during a continuous shot (i.e. not on a cut), suggesting that lengths of stock had been joined before exposure.

The use of editing as a deliberate narrative device as distinct from a technical exigency – i.e. juxtaposing images in order to convey a deliberate message to the viewer – developed and evolved gradually during the 1900s and 1910s. Individual, edited films of more than a few minutes in length did not start to emerge until the late 1900s, though the systematic use of creative editing becomes more and more apparent in the Mitchell and Kenyon Collection as the decade progresses. The greater proportion of films from the 1900–2 period consists either of long, continuous shots, with the only edits being either 'jump cuts' (i.e. when cranking was stopped and resumed after a time delay without moving the camera – several examples can be seen in the second half of the Middlesbrough church film) or when two or three 'scenes' were joined to form a finished film. A typical example of the latter can be found in M&K 219: *A Trip to North Wales on the St Elvies* (1902), which consists of three shots taken from a boat, showing the shoreline. The breaks were presumably to reload the camera.

By the middle of the decade, Mitchell and Kenyon's editing had become a lot more sophisticated. The football films are among the most polished examples, possibly because their subject matter – fast-moving action happening within a predefined, enclosed space – lent itself especially well to the use of camera movement and sequential cutting to illustrate the progression of play. A convincing demonstration of this can be found in M&K 136–8: *England v. Ireland at Manchester* (1905) which, it could be argued, even attempts a rudimentary version of 'classical' continuity editing, which emerged in the late 1910s. In one sequence we see the England goalkeeper from a reverse angle, anticipating a shot. The film then cuts to an approaching Irish striker (suggesting that two cameras were used, as the lens used for the second shot appears to be longer), followed by a further cut to the converging English defenders. Remarkably, this sequence includes cuts on action and obeys the 180-degree rule, though this could be accidental.

PROCESSING AND DUPLICATION

The services provided by a film laboratory are essentially twofold: to process exposed film and to produce duplicate copies for cinema exhibition. Nowadays various control mechanisms exist to ensure the quality and consistency of these procedures, e.g. sensitometry, chemical analysis of the developers and fixers and accurate control of exposure in printing. None of these existed in the 1900s. In fact, most of this work was carried out by the film-makers themselves, although we do not know whether Mitchell and Kenyon did this or outsourced it. One writer noted that, even as late as 1930, 'very little was known of the laws of nature which govern the making and processing of cine film.' He continues:

> Processes in these early days were essentially unstable and the causes of fluctuations in activity were unknown. This situation gave rise to many 'old wives' tales', some of which were so firmly held as to constitute, in later days, a real brake on progress.[17]

This impression is supported by the findings of the archivist John Reed, who, when restoring a feature film from 1918, noted evidence of careless film handling and 'poor processing consistency' in surviving elements.[18] Film processing was typically done using the 'rack and tank' method. Working under a red safelight, technicians would wind the exposed orthochromatic stock onto a large cylindrical rack which would then be mounted above an open tank containing the developer. The film would be periodically immersed in the tank as the rack was rotated, which would continue until the developed image was visible under the safelight. The rack would then be moved to a tank containing the fixer, after which the processed film was dried and unwound. Systematic control of the composition and temperature of the chemicals (both variables affecting the processing time) was simply non-existent during the 1900s (automated developing machines were not commonplace until the 1930s). Film-makers of Mitchell and Kenyon's generation, therefore, had little control over subtleties of contrast and density. Indeed, it is likely that the new Mitchell and Kenyon preservation elements and viewing copies enable us to see a *higher*-quality image than original audiences would have done.

Printing–duplication by exposing an image of the processed film onto new stock – was also a primitive operation. In the very early days, cameras doubled as printers. Prestwich Model 1 at Bradford has slit holes in the top and bottom of the case, to enable an exposed and processed element to be passed through the mechanism in contact with raw stock. Although purpose-built printers began to be marketed during the mid-1900s, it is unlikely that the Mitchell and Kenyon films were duplicated for exhibition using anything more sophisticated. It would certainly have been impossible to carry out any of the image enhancement which is now possible at the printing stage.

PROJECTION

Projection technology during the Mitchell and Kenyon period typically consisted of a mechanism attached to the same light source used to project lantern slides. The key difference from the light used in today's projectors was that it was produced chemically rather than electrically, by means of a flame from a cylinder of hydrogen reacting with a stick of lime (i.e. limelight). Unlike in exposure or printing, this generated intense, sustained heat. This placed significant demands on the projector's intermittent mechanism. Although, as Salt notes, projectors of the period generally used the same sorts of intermittent mechanisms as found in cameras from the period,[19] they tended to fail from heat exposure. Another point to bear in mind was that during the 1900s, film exhibition was generally itinerant. Purpose-built cinemas were the exception rather than the norm, so projector components had to be portable. This combination of the combustibility of nitrate, the volatility of the chemicals used to generate limelight, the fragility of early intermittent mechanisms and the need for portability imposed restrictions: screenings tended to be short, the picture relatively dim by today's standards, and the audience size small. All this was to change with the evolution of the 'Maltese cross' intermittent mechanism in the 1910s, the emergence of carbon arc (electric) illumination and the gradual move from itinerant exhibition to purpose-built venues (encouraged, in Britain, by specific health and safety legislation), but in the period Mitchell and Kenyon were operating, this was all yet to come.

CONCLUSION

From the evidence in the newly discovered films, it appears that Mitchell and Kenyon successfully exploited the rapidly expanding possibilities of the technology at their disposal, yet also had to work within its limitations. As far as the evolution of British moving image technology is concerned, the discovery of this Collection hasn't necessarily forced a re-evaluation of Rachael Low's contention that Mitchell and Kenyon 'made a solid contribution to the considerable British output of the time, but do not seem to have exerted any influence on the development of cinema technique.'[20] On the one hand, they purchased what was probably the most technically advanced model of camera on sale at the time, and used it to its full potential. They also took advantage of the wide lens apertures and 'telescopic' focal distances available in the commercial marketing of their films. They may also have been slightly ahead of their time in their use of editing. On the other hand, they were clearly constrained by the health and safety risks then inherent in film exhibition, hit-and-miss laboratory procedures and the absence of a comprehensive 'language' of film editing which would have enabled them to play a more interpretative role toward their subjects. Furthermore, there is no evidence that they sought to take any active steps to break free from these constraints. It would be overly negative to conclude that technology was a 'real brake on progress' for Mitchell and Kenyon. Rather, their career is an illustration of what was then the state of the art, warts and all.

NOTES

1. John Barnes, *Filming the Boer War* (London: Bishopsgate Press, 1992), p. 8.
2. Despite the inherently dangerous nature of its main raw material the film industry in Britain was not subject to any legislative regulation until the Cinematograph Act of 1909.
3. Cecil M. Hepworth, *Animated Photography: The ABC of the Cinematograph* (London: Hazell, Watson & Viney Ltd, 1897); *Came the Dawn: Memoirs of a Film Pioneer* (London: Phoenix House, 1951).
4. Earl Thiesen, 'The History of Nitrocellulose as a Film Base', *Journal of the Society of Motion Picture Engineers*, vol. 20 (1933), pp. 259–62.
5. John Barnes, *The Beginnings of the Cinema in England* (Newton Abbot: David and Charles, 1976), pp. 66–70.
6. H. Mark Gosser, 'The *Bazar de la Charité* Fire: The Reality, the Aftermath, the Telling', *Film History*, vol. 10, no. 1 (1998), pp. 70–89.
7. R. J. Hercock and G. A. Jones, *Silver by the Ton: A History of Ilford Ltd., 1879–1979* (Maidenhead: McGraw Hill, 1979), p. 51.

8. C. E. Kenneth Mees, 'History of Professional Black-and-White Motion Picture Film', *Journal of the Society of Motion Picture Engineers*, vol. 63 (1954); reproduced in Raymond Fielding (ed.), *A Technological History of Motion Pictures and Television* (Berkeley: University of California Press, 1967), p. 125.

9. Barry Salt, *Film Style and Technology: History and Analysis* (2nd edn, London: Starword, 1992), p. 31.

10. Barnes, *The Beginnings of the Cinema*, p. 184.

11. Ibid.

12. H. Mario Raimono Souto, *The Technique of the Motion Picture Camera* (4th edn, London: Focal Press, 1982), p. 20.

13. Brian Coe, *The History of Movie Photography* (London: Ash and Grant, 1981), p. 82. This book contains an illustration (p. 80) which is captioned as a Cinecamera; but an identical model held by the National Museum of Photography, Film and Television (NMPFT) (K3273) is catalogued as a Model 4. As a description of the Model 4 in Barnes (1992) corresponds with Bradford's camera, it would seem safe to assume that the caption in Coe is a mistake.

14. Barnes, *Filming the Boer War*, p. 110.

15. Salt, *Film Style and Technology*, p. 33.

16. W. K. L. Dickson, 'A Brief History of the Kinetograph, the Kinetoscope and the Kineto-phonograph', *Journal of the Society of Motion Picture Engineers*, vol. 21 (1933), reprinted in Fielding, *A Technological History*, pp. 11–12.

17. F. P. Gloyns, 'Processing over Fifty Years: The Work of the Film Laboratories', *The British Kinematograph Sound and Television Society Journal*, vol. 61, no. 1 (January 1981), p. 34.

18. John Reed and Gwenan Owen, 'Uncanning the Uncanny', in David Berry and Simon Horrocks (eds), *David Lloyd George: The Movie Mystery* (Cardiff: University of Wales Press, 1998), p. 87.

19. Salt, *Film Style and Technology*, p. 33.

20. Rachael Low and Roger Manvell, *The History of the British Film, 1896–1906* (London: Allen and Unwin, 1948), p. 23.

II
The Films in Context/The Film Text

4 From the Factory Gate to the 'Home Talent' Drama: An International Overview of Local Films in the Silent Era

Stephen Bottomore

Until quite recently, locally produced films were scarcely discussed or even recognised in film history. But this is changing. Partly because of the re-emphasis that historians are placing on itinerant film-making, and the rediscovery and conservation of the Mitchell and Kenyon Collection, local films are now seen as a major genre in early cinema. Furthermore, due to a growth in regional archives and an interest in 'orphan films', we are rediscovering local films from throughout the silent era, in strange varieties, including local dramas. In this chapter, I will provide an overview of these kinds of films, with an emphasis on the early era, and will examine some definitions of locals, describe variations in the genre(s), and discuss the economics of their production and their historical evolution over time.

To begin with, what is a 'local film'? We need to be quite careful about a definition, because several kinds of films may be called 'local' for different reasons. For my purposes here, local doesn't just mean a film which is made about a local area. I define a film as 'local' only if there is considerable overlap between the people appearing in the film and those who watch it or are intended to watch it.

By this definition certain kinds of films are excluded and others are only partially included. Excluded, for example, are those films made for what I call 'municipal advertising'. That is to say the 'come to our city' kind of films, such as *Blackpool: The Wonderland by the Waves* (1912) or *Denver in Winter* (Buckwalter, 1905). There were literally dozens of these kinds of films made from the turn of the century in the USA and Britain and probably elsewhere too.[1] But, even though these films were often made by locally-based production units and/or were about a defined local area, the primary *audience* was from out of the area: people who might come and visit the town or locality, either as tourists or as immigrants or business investors. On the other hand, some *local newsreels*, showing events such as pageants, local sports, inaugurations of city halls and the like – may be seen as partially 'local' films, for some of their audiences were the same people who had been filmed.[2] Obviously some indistinctness in the borderlines of definition may be expected.

ORIGINS

Local film-making began very early. There is evidence that the Lumière cameramen shot films which were later shown in the same communities, sometimes at the request of local people, as early as 1896.[3] The same year the Gaumont company in France advertised its combined camera/projector to showmen with the words: 'Do you want to be a sensation and a success? Get animated pictures for your show, using local views that you can easily take with a Chronophotographe Demeny.'[4]

Meanwhile in the US the Edison Company also experimented with local production: a cameraman filmed in Harrisburg, Pennsylvania in December 1896 and later showed the film in the same town. The local paper enthused: 'It will be a strange and novel sight for our townsmen to see themselves pictured the same as in everyday life and many a well-known personage will be easily recognized …'[5]

Local filming continued sporadically in the US through the early years of the twentieth century, by exhibitors/film-makers such as Lyman Howe.[6] Local films were made in several other countries in the first decade or so, though not all countries were in at the initial stage: in Germany there is little evidence of the genre until 1904, and in Sweden examples only seem to appear from 1907.[7] It appears that the most active nation in this regard may have been the British.

In Britain the vogue for local films seems to have begun around 1900, and the heyday was in 1901 and 1902. Their prominence in the Mitchell and Kenyon Collection is one confirmation of the popularity of local films, and corroboration comes from the contemporary trade press. One writer noted in this period that 'comic and local pictures are the ones which are the most appreciated'.[8] Another trade commentator added that local films were 'always an attraction' – he was referring to the city of Bradford, where the opportunity to 'see yourself' on screen became such a vogue that people would apparently say to one another: 'Do you know that you are on the curtain at St George's Hall'.[9] The appeal was strong in London too, and at the newly opened Mohawks Hall one trade journal noted in 1901 that 'local pictures always prove a strong draw … and … on the occasion of our visit, it was quite apparent that they [the audience] could not have too much of them.'[10]

Such films were often commissioned by travelling showmen or even made by the showmen themselves.[11] The popularity of these films may have affected the seasonal pattern for entertainment. It was usually assumed that the winter months were most profitable for indoor entertainments, but one showman claimed that, because these local films were so appealing to audiences and were best taken in bright weather, the summer was the most lucrative time for the exhibition business.[12] The popularity of local films continued up to World War I, even as fiction films were appearing on the market in ever greater numbers. Both Warwick and the Sheffield Photo Company were making local films in 1906, and the following year a trade journal claimed that locals 'are the biggest "draw" a house can have'.[13] The vogue continued through 1912, when the standard work on cinema management stated that:

> There can be no two opinions as to the value of the local topical film as a means of filling your theatre. Everyone loves to see himself, or herself, or friends, or children, on the screen, and the local topical is the best means of gratifying this desire.[14]

FACTORIES AND CHURCHES

Many of the first local films belonged to a genre which has come to be called the 'factory gate' film. This involved filming workers as they departed from their factory or workplace, then later attracting the workers to the film show to see themselves on the screen. One could argue that this is the oldest of all genres as the Lumières' *Sortie de l'Usine* of 1895 was nothing if not a factory gate film, but as a regularly produced genre in Britain it seems to date from about 1899. People were always filmed leaving the factory rather than entering so that faces could be seen clearly and so people could recognise themselves, because recognition – and the emotional or comic possibilities that went with it – was an important element in the appeal of these films. A typical example of the fun of identification came in Britain in 1902, when Alf Ball, a cinematograph showman based in London shot two films in Reading 'taken in the city centre and biscuit factory, which evoked shouts of the audience on recognising familiar scenes and faces'.[15]

Factory gate films were also produced in France: a typical example was made in Lorraine in May 1904, when a camera operator from a fairground show filmed outside a tobacco factory as workers emerged at midday: the workers are described in a local report as laughing, making jibes etc. during the filming. In France, as in the UK, the possibility of recognising friends – 'sometimes in a funny or grotesque posture' – was a great attraction and sometimes made such films the 'clou' or hit of the show.[16] A variation on the 'factory gate' genre became well known in France, in which the local showman filmed people coming out of church after Mass – which we may call the 'sortie de l'église' subject. Examples are known in Lorraine from as early as 1900, and the possibility of seeing friends was still a principal appeal, as a press report noted of a 1906 film of people coming out of Verdun Cathedral. When it was shown, 'Everyone recognised a relative or a friend, and so cries of recognition were coming all the time.'[17]

As we have seen, many of those filmed found it amusing to be seen subsequently on the screen, but not everyone was as acquiescent. Early indications of this came in 1904 when there was a report in a French fairground magazine about two separate incidents, in Toulon and in the Loire region, of people objecting to having moving images of themselves put on display in fairground cinema shows.[18] Things became more serious when a travelling showman, Abraham Dulaar made a 'sortie de l'église' subject in Narbonne on 29 January 1905, filming people coming out of Mass at the Saint-Just Church. One person, known anonymously as T… was later recognised on screen and objected to his/her image being put before the public in this way. T sued the showman, on the grounds that ownership of his/her image had been violated. There was a court case, the judge eventually deciding against T, on the grounds, firstly, that the filming had been done openly – there was, for example, a sign on the camera stating its purpose; and secondly, that French copyright law only protects the fruits of work or talent – and to walk in public is neither.[19]

It was an interesting and significant case, and the judgment effectively gave the green light for local film-making in France – though the decision was effectively overturned by another court judgment in 1911. However, in this same year, as France backed off, matters went the other way in the US, when an American court made what was effectively a converse ruling: Judge Stearns of the Supreme Court deciding that 'photographers may take pictures at will on the public highways.'[20] Perhaps this is one reason why local film-making only seems to have taken off strongly in the US from about this time, though the American local film was to develop in different guises from the basic factory gate film, as we shall see later.

ECONOMICS

One cannot understand much about local films without reference to the economic circumstances of their production and exhibition. Yet local films apparently make little sense in the context of conventional assumptions about the economics of the film industry. Much of the success of cinema as a medium may be attributed to what one might call 'multiplication factors'. A film – let's say a feature film for the sake of argument – is an expensive commodity to produce. However, once the negative has been made, the remaining processes of print-making and exhibition are all relatively low cost, and are potentially sources of immense revenue. This is because from one negative many prints may be made, each of which may be projected hundreds of times for many months, to hundreds of spectators each time. So even if each spectator only pays a nickel, the product of multiplying many spectators by many screenings by many prints means that the dollars can rapidly accumulate. (This is why film producers can afford to travel in Rolls Royces and smoke expensive Havana cigars.)

The various factors to be multiplied vary considerably in size between different genres. For example, fewer prints would be made for non-fiction or educational titles, though on the other hand the shelf-life might be quite long for these kinds of films, so the number of projections per print could therefore be quite high. On the other hand, for newsreels, while many prints might be made, there will be a short shelf-life and fewer screenings per print because news rapidly goes out of date.

As far as the local film goes, the factors to be multiplied are different again, and generally all are smaller. By definition local films are only ever likely to appeal to a small number of people for a very limited time: in the case of a factory gate film, half a dozen screenings in a single hall is about all one could hope for. The local film, in short, minimises the multiplication factors (i.e. the economic benefits of mass production) which sustain most forms of film production, and it would seem, on the face of it, to be rather a poor commercial prospect. And yet, despite this, the local film proved quite durable as a genre and clearly enjoyed some business success. The main reasons why locals can succeed as a genre are simple, and involve two basic strategies: keeping production costs low and maximising the number of people filmed – and hence the audience.

Showmen would achieve the latter – getting 'bums on seats' – by going to film in areas with the largest number and density of people. The aim in filming was always, as an exhibitors' manual advised, 'the inclusion of as many faces as possible' in the picture. To be sure of achieving this, showmen were advised to 'boom' the planned filming in advance, as the camera was an 'irresistible attraction' if people knew it was coming.[21] The manual added:

> … People will flock round the operator's stand when he is taking the film in the hope of being included in the picture, and each one is a sure patron on two or three succeeding evenings when the film is screened at the theatre should he be able to discern himself in the crowd. Such is human nature![22]

Local film-making was essentially a circular process: people first appeared in front of the camera and then some of those same people paid to sit in front of the screen. The latter was of course the important thing for showmen, and there were a variety of strategies to attract spectators to come to see local films. It was sometimes worth offering cash prizes for self-recognition: for example, in 1908 one manager gave 5s every night to whoever could spot himself on the screen.[23] This cash offer would work as bait even if the filming itself were a ruse, which it sometimes was. For example, showman John Codman would tour through a locality cranking an empty camera at the crowds and shouting 'Come and see *yourselves* on screen, tonight and tonight only! A handsome prize for those who can claim to have recognised themselves!'[24] This need for many faces helps to explain why the local film was more common in densely populated Britain than in some other countries. It also explains why showmen so often filmed in industrial areas where hundreds of workers could be filmed streaming out of factories.

The other economic essential of local film-making – keeping production costs low – could normally be achieved because filming could be done very quickly with few direct costs. Usually the only expenses were hiring the cameraman (for a day or less) and paying for the film to be developed. A number of firms in Britain, including Warwick, Hepworth and of course Mitchell and Kenyon, offered to film locals for showmen at quite low rates (and similarly low-cost filming options for locals were offered in the US by 1911).[25] In the UK, between 1901 and 1905, it cost around 10s a day to hire a cameraman and from 4½d to 8d a foot to develop and print the film.[26] This would mean that a local film of a hundred feet could easily cost less than £4 to produce, which was not significantly different from the cost of buying a normal, commercially produced film, though one has to remember that the latter had a much longer shelf-life and wider appeal (more of those 'multiplication factors'). It is worth adding too, that by 1912 some commentators put the costs much higher – as much as £10 to £15 to make a local.[27]

Costs could potentially be reduced by the showman shooting the film himself and trade papers sometimes recommended that exhibitors buy cheap cameras to enable locals to be made on this do-it-yourself basis.[28] As early as 1901, some people claimed that it was cheaper in the long run to buy a camera than to hire a cameraman for locals, and the Prestwich camera may have led the field for these purposes.[29] By the early 1910s the market for such cameras was opening up in the US. From January 1913, the Williamson company of London had its 'Compact Marvel' camera on sale for $150 and within a year a New York firm was selling a camera for half that price.[30]

MORE ECONOMICS

Local films continued to be made for many years in many different countries and regions, and so, presumably, must have had *some* economic benefit for showmen.[31] Certainly, several commentators claimed that the novelty of locals boosted the revenues of a film show, and even if this were only for a few days or a week, that would be enough to pay for the day's filming. There may also have been indirect benefits, one of them possibly being that local films attracted people who otherwise wouldn't go to the cinema at all. French commentator Charles Mendel suggested that showing films of people coming out of a factory or on a busy town street would pack a cinema, 'and the public, having once taken the road to the picture show, returns willingly time after time.' In other words, even if the local film itself didn't make much money, it could act as a kind of 'loss leader' to attract people to a cinema for the first time, who might then develop the cinemagoing habit.[32]

Yet not everyone agreed about the economic benefits of locals to showmen. In 1909 a writer in the *Moving Picture World* suggested that at a time when regular films cost so little to hire, local pictures were more expensive to make than their receipts warranted. He underlined the undeniable fact that locals appealed only to a small audience pool and had a short lifetime:

> A local picture used by a nickelodeon will not be used by a competing house in the same town, and no matter how much interest may attach to the picture locally, it would put to sleep an audience fifteen or twenty miles away. Local subjects are practically topical subjects. Like newspapers, they are looked over and then thrown upon the scrap heap.[33]

However, this same writer had to acknowledge that there was still an appetite for locals – an 'almost reckless' craze, he called it – among nickelodeon showmen. Some exhibitors were even requesting that the film distributors which supplied them with commercial films, should also send cameramen to film local events, claiming that such locals would double or even triple their receipts for a week.[34] The renters wanted none of this, fearing no doubt that having to make locals might disrupt their businesses and turn them into part-time producers instead of distributors *per se*. Yet claims continued to be made that local films could bring in box-office rewards. One expert in 1914 cited the example of a certain British film of a parade of schoolchildren, which had attracted both parents and relatives, and so packed a hall twice nightly for a fortnight.[35] A humdrum local parade might seem an unlikely box-office winner, yet stories in the trade press at this time show that a significant amount of local production in Britain involved filming processions, parades and pageants. In just one week of June 1914 Gaumont's branch in Manchester filmed five different children's processions in the city and surrounding area and the resulting films were then shown the same night in picture theatres and music halls in the district.[36] Incidentally, such films of local pageants were sometimes thought to have a wider appeal than the purely local situation and were offered for sale on the general market as early as 1906.[37]

Some wily showmen tried to boost revenues by including aspects of self-advertisement in the local films which they commissioned or made. In a few Mitchell and Kenyon films, for example, posters for the firm's own local cinematograph shows can be seen, and some of their fairground films include shots of the frontages of cinematograph shows.[38] This strategy of 'product placement' continued when exhibition shifted to permanent sites. A British film from approximately 1913 preserved in the NFTVA shows dozens of children filing through the streets in Newbiggin-by-the-Sea and past the front of the Empire cinema. Presumably the film was commissioned by the cinema's proprietor as a way of attracting the children and their parents to see the film, and also to give his theatre additional publicity.[39] There are other similar films held in British regional archives, showing children waiting outside cinemas or parading past. Showmen in the United States (the home, after all, of marketing and 'boosting') also drew on this practice. In 1914, a movie theatre proprietor in a small town in Maine got a friend with a movie camera to film the audience coming out of his theatre, showing the films there the following week.[40] There are examples from other countries, including Brazil, where in 1912, the people going in and out of the Rio Branco cinema in Manaus were filmed and then the film shown in the same cinema.[41] In this and the other cases, the local film acted to advertise the very venue, in which it was being screened.

Showmen also tried to use local films to establish friendly links between the theatre and audience members, and would inform people whom they had filmed about planned screenings. For instance, in 1913 the Lawler Brothers Amusement Company sent personal letters to the children who had appeared before their camera in one Vermont town, informing them that the moving picture would be shown at the Princess Theatre, and adding 'I sincerely trust that you and your little friends will enjoy it.'[42]

TOPICALITY

The films I have mentioned of children's processions and local pageants suggest a move away from the basic see-yourselves-on-the-screen genre – the 'factory gate' and 'sortie de l'église' models – towards local films of wider topical interest. A recommendation for this kind of film had appeared in a photographic review as early as 1897:

> When any local events of more than usual interest, such as processions, fairs or sports, take place, the dealer should be on the spot with his kinematograph and take animated photographs of the same. Such films will be profitable stock for future e.g. visits of royalty, the return of a prominent townsman etc.[43]

Films of local current events started appearing from the late 1890s onwards, as Vanessa Toulmin has shown in her examination of the work of Mitchell and Kenyon, who made films of sporting events, local customs, and tram rides.[44] The main audience for these films would still be local people, though the reels might enjoy a sale outside their original area (and therefore, according to my definition, are less 'local' than the factory gate films, which appealed purely as 'come and see yourself' subjects, and would have little appeal beyond the community of people originally filmed). 'Local topicals' remained an important part of local film-making in the UK for years. Examples are preserved in several of Britain's regional film archives in considerable numbers, dating from the 1910s to the 1960s, though their heyday was probably in the 1920s and 1930s. Typical subjects were processions, gala days, sports meetings, outings, inaugurations and unveilings of war memorials.[45] To give some idea of numbers, the Scottish Screen Archive, for instance, holds over 300 'local topicals', and in New Zealand such local films became a dominant genre of national production in the 1920s.[46] Incidentally, one British trade commentator in 1908 suggested that lantern slides, taken

M&K 15: *The 'Hands' Leaving Work at North Street Mills* (1900), commissioned by Captain Thomas Payne to be shown at the annual Chorley Fair held in September.

by showmen of local events, were a low-cost alternative to films, and would still attract the crowds, though it's not clear how established a practice this became.[47]

Some showmen, in their evolving roles as regional cameramen, also tackled more up-to-the-minute, 'hard' news stories on occasion: for example, in 1908 a film about the survivors of a railway accident was filmed by a fairground operator and screened in the Nantes region of France.[48] In the US, a number of regional film production companies came into being to film such news stories, as well as making industrials and the like.[49] In Europe, there were also some attempts at more regular regional production. In 1906 a producer in Italy made a film of the local people and places of Livorno, which he screened as 'Livorno cinematografata', and the same producer then went inland later that year to make 'Regio Emilia cinematografata'. In 1910 and again in 1911, a 'Giornale cinematografico di Ferrara' was designed to attract local spectators.[50] The first newsreels proper were being released by this time (1910 onwards), and they too inscribed an element of 'localism' in their structures: both Gaumont Actualités and Pathé Journal divided up their newsreel issues by geography, Gaumont for example giving Paris news first, then French news, then world.[51]

The next variation to emerge was the purely local or regional newsreel, mainly a US development, which has been little studied by historians to date. The first regional newsreel seems to have been the *Los Angeles Weekly* which began in 1912, and in addition to a hard news component – it covered events in the LA region – there was also a reminder of the old factory gate genre, in that each week a scene was taken for the *Weekly* in the crowded shopping district, showing 'as many faces as possible'. The belief was still firm that: 'people will always turn out to see a film in which there is a chance to see themselves.'[52] Local newsreels soon became quite a vogue. From 1912 to 1914 – a mere three years – I have logged the arrival of no fewer than eighteen regional newsreels in the US.[53] However, because many of these were organised on a regional rather than strictly local basis, they do not qualify in our strict definition of 'local' film (in which there is significant duplication between the people filmed and the audience).

LOCAL DRAMAS

Like local newsreels, locally produced dramas have been neglected by historians, though such films were at one time widely known in moving picture theatres in the United States. Interestingly though, the earliest reference I have found to such a film was from the other side of the Atlantic. In September 1913, *Moving Picture World* noted that a 'new kind of local picture' had appeared in the UK:

> At Reading last week a local showman secured the services of the Reading Thespian Society in a scenario, in which a local dude persistently follows a charming local lady. This novel attraction, although hackneyed in design, proved an immense draw, for the sole reason that the scenes and characters were well known to the audience.[54]

Sadly there are no more details of this British experiment but by the following year the idea was becoming established in the US. In the summer of 1914, a film was made in South Dakota entitled *It Happened in Joyland*. Though little further information is available, we do know that the film featured a local cast. Later in the year the idea had spread to other parts of the country: *When the Tango Craze Hit Lexington* was produced with local people from that city, and in Winona, Wisconsin they filmed two local comedies.[55]

As with America's regional newsreels, these local dramas were sometimes made with the involvement of the provincial newspaper, and sometimes involved a competition. In August 1914, for example, the *Dayton Journal* organised two linked competitions for its readers: first, a prize for the best scenario sent in, which would then be filmed starring the winner of the second, – for the most beautiful local girl.[56] An even more ambitious contest took place in Chicago later that year run by the *Chicago Herald*, which launched a highly publicised search for 'the prettiest and most popular girl in Chicago'. The forty finalists (ten from each of Chicago's districts) would be screen-tested and the test sequences included in the *Herald*'s own weekly newsreel, the *Herald Weekly*, and therefore seen by thousands of people in the city's movie venues. The winning girl, as voted for by the audiences, would be given the opportunity to play the part of Sue in a scenario, *Who Is Sue?* to be produced by the Essanay Company.[57] The idea caught on, and the *Omaha World-Herald* sponsored its own contest – another double one, for a scenario and for female leads – and the resulting three-reeler premiered in Omaha in June 1916.[58] [See Table 1]

As so often in cinema history, this 'new' genre contained elements which had been present in earlier media practices. Competitions had been run in newspapers and in other contexts, and there had been beauty contests of many kinds since the late nineteenth century. Even in motion picture theatres a kind of beauty contest had been staged in the form of 'baby shows', in which photographic slides of babies, entered by their parents, were projected on the theatre screen, and the audience voted for the most appealing one. This may have been quite a widespread practice in the US, for by 1909, slide companies were advertising their services to make up the slides for these competitions.[59]

Table 1: Local dramas produced in the US from 1914

Title	Town/State	Date
Present and Past in the Cradle of Dixie	Montgomery, Alabama	1914
Who Is Sue? [*Chicago Herald* contest film]	Chicago, Illinois	1914
[*Dayton Journal* contest film]	Dayton, Ohio	August 1914
It Happened in Joyland	South Dakota	Summer 1914
The Mine Owner's Daughter (involving Vachel Lindsay)	Springfield, Illinois	1914?
Two local comedies	Winona, Wisconsin	1914?
When the Tango Craze Hit Lexington	Lexington, Kentucky	Late 1914
The Man Haters	Muncie and Anderson, Indiana	1915
[*Omaha World-Herald* contest film]	Omaha	1916
Home Talent motion picture (multiple versions)	Midwest	Late 1910s
Our Gang (multiple versions)	South Carolina	1926
The Movie Queen (multiple versions)	New England	1930s

NB Many other local dramas were made
in the 1920s to 1930s

A similar idea transposed to the film medium took place in Barnsley in England in 1913 where a film of the best-looking local children was planned.[60]

But local film dramas were far more ambitious than these previous forms, and some dramas of this kind have survived. One extant example is *Present and Past in the Cradle of Dixie*, a two-reel film made in Montgomery, Alabama in 1914, about a New England man who falls in love with a Southern belle. It featured a cast of leading citizens from Montgomery and included reconstructions of historical scenes from the time of the Confederacy. Like some other local dramas, this film was intended both to promote the city and its sights for out-of-state advertising, and for showing to local audiences.[61] Another surviving example is *The Man Haters*, a local drama made in Muncie, Indiana in 1915, after a newspaper competition to find 'stars' who would appear in the film. In the same month the producer, Basil McHenry, made another version of the film (also extant) in the nearby town of Anderson, Indiana, with local people from that town.[62]

This concept of making multiple versions caught on, and it clearly had potential to reduce costs. Producer Richard E. Norman specialised in making these kinds of films in the late 1910s (before moving into another niche market, 'race films', in the 1920s). He travelled the Midwest, making multiple versions of the so-called 'Home Talent motion picture'. The town-specific versions of these films were designed to highlight 'municipal progress' and often showed an engaged couple who were looking for items for her trousseau. In this way, as the couple visited the town's shopping streets, the film served as advertising for the local shop owners, especially as, after the initial screenings, the town would retain the film and could use it for promotional efforts.[63]

The starring couples in these films were often chosen as the most eligible sons and daughters of the town's leading citizens and a glorification of the local elite was apparently a common pattern.

Even Vachel Lindsay, eminent poet and pioneering film critic, got himself involved in one such production, *The Mine Owner's Daughter*, which was made in Lindsay's home town of Springfield, Illinois, 'using our social set for actors', and these 'actors' even included the governor's son. Lindsay was quite open in admitting that, as with Norman's films, this enterprise was 'backed by the local commercial association for whose benefit the thing was made'. Who knows, perhaps it was made by the aforementioned Richard E. Norman himself?[64] Sometimes these films were less than a triumph at the box office, and it was reported in October 1915 from the Midwest that two badly made local dramas had totally 'bombed' with their home-town audiences.[65]

Local dramas became quite prevalent across America through the rest of the 1910s, into the 1920s and as late as the 1940s, though they didn't always put as much emphasis as Norman did on commercial promotion and on featuring 'leading citizens'. For example, a version of *Our Gang* was shot in South Carolina in 1926, while in Nebraska there are records of several local dramas being shot at county fairs and the like, to be shown at the end of the fair's run. [66] By the 1930s, these films were virtually into mass production, and in New England a producer travelled the region shooting a plot called the *The Movie Queen* in numerous different towns. The roles were played by local people and the films (some surviving) premiered in the towns' theatres almost immediately after processing.[67]

Present and Past in the Cradle of Dixie (1914,) a film made in 1914 about Alabama's secession from the Union, featuring a cast of local citizens from the town of Montgomery.

CONCLUSION

It is becoming apparent from research in several countries that local films were an important genre almost from the beginnings of cinema. It is also apparent that the genre splits into a number of subgenres, including such types as factory gate and 'sortie de l'église' films, as well as local topicals, local newsreels and local dramas. The common factor, as I have suggested above, is that these films had a significant overlap between the people or community who were filmed and the subsequent audience for the film (i.e. the film should include recognisable people). As ever there are bound to be some problems of definition, notably with types of films which don't quite meet the criteria and one can imagine that certain municipal advertising films, some semi-amateur productions and certain kinds of news films might shade over into locals. Nevertheless the basic criteria I believe are useful.

I believe that these films offer a certain challenge to the conventional economic models of the film industry, in that here we have a genre which is sustained not by a mass, widespread, even international, audience, but by a very circumscribed one. This is not the only incongruity of local films. Cinema historians have always liked to divide the film industry into three categories of production, distribution and exhibition, but local films subvert this tripartite division, because the producer is often the exhibitor and there isn't any distribution involved at all. Categorisation was looser in the early years of cinema, but even then some people preferred clear dividing lines between things. The exchange men in 1909 who (as I've noted above) objected to being asked to make local films for their exhibitor clients were an advance guard for the compartmentalisation of the industry: they wanted to be distributors, and not part-producers as well. Film historians have perpetuated this propensity to pigeon-hole the film industry, and perhaps have overlooked locals partly because these films do not fit into the conventional tripartite model of the film industry. It is largely thanks to the rediscovery of many extant local films in the archives – notably the Mitchell and Kenyon Collection and Scottish and New Zealand local films shown at Pordenone, and the various offerings at the Orphans film symposia – that we have been forced to realise that there is another, rich layer in the archaeology of cinema.

POSTSCRIPT

Since completing the chapter above, I have come across a number of further references to local film practices. Local films were made and screened all over the world, including in the main towns in Algeria: in March 1907 the local press drew attention to showings exclusively of films of life in Oran where 'you can go and recognise yourself'.[68] In England, one film pioneer in Beverley, East Yorkshire, Ernest Symmons, was making local films from 1911, and even branching out into comedy using local performers; he continued as a local cameraman/showman until the 1950s.[69] In Switzerland, a family of itinerant showmen/film-makers, the Leuzingers, were making films of local public events such as carnivals by the 1920s, and then screening them to the populace – fifteen of their films have survived.[70]

In the United States, the trend for films to advertise local businesses was well established by 1915, though one local newspaper attacked the practice as unproductive for the enterprises which were so featured – but perhaps the real reason for this critique was that such films threatened to take the money which formerly went into newspaper advertising.[71] Also in the US, I have found a further reference to the making of local dramas: in the summer of 1916 director Donald Ryan, with cameraman Frank Bender, were said to be 'working through' northwestern Pennsylvania, 'producing amateur photoplay comedies in which the beaus and belles of the different towns are featured'. Ryan was working for the McHenry Film Corporation of Akron, Ohio, presumably run by the same Basil McHenry who, the previous year, was making the local dramas in Indiana which I've described.[72]

I have no doubt that, now this subject of local films has been put on the film historiographical map, more and more references to local film-making will start to be unearthed by historians everywhere.

NOTES

1. The production of these city-boosting films grew through the first decade of the twentieth century and my research suggests that 1911 was probably a peak year for early US production. Watterson R. Rothacker was the chief exponent of such films. I plan to write an article on this subject in future.

2. For example, T. J. West, while exhibiting in Coventry, shot a film of the city's football team in a match with Stafford: 'Showmen's Notes', *Music Hall and Theatre Review* (*MHTR*), 28 November 1902, p. 357.

3. A Montpellier newspaper noted in mid-1896 that, responding to the requests of many local 'cinématographe' enthusiasts, Lumière operators had taken several views of the city to show to the local people. See Jacques and Marie André, *Une Saison Lumière à Montpellier* (Perpignan: Institut Jean Vigo, 1987) p. 88.

4. The ad is reproduced in Marie-Sophie Corcy *et al.*, *Les Premières Années de la Société L. Gaumont et Cie. Correspondance Commerciale de Léon Gaumont 1895–1899* (Paris: AFRHC etc. 1999), p. 135 (author's translation). The Chronophotographe is pictured in *La Nature*, 21 November 1896, p. 392.

5. David Nasaw, *Going Out: The Rise and Fall of Public Amusements* (Cambridge, MA: Harvard University Press, 1999) p. 148 (quoting Allen, *Vaudeville and Film*).

6. Charles Musser and Carol Nelson, *High-Class Moving Pictures: Lyman H. Howe and the Forgotten Era of Traveling Exhibition, 1880–1920* (Princeton, NJ: Princeton University Press, 1991), pp. 109–11, 149–52. Local views were also taken by William Paley in Worcester in 1900 which attracted enthusiastic audiences in the town. In 1901, Lyman Howe enticed inhabitants of Wilkes-Barre to his shows with shots of the town that had been taken a few weeks before by a cameraman he had hired for this work, and he did the same in Troy in 1902. By 1904, having acquired his own camera, he filmed local scenes in Wwilkes-Barre himself to show in the town. In 1904 and 1905, Vitagraph were making local filming a central plank in their programming: filming scenes such as a fire brigade turnout some days in advance of visits by their exhibition units. They also filmed employees leaving a factory, with their publicity urging workers to come to the show to 'see yourself as others see you', resulting in big ticket sales. William Steiner's company was also taking local views about this time.

7. In Sweden, from 1907 to 1910, Svenska Bio took several local films. See Pelle Snickars, 'Im Zeichen Der Bricolage – Produktions- und Programmstrategien der Schwedischen Filmkultur um 1910', *KINtop*, vol. 11, 2002, pp. 88–90, 98. One of the earliest cited locals in Germany was a church 'sortie' film: people coming out of Trier Cathedral in 1904. See Uli Jung, 'Local Views: A Blind Spot in the Historiography of Early German Cinema', *Historical Journal of Film, Radio and Television*, vol. 22, no. 3 (2002), pp. 253–73.

8. 'Showmen's Notes', *MHTR*, 18 July 1902, p. 47, concerning film shows in Leeds.

9. *The Showman*, 4 October 1901, p. 58. See also *The Showman* in 1901: 15 February, p. 115; 14 June, p. 389; 16 August, p. 521; 27 September, p. 42.

10. *The Showman*, 16 August 1901, p. 521.

11. Vanessa Toulmin, '"Local Films for Local People": Travelling Showmen and the Commissioning of Local Films in Great Britain, 1900–1902', *Film History*, vol. 13, no. 2 (2001), pp. 118–37.

12. The showman, Arthur Rosebery of the Thomas-Edison Animated Photo Co., said that the summer time was best for exhibition because then 'we can take a picture in the afternoon, and show it in the evening, and people come to see themselves in it.' Quoted in 'A Cinematograph Case', *The Era*, 12 April 1901, p. 20. It should be noted though, that this witness was biased, as his company was claiming damages for having missed a booking for the summer season.

13. Two testimonies to the popularity of local subjects appear in *Optical Lantern and Cinematograph Journal* (*OLCJ*), November 1904, pp. 13–14, 22. And *OLCJ*, September 1906, p. 201 notes that the Sheffield Photo Company specialises in local subjects, and they have a 'travelling darkroom plant always ready for this class of work'. *Cinematography and Bioscope Magazine*, December 1906, affirms that local films are still

popular and the Warwick Co. still take them. See also *Kinematograph and Lantern Weekly* (*KLW*), 23 May 1907, p. 19, which says that local films are the 'biggest draw'.

14. 'The Value of Local Topicals', Chapter 15, in *How to Run a Picture Theatre* (London: E. T. Heron & Co., 1912), pp. 121–5.

15. *MHTR*, 9 May 1902, p. 301 re 'Professor' Ball at Reading fair. See also *Optical Magic Lantern Journal* (*OMLJ*), January 1901, p. 2, for a description of an enterprising cinematographer who had taken a film of factory workers leaving for lunch. The film was later shown in the town and great amusement was caused by one spectator 'who recognising himself shouted out to a companion, "Lor Bil', that's me with the square basket!"'

16 Such a film, for example, was a great hit in February 1903 in one small French town, because of this recognition factor. See Pierre Berneau, 'Histoires des Cinémas d'Angoulême de 1896 à 1940 d'après la Presse Charentaise', *Bulletin et Mémoires: Société Archéologique et Historique de la Charente*, no. 2 (1988), p. 122.

17. Blaise Aurora, *Histoire du Cinéma en Lorraine: Du Cinématographe au Cinéma Forain, 1896–1914* (Metz: Editions Serpenoise etc., 1996), pp. 173–9. The first local film made in Lorraine (by fairground showmen) showed people coming out of the church in Camby in 1900; there were also two factory gate ('sortie de l'usine') films in 1901. Aurora lists several of these kinds of films, 'sorties' from both churches and factories, produced up to 1910.

18. See *L'Avenir Forain*, 1904, p. 1. I have found one report in Britain (written by the cameraman) of the apparent hostility of a crowd as they were being filmed. See 'Experiences in Animated Photography', *The Showman*, 3 January 1902, p. 272.

19. The judge's decision was delivered on 4 March 1905. See Jacques Deslandes and Jacques Richard, *Histoire Comparée du Cinéma – vol. 2. Du Cinématographe au Cinéma 1896–1906* (Paris; Tournai: Casterman, 1968), pp. 523–8.

20. 'Foreign Notes of Interest', *Moving Picture World* (*MPW*), 12 August 1911, p. 360. The Court of Appeal in Paris's decision about photographic rights stated that all negatives taken by a photographer are his property, but he cannot make prints or exhibit them without the consent of the sitter even if no sum has been paid for the taking of the negative. The US decision was in the context of a report that there had been disturbances in Newport, RI as photographers and cameramen tried to photograph the sights there. The report added that, 'many cameras have been smashed by irate proprietors': 'New England', *MPW*, 15 July 1911, p. 52.

21. *How to Run a Picture Theatre*, p. 122.

22. Ibid.

23. See *Bioscope* (*Bios*), 10 December 1908, p. 13. See also H. H. Fullilove, *Animated Pictures: The World before Your Eyes*, 1964 (manuscript in BFI). A show in Brainerd, Minnesota also offered prizes to people who spotted themselves: *MPW*, 1 August 1914, p. 722.

24. John M. East, 'The Codmans', *The Silent Picture*, no. 13 (1972), pp. 24–6. Others also recalled this con trick. Alfred Claude Bromhead, 'Reminiscences of the British Film Trade', *Proceedings of the British Kinematograph Society*, no. 21 (1933), p. 6. In 1913 a gang of swindlers in New England would come to a town and set up a dummy camera with no film inside, solicit deposits from the businesses that they 'filmed', and then vanish. 'Swindlers doing "local stuff"', *MPW*, 6 September 1913, p. 1054.

25. Firms such as the Advance Motion Picture Company had several contracts to film locals in Midwestern states by 1911. For example they were commissioned by a theatre circuit in Aurora, Illinois to film a parade and the fire department, and other city scenes for showing in the circuit's theatres: *MPW*, 14 October 1911, p. 133. The Superior Film Mfg. Co. also hired cameramen out, to make local and municipal-boosting films: see pictorial ad in *MPW*, 6 December 1913, p. 1226.

26. *The Era*, 5 April 1901, p. 32: the Warwick Co. notes that it has reduced prices for taking local ('private') films to 5d a foot; *The Era*, 20 June 1903, p. 28: the Sheffield Photo Company says it charges 4½d. to print and develop showmen's films and twice that rate to supply the cameraman too; *OLCJ*, November 1905, p. 2 says it costs 10/6 a day for the cameraman and 8d a foot for the film; *OLKJ*, October 1906, p. 221 notes that one can hire a cameraman for 10s a day, and several cheap cameras were now available for filming local events.

27. *How to Run a Picture Theatre*, p. 121.

28. Showmen, being untrained, might not have been the best cameramen, but it seems that even professional firms hired to produce a local film might turn out sloppy work. See 'World of Finance', *Bios*, 22 January 1914, p. 353: a court case in which the clients complained that the film of their annual outing, made by a cameraman from Cunard Films, was badly shot.

29. *The Showman*, 9 August 1901, p. 509; Toulmin, '"Local Films for Local People"', pp. 131–2.

30. *MPW*, 24 May 1913, p. 814 claims that many Compact Marvels have been bought by exhibitors. See another ad for a camera for exhibitors in *MPW*, 22 February 1913, p. 765 and p. 793; and a similar in *MPW*, 3 May 1913, p. 533. Hugh V. Jamieson was making locals in the pre-World War I era, using a Williamson camera: see *SMPE Journal*, November 1974, p. 912. The Motion Picture Camera Company of New York advertised a $75 camera in *MPW*, 27 January 1914, p. 462.

31. Locals were made as far afield as Australia (a cinematically adventurous country from the outset): for example, *Adelaide in a Hurry* (1911) was filmed on a city street to attract people to see themselves at the show in Adelaide Town Hall. See W. Dylan Walker, 'The Rise of Popular Culture – Adelaide Cinema 1896–1913', in A. D. McCredie (ed.), *From Colonel Light into the Footlights: The Performing Arts in South Australia from 1836 to the Present* (Norwood, S.A.: Pagel Books, 1988), p. 380.

32. Charles Mendel, 'The French Cinematograph Trade', *Bios*, 26 October 1911, p. 221.

33. 'Local Pictures', *MPW*, 28 August 1909, pp. 277–8.

34. 'Local Pictures', pp. 277–8.

35. 'A New Field for Exhibitors. The Taking of Local Topicals and Their Market Value, by One Who Has Tried It', *The Cinema*, 12 February 1914, p. 27: notes the costs involved and that these films will greatly boost a theatre's revenue, e.g. A 100 ft film can be made all-in for less than £2. It adds that 'the topical gazettes' will sometimes buy local news event films.

36. 'Trade Topics', *Pictures & Pleasures*, 15 June 1914, p. 2.

37. Films of pageants included: Warwick Pageant: *OLCJ*, July 1906, p. 170; Bath Pageant: *Bios*, 25 February 1909, p. 9; Penn Pageant: *MPW*, 9 November 1912, pp. 574–5, 649, 684–5.

38. See M&K 58: *Pendlebury Colliery* (1901), for an example of Sedgwick's Animated Pictures on M&K 772: *Sedgwick's Bioscope Showfront and Stage Show* (1901).

39. NFTVA title: *School Children's Cinema Outing*. Until the discovery of the Mitchell and Kenyon Collection and the increasing sensitisation of historians to these issues, few local films were known to be extant. This is an example of a previously existing film, only now recognised as a local.

40. As they were filmed, the patron-extras were told to 'not stand still but keep moving' and 'don't forget your facial expressions'. Cited in Kathryn H. Fuller, *At the Picture Show : Small-Town Audiences and the Creation of Movie Fan Culture* (Washington, DC: Smithsonian Institution Press, 1996), pp. 130–1. That same year in Arkansas City, Kansas youngsters were filmed in front of a local cinema as part of publicity for a municipal cleanup campaign: *MPW*, 8 August 1914, p. 851.

41. Selda Vale da Costa, *Eldorado Das Ilusões: Cinema & Sociedade: Manaus, 1897–1935* (Manaus: Editora da Universidade do Amazonas, 1996), p. 272.

42. 'School Friendship Book' for a girl named Eleanor Rogers, listed on eBay, September 2003.

43. 'How Dealers Can Make Money out of Kinematographs', *Photographic Dealer*, August 1897, pp. 168–9.

44. Toulmin, "'Local Films for Local People'". Some tram ride and similar films involved 'product placement', the showman, for example, filming posters for his own shows.

45. Such films are sometimes mentioned in the trade press. A film showing a commemoration of Robert Burns' grave was commissioned by a local Scottish cinema manager and filmed by a Gaumont operator: 'Round the Scottish Renters', *KLW*, 5 February 1920 (courtesy Janet McBain); see also 'The Local Topical as a Business "Booster"', *Cinematograph Exhibitors' Diary*, 1926, pp. 121–3.

46. Local films are held in the following UK archives: the North West, East Anglian, Scottish and Wessex film archives, and SEFVA.

47. 'Local Slides as Money-makers', *KLW*, 2 July 1908, p. 161.

48. Frederic Monteil, *La Belle Époque du Cinéma et des Fêtes Foraines à Nantes (1896–1914)* (Nantes: Ouest Editions, 1996), pp. 104–5: Monteil calls these cameramen 'opérateurs-reporters' (he gives no names).

49. For example, the St Louis Motion Picture Co. filmed a fire in the city 'while the ruins were still warm' and this was shipped immediately to be shown in Kansas City in the same state: *MPW*, 18 April 1914, p. 381.

50. Aldo Bernardini, *Cinema muto italiano: i film 'Dal vero', 1895–1914* (Gemona: Cineteca del Friuli, 2002), pp. 73, 78, 169.

51. For example, Gaumont: *Cine Journal*, 18 March 1911, n.p.; Pathé (le 'Roi de l'actualité'): *Cine Journal*, 1 April 1911, n.p.

52. 'A Local Photographic "Weekly"', *MPW*, 25 June 1912, p. 1219; *MPW*, 6 July 1912, p. 35. It was to be issued from 17 June by the Sunset Motion Picture Co.

53. I plan to write an article on this subject.

54. 'British Notes', *MPW*, 13 September 1913, p. 1164.

55. Joyland: *MPW*, 8 August 1914, p. 850: I can find no further information about this at the South Dakota State Historical Society website. Tango: *MPW*, 19 December 1914, p. 1709: this film was apparently to raise funds for baby welfare. See David O. Thomas, 'Winona Nickelodeon Theatres 1907–1913: The Battle for Local Control', *Marquee*, vol. 13, no. 1 (1981), p. 16. Thomas stresses the importance of 'localism' in the development of film exhibition in Winona. The same vaudeville man who made these comedies also launched a local Winona newsreel.

56. The film was to be produced by a Cincinnati firm: *MPW*, 1 August 1914, p. 722.

57. *MPW*, 12 December 1914, p. 1502; *MPW*, 19 December 1914, p. 1659.

58. Information from Paul J. Eisloeffel, Curator of Audio-Visual Collections, Nebraska State Historical Society in AMIA-Listserv, 4 December 2001.

59. The Brayton Manufacturing Company offered this service: *MPW*, 15 May 1909, p. 632; as did the Novelty Slide Company: ad, *MPW*, 19 June 1909, p. 841. Sometimes local projectionists made the slides themselves: *MPW*, 21 November 1914, p. 1074; see also *MPW*, 12 September 1914, p. 1535, col. 3.

60. See *Bios*, 5 June 1913, p. 700.

61. Information in letter from State of Alabama, Department of Archives and History, 16 September 1994. See Tanya L. Zanish, 'Present and Past in the Cradle of Dixie', *Alabama Heritage*, vol. 27 (Winter 1993), pp. 25–8.

62. Nancy Turner, *'Having Fun with It' : The Man Haters Project* (Muncie, IN: Ball State University, 1996), pp. 14 and *passim*. The film's title was a spoof on several commercial films with 'woman haters' in the title released from 1912.

63. Matthew Bernstein and Dana F. White, '"Scratching around" in a "Fit of Insanity": The Norman Film Manufacturing Company and the Race Film Business in the 1920s', *Griffithiana*, nos. 62–3, 1998, pp. 81–127. Norman edited the films himself, into say a 1,000' final length, often incorporating existing footage.

64. Vachel Lindsay, *The Art of the Moving Picture* (New York: The Modern Library, 2000 [orig. 1915]), p. 102 (Chapter 11). Like other such local dramas, this film is not listed in Einar Lauritzen and Gunnar Lundquist, *American Film-Index* (Stockholm: Film-index, 1984).

65. 'Do Local Films Pay?', *MPW*, 16 October 1915, p. 485. The films had been made in towns in Illinois and Indiana.

66. Ernest Alfred Dench, 'Writing a Local Photoplay' in his *Motion Picture Education* (Cincinnati, OH: Standard Book Publishing Co., 1917), pp. 268–82. Dan Streible, 'Itinerant Filmmakers and Amateur Casts: A Homemade "Our Gang", 1926', *Film History*, vol. 15, no. 2 (2003), pp. 177–92. The film was made in Anderson, SC, sponsored by the city's movie theatre.

67. Information from Dwight Swanson, Northeast Historic Film: AMIA-Listserv, 3 December 2001.

68. Younes Dadci, *Première Histoire du Cinéma Algerien, 1895–1979*, 3rd edn (Paris: Editions Dadci, 1980), pp. 175–6.

69. Peter H. Robinson, *The Home of Beautiful Pictures: The Story of the Playhouse Cinema, Beverley* (Beverley: Hutton Press, 1985), pp. 13–17, 87–94.

70. M. L.Farinelli, 'Un Trésor Régional: Les Films Leuzinger', in Rémy Pithon (ed.), *Cinéma Suisse Muet: Lumières et Ombres, Médias et Histoire* (Lausanne: Éditions Antipodes; Cinémathèque Suisse, 2002), p. 152.

71. 'Do Local Pictures Pay?', *MPW*, 31 July 1915, p. 846.

72. 'Ryan Making Amateur Photoplays', *MPW*, 15 July 1916, p. 371.

5 Pictures of Crowd Splendor: The Mitchell and Kenyon Factory Gate Films

Tom Gunning

> The apparition of these faces in the crowd;
> Petals on a wet, black bough
> Ezra Pound 'In a Station of the Metro'

The twentieth century might be considered the century of the masses, introducing mass production, mass marketing, mass communication, mass culture. We could describe this transformation as the entrance of the working class (putatively the driving force of any age, but often eclipsed in the realm of official representation) onto a new stage of visibility. But this entrance was not uncontested and often met with a reaction to such a supposed influx of vulgarity, as new hierarchies of space, time and bodily function sought to shore up apparently crumbling structures of social control.

This reaction appears already at the end of the nineteenth century in a letter written by the young Sigmund Freud to his fiancée Martha Bernays, commenting on her description of the Wandsbeck Fair: 'But, no beloved, you are quite right, it is neither pleasant nor edifying to watch the masses amusing themselves.' Yet typically, even at this early date, Freud does not feel entirely comfortable about the superiority implied by his comment. He sees the masses' thirst for pleasure as a result of their oppression, 'for being a helpless target for all the taxes, epidemics, sicknesses and evils of social institutions,' and adds 'they have more community spirit than we have.'[1] Anticipating his later theories by several decades, he speculates on the negative effects of repression on the middle class, the price paid for their gentility and class difference, observing, 'the mob gives vent to its appetites and we deprive ourselves.'[2]

In the late nineteenth and early twentieth century the masses, – the crowd, the mob, the larger proportion of the human race – became not only more visible but a subject for investigation, discipline, apprehension and fantasy, viewed primarily from a middle-class or elite viewpoint. As Raymond Williams pointed out in his *Keywords*, the ambivalence towards the masses becomes explicit in 'two disintinguishable kinds of implication. Masses (i) is the modern word for *many-headed multitude or mob*: low ignorant, unstable. Masses (ii) is a description of the same people but now seen as a positive or potentially positive force.'[3] While these differing understandings of the term primarily represent opposed positions, conservative and progressive, the new century also witnessed a mixed reaction similar to that expressed by Freud, a desire on the one hand to maintain a distance from the working class, a distance which new modes of interaction seemed to undermine, as well as a sense that in their pleasures the working class might possess something left undeveloped or repressed in the lifestyles of the better classes.

As it moved toward a dominant mass medium in its first decades, the cinema too was viewed with suspicion and fear, investigated for its effects (physical, psychological and social) as well as being seen as potentially a transforming force, providing in both cases a prime canvas for projected fantasy. The privileged relation between the new medium of moving pictures and the working class that formed an important part of the imaginary history of the cinema has been questioned in recent years. Historians investigating the opening nights of the cinema, its premieres around the world in the 1890s, discovered elite audiences in sumptuous vaudeville palaces or music halls receiving a technological marvel of special interest to an educated populace. In America the nickelodeon, the poor man's theatre appearing around 1906, has been redefined as a brief transitional point in the film industry's continual solicitation of a middle-class audience, while the succeeding period of stardom, picture palaces and feature films has been understood as the triumph of bourgeoisification of the cinema that absorbed, but also eclipsed, the working class.

However, I strongly believe that, pushed even further, the history of the cinema will always reveal an important relation to the working class, both as an audience and as a subject of representation. The portrayal of the masses, particularly in the modern form of the crowd, posed a challenge to the traditional arts of painting or literature; the naturalist novel and, successively, Impressionist and Futurist painting partly arose from this challenge. But, as Louis Lumière claimed, the cinematic apparatus could 'represent the movement of the streets, of public places, with truly astonishing fidelity.'[4] Thus the cinema appeared as a medium seemingly created to capture what film historians Jacques and Marie André referred to as 'crowd effects',[5] picturing not only the crowd, but their gait, bearing and cadence as they moved through public spaces. The ability of the cinema to capture contingent happenings in all their details, seeming to sacrifice principles of selection and hierarchy found in traditional images, gave its images a democracy of composition that matched the subject. Further, the extraordinary films that form the topic of this chapter, the Mitchell and Kenyon factory gates, involve a rather unique perspective: films of the working class – filmed primarily to be seen by the working class.

The premieres of the Vitascope, Cinématographe or Biograph attracted an upper middle-class audience; but as opposed to these media-saturated first nights, the period of cinema's pervasive movement through the fairground and show culture of Europe not only represents an arguably more important entrance of cinema into the daily life of the modern age, but one focused on the working classes. Fortunately for film history this fairground culture has aficionados and passionate chroniclers, who have searched the records of showmen and the archives of local newspapers. This era of cinema not only claims attention on its own grounds, but provides us with the most unforgettable images of the working class in early cinema, the factory gate films, especially the films of this genre produced by the Mitchell and Kenyon Company in the north of England at the turn of the century.

The factory gate genre could be said to begin with the film(s) of the workers of the Lumière Company leaving their factory in Lyon. If we view the genre simply in terms of action and location, this origin holds. The gate opens (at least in some versions of the three films the Lumières made of this subject in 1895), the workers emerge and (in some versions) the gate closes. However, the relations between crowd and camera and – most important of all – audience and film in the Lumière films contrast with Mitchell and Kenyon's films.

In 1895 the Lumière Company shot three films of workers leaving their factory.[6] According to testimony by François Doublier who later served as cameraman for the company (and who claims he appears in one of these films as the worker on the bicycle), the camera was placed in a building across the street from the factory, shooting through a window, 'in order not to distract the crowd.'[7] Indeed the workers seem to regard the camera with studied indifference – so much so, in fact, that Lumière scholar Bernard Chardère believes that they must have been directed *not* to look at the camera.[8] Further, the workers were not the intended primary audience of this film (although Doublier does indicate there was a screening for them a few days after the filming). The films were shown in private screenings to amateur photographers and to an organisation interested in the promotion of French industries before the film's commercial premiere at the Grand Café in December of 1895. In other words, it was presented to elite audiences in order to demonstrate the success of the latest Lumière photographic experiment, for which the workers were guinea pigs, rather than the intended audience.

The two earlier (but until recently little known) versions of the Lumière factory gate film included a marked moment of class differentiation as the crowd of workers parts to let a carriage carrying the Lumières themselves pass through in stark contrast to the workers on foot or bicycle. Mitchell and Kenyon films also often seem to show people of different classes – if dress codes are legible – with some workers in collarless shirts and caps, while clerks, perhaps, appear in white shirts, ties and straw hats. Other better-dressed folk also appear, whether family or friends of factory managers or owners, showmen or their relatives, or simply workers in their Sunday best, only a cultural historian with a better knowledge of sartorial codes than I could tell for sure. But if owners or managers do appear in these films, for the most part they seem to mingle with the crowd. Exceptions occur, M&K: 673 *Jute Works Barrow* (1902) opens with a separate brief shot of three men in top hats, wearing long coats and carrying canes or umbrellas, the camera panning with them as they walk in cadence along the exterior wall of the factory. They pass out of the frame as the camera pans further along, pausing at the gate. It is hard not to assume that these men are owners or managers.

M&K 58: *Pendlebury Colliery* (1901), showing the advertising poster for Sedgwick's Animated Pictures in August 1901.

The genre of the factory gate as it evolved after the Lumières, melded the idea of reception with production. These films were intended primarily to be seen by those who appeared in them. A showman set up the camera outside factory gates some time in advance of a screening of films. The film being shot was announced as something that would be featured in a forthcoming show. In M&K 58: *Pendlebury Colliery* (1901), we see a placard held by a showman's assistant announcing the programme of living pictures and magic lantern views (featuring the passion play in sixteen scenes) in which presumably the film then being shot would also be featured. Whether placards were the main way in which this information was conveyed, or the leaflets that we can see being handed out in such films as M&K 93: *Pay, Factory Gate* (c. 1900) or M&K 409: *Employees Leaving Alexandra Dock* (1901), or even through an oral announcement made by showman and /or camera operators at the moment of filming, the purpose behind all of these films lay in attracting audiences to living picture shows with the promise of seeing themselves and their co-workers on the screen.

This practice was widespread and international, although we have perhaps the most abundant evidence of it in the industrial north of England. The factory gate genre depended on a close relation between exhibition and production; thus film showings could be adapted to local audiences. An advert from the Cecil Hepworth Company in 1901 proclaimed:

> To Showmen.
>
> The most popular Cinematograph Film in a Travelling Show is ALWAYS A LOCAL PICTURE containing Portraits which can be recognised. A Film showing workers leaving a factory will gain far greater popularity in the town where it was taken than the most exciting picture ever produced. The workers come in hundreds, with all their friends and relations, and the Film more than pays for itself the first night. In other words this is The Greatest Draw you can have and it is Our Business to Provide it for you in Advance, for each Town you visit.[9]

Cinema, from its origins, displayed an international consciousness, from the peripatetic Lumière cameramen, who toured the globe gathering exotic images, to the slogan used by several early film companies: 'We Bring the World within Your Reach.' But early cinema also marked the era of local cinema, the travelling exhibitor and the fairground cinema, especially during the period between cinema's highly publicised premieres and the dawn of new permanent theatres shortly before World War I. The lure of virtual world tours and glimpses of distant, exotic places marked the global aspect of early cinema, while the gasp of recognition and the naming of familiar faces or places characterised its local identity.

This cry of recognition which baptises this cinema of locality, as the amazement of a direct connection marks the viewing process, appears in two descriptions of screenings:

> 'Lor', Bil', that's me!' – An enterprising cinematographist, who was giving a series of lantern entertainments in a town up north exposed a film at the gates of a large factory as the men were coming out for their dinner hour. This was in due course projected on the screen, when great amusement was caused to the audience by an enthusiastic member, who on recognizing [sic] himself in the picture, shouted out to a companion, 'Lor', Bil', that's me with the square basket!' We are informed that this small incident was the means of bringing a huge audience on the following evening of men engaged at the said works, and after this particular film had been projected, they insisted on an encore, which was of course honoured.[10]

> The big draw was a local film of the Belper mill hands leaving work; and I must say it was rather amusing to be inside when they were showing this one, as you kept hearing the refrain (ad lib.), 'O there's our Mary!', 'O, that's little Sally Smith!' etc.[11]

This calling out of names does not represent a naïve response to the motion picture illusion, although it does reveal an audience not yet subject to the discipline of spectator behaviour already rampant in the legitimate theatre, but not yet present in the film show or music hall. Rather, the viewer in a canny manner participates in the film screening, becoming aware that the film directly addresses her ('Watch me! Do you know me?') and responding to it. Viewer and film share a dialogic relation.

These films, and especially the treasure trove of Mitchell and Kenyon productions discovered and restored recently in such extraordinary condition, represent invaluable works of art as well as documents of history: an image of the working class as they move from the factory space into the space of their daily life. The films' variety, their constantly shifting centres of interest, provide a pleasure that is certainly both aesthetic (they are beautiful and capture the combination of motion and a moment unique to cinema) and filled with information. It is devoutly to be wished that historians of daily life, of costume, or working-class culture and even of the history of the body (ranging from observing the signs of rickets in the adults and children to describing the confident swagger or oppressed gait of the various workers we see) will comb through these films and interpret for us such things as the variety of headgear (from hats to shawls, from caps to top hats), and even give us some sense of how the different factories and their localities are reflected in these things.

Although an appreciation of these films depends partly on knowing their context, they are not simply documents for specialists, whether historians of culture or of early cinema. They address us directly; we participate in their humanity and their spontaneity. These workers still look us in the eyes, whether expressing curiosity, good humour or smouldering anger. It is as a filmic experience, which is also a moment snatched from history, that I will approach them.

I have claimed, in my discussions of early cinema as a cinema of attractions, that the relation between viewer and film in cinema's early era predominantly involved a direct address.[12] Nowhere is this clearer or more literal than in these films, as people were shot in order to be recognised, filmed for the pure delight of seeing themselves and others. We can no longer hear the cries that welcomed these images at the turn of the century; one side of the dialogue has been silenced. But, as historians, we have a responsibility to recall and channel those departed voices, or at least to search for their echo in the images that, thankfully, have survived. If we cannot hear the audience, we nonetheless have the faces, expressions, glances, bodily carriage and gestures that delighted them. Unmoored from their original exhibition context, these films still offer both a unique image of the working class at the turn of the century and rich moments in the history of the cinematic image: fragments of history, containing the contingencies of the 'everyday' a century ago. If not quite in the same way, they beckon to us as well today, calling on us to recognise them.

Cinema creates a gap in time between filming and screening. The audience responding verbally to Mitchell and Kenyon films belonged to the culture of music hall and popular theatre in which audience and performers acknowledged each other. Although the early cinema of attractions preserves moments acknowledging the audience (Méliès bowing as he presents an illusion, a clown sharing a joking smile and look with the audience), the presence of the camera necessarily entails the audience's absence. Audiences may have felt themselves solicited by performers on the screen, but they also realised no one could hear their applause or catcalls. Only the local films could truly heal this breach, or rather exploit it. People might not only recognise their co-workers and friends on the screen, but, like the man with the square basket, themselves. Many of the people in these films look directly at the camera as if in anticipation of recognition to come. This frank glance or even stare at the camera gives these films a large degree of their power.

Part of the richness of these films lies in their variety, so almost any statement I make about them could be reversed by another film (or even sometimes in the same film). While frank engagement of the camera is characteristic, this engagement runs a gamut of styles and attitudes. While these films abound with broad smiles, necks craned to see the camera better, flirtatious poses, waves of hands and caps, bits of performances and attempts to attract attention, we also find their opposites. People hide their faces behind hands or shawls, ignore the camera, regard it sullenly if at all, or stare at it without delivering a quiver of recognition. This range of reactions constitutes part of the drama of these films, seeing how an oncoming sea of faces reacts to this elementary encounter. We can speculate on the meaning of this range: oppressive working conditions, an invasion of privacy, suspicion of technology or of anything the management arranged (or at least allowed). Likewise, the more lighthearted responses contain a mixture of sarcasm, burlesque, and mockery, as well as a sense of fun, amusement and earnest curiosity. The encounter runs two ways, the passing parade of onlookers strives to get a good look at the camera, as well as forcing it to imprint their faces on the film. One would give a great deal to get the reverse angle of these films and be able to discover more about what the cameramen were doing to draw attention and who else and what else stood beside them (assistants, showmen, placards, entertainers?)

These films capture a moment of self-presentation of workers (and often their families, children mainly, who seem to have come to the gate to greet parents or relatives, possibly bringing lunches) leaving a modern factory. If the films seem disarmingly simple, we must keep in mind that every aspect of this moment carries the freight of history as well as the liveliness of immediacy. The reaction to the new medium itself – a mixture of curiosity, amusement, suspicion and a surprising degree of indifference, – flashes across the screen. Particularly in the films which literally open with the opening of the gate (such as M&K 6: *Haslam's Ltd Colne* (1900); M&K 39: *Ormerod's Mill, Great Moor Street, Bolton* (1900), we experience the workers passing out of the factory confines into a larger world, with many (mainly younger) faces expressing the delight of kids let out of school, crossing a threshold that marks a change in behaviour, a certain release.

The range of self-presentation immediately grabs our attention. Although many of the passersby refuse to play the game, many seize on the encounter with the camera as a chance to leave an impression. In numerous films, young boys crowd the foreground. Are they young workers, children of workers, or just boys who have happened by, attracted by the new technology? Sometimes they pass out leaflets, doubtless advertising the coming spectacle, while in M&K 409: *Employees Leaving Alexandra Dock*, and M&K 612: *Street Scenes in Halifax* (1902), a number of paperboys hawk their wares. Boys seem to delight the most in being filmed; they hang around in front of the camera, while the adults hurry through the frame, clearly having some place to go, the boys either have the time, or simply take the time, to linger. In M&K 673: *Jute Works Barrow*, one boy hops for the camera while another thumbs his nose, while in M&K 6: *Haslam's Ltd Colne*, they throw rocks or snowballs, as they parade around, and in M&K 609: *Street Scenes in Halifax* (1902), several of them play leapfrog. In M&K 64: *Storey's Moor Lane Mill, Lancaster* (1902), one boy (a worker?) even emerges holding a hand camera and snaps a photo of the off-screen movie camera, while a boy in M&K 61: *Pendlebury Spinning Co.* (1901), hoists his puppy into the camera's view. A well-dressed boy with an umbrella insists on returning again and again to the foreground in M&K 761: *Haslam's Ltd Colne* (1900), as a more roughly dressed kid takes snuff (or simply picks his nose) the film ends.[13]

Do these children recognise the motion picture camera as another newcomer to the world, young and irresponsible like themselves? Risking what sound like gender clichés, the little girls show different ways of captivating the camera than the boys, less swaggering and physical action or nasty

M&K 61: *Pendlebury Spinning Co.* (1901), filmed in July 1901 James Kenyon can be seen in the centre of the picture directing the eager crowds.

behaviour, more determined circulation in front of the camera with a charm of expression, such as the little girl in the fancy hat who keeps re-appearing in M&K 673: *Jute Works Barrow*, or the little girl in M&K 39: *Ormerod's Mill, Great Moor Street, Bolton*, who pauses in front of the camera and wraps a huge shawl about her diminutive body. M&K 612: *Street Scenes in Halifax*, demonstrates the magnetic attraction the camera exerted on these children, as they throng about the camera apparently mounted on the back of a cart and, when the vehicle bearing the camera begins to move, run along to keep pace with it.

This is not to say that adults do not display strong reactions to being filmed, including studied indifference or even opposition. In M&K 602: *Parkgate Ironworks* (1901), one young man is seen making the traditional two-fingered rude gesture to the camera. In M&K 58: *Pendlebury Colliery*, one man pointedly walks against the flow of motion – to express contempt towards the filming or to make sure he stands out from the crowd? A woman on the sidewalk in M&K 673: *Jute Works Barrow*, waves at the camera and then does a couple of dance steps. Men and women carry their babies or small children, hoisting them up to either get a better view or become more clearly seen.

One gets the impression of an unending sea of humanity continually breaking against the camera. Following the aleatory logic of many early actuality films, these films present a generally static frame through which an endless succession of characters and events seem to pass (a few pans and the camera mounted on a vehicle in M&K 612: *Street Scenes in Halifax*, provide exceptions, but still show the same principles of composition). Master film-maker Robert Bresson once described his style as consisting of 'infinite surprises within a finite frame.'[14] Understood differently, this phrase captures the wonders of these films: a firm quadrangle encloses, but cannot contain, a world of unpredictable vitality and motion. From the background, from the sides, sometimes from the foreground, the masses surge into view, barely pausing for us to get a vivid image of them before they move out of sight. The films practically demand repeat viewings, like the encores called for by the original audiences.

While these moving images remain unpredictable (one never knows where the centre of interest might appear, as our attention migrates from this face to that gesture, from this gruff old man's brusque swing of an arm to a glimpse of a face we think we could love), a degree of control also appears. In several films men appear who are directing the action. These directors are either show-men involved in the production and exhibition of the films or Mitchell and Kenyon employees who are arranging the shots for the cameraman. These figures are different from film to film reflecting the variety of showmen.

In M&K 58: *Pendlebury Colliery*, a man, who we know was Sedgwick the proprietor of a cine-matograph show, repeatedly points at the camera, apparently attempting to increase the reaction of the passing men, who thus far have shown little interest in it. After a break in filming we see the same man standing with the crowd. He starts them moving again, and points towards the camera, continuing to motion and even push folks a bit as they begin walking. Apparently even the atten-tion paid to the camera and the process of walking past it, seemingly spontaneous actions, needed coaching and direction. In M&K 61: *Pendlebury Spinning Co.*, a bearded man in a bowler hat not only wades into the crowd, waving them along, but grabs a woman by the arm as if trying to get her out of the way and then they both laugh broadly at the camera. This vivacious figure is, in fact, James Kenyon himself; his sense of ease in moving among the crowd a remarkable aspect of early showmanship.[15]

These traffic directors love the camera almost as much as the boys, often lingering and clown-ing around in a similar manner to their younger cohorts. The man who introduces M&K 336: *Poole's Clitheroe* (1901), is a showman, and the film opens with him alone in the frame repeatedly bowing and tipping his hat to the camera. Then, with a break in filming, the crowd suddenly appears, like a Méliès magic trick, as if the showman's hat trick made the masses materialise. Are both the men clowning around and engaging in mock fights in M&K 609: *Street Scenes in Halifax*, showmen, or only the mustachioed man who bobs his head into the camera?

Some figures appear more ambiguous, such as the man with hat, tie moustache and cane who repeatedly wanders back into frame with an air of authority in M&K 409: *Employees Leaving Alexandra Dock*, but rarely seems to direct any action except perhaps towards the end when he points at the camera and seems to clear space for a wagon to pass.[16] Perhaps oddest of all is the very short man (possibly a midget) in M&K 64: *Storey's Moor Lane Mill, Lancaster*, who wanders in and out several times, sometimes smoking a large cigar. He rushes up and speaks abruptly to a little girl at one point, who recoils with fright, and then appears at the end of the film as the crowd gathers near the gate as it closes. It could appear that he was simply attracted to the camera or was recognised as an attraction for the film and encouraged to walk back in.[17]

Despite these occasional overt gestures of direction and control, the frame remains filled with momentary attractions that grab our attention, then pass away beyond our reach. Even with repeated viewings we could never get it all, we will always miss something. The fact that there will always be more than we could see, understand or embrace, makes these films, for me at least, among the most exciting works in the history of film.

M&K 336: *Poole's Clitheroe* (1901), showing one of the showmen from Poole's Myriorma in Clitheroe posing for the camera.

To find in early cinema a promise that remains unfulfilled might seem a romantic gesture. But a mystery and fascination rooted in the material and everyday lies in these films that waited so long to be rediscovered. It may be an exaggeration to claim the Mitchell and Kenyon Collection as equivalent to such major archaeological discoveries as the Dead Sea Scrolls or the Nag Hammadi codices. After all, the films are in many ways similar to other early actuality films that remain lying neglected in archives. But hopefully, these films, like the recently restored 68mm films of the Mutoscope and Biograph company, will enable a broader range of viewers than archivists and specialists in early cinema to discover the fascination that the cinema exerted when it first appeared – as well as the value it has gained over the century since the films were first made – this ability to give us a glimpse of a corner of the world as it appeared on some morning, evening or afternoon when the gates were flung open and a sea of humanity rushed out to meet, and be met, by the century's newest medium.

America's first theorist of the cinema, the poet Vachel Lindsay described what he called the 'picture of Crowd Splendor' in his 1915 book, *The Art of the Moving Picture*:

> the sea of humanity is dramatically blood-brother to the Pacific, Atlantic or Mediterranean. It takes this new invention, the kinetoscope to bring us these panoramic drama elements. By the law of compensation, while the motion picture is shallow in showing private passion, it is powerful in conveying the passions of masses of men.[18]

Lindsay held utopian hopes for the cinema that, like his socialist ideals, might be seen today as naïve. For him, the two were intertwined:

> The World State is indeed far away, But as we peer into the Mirror Screen some of us dare to look forward to the time when the pouring streets of men will become sacred in each other's eyes, in pictures and in fact.[19]

Today we may look into that screen and see both forward and back, to revision the forgotten future early cinema imaged and promised. These extraordinary films allow us to do that.

NOTES

1. *The Letters of Sigmund Freud*, ed. Ernst L. Freud (New York: Basic Books, 1975), p. 51.
2. Ibid., p. 50.
3. Raymond Williams, *Keywords: A Vocabulary of Culture and Society*, (rev. edn, New York: Oxford University Press, 1985), p. 195.
4. Louis Lumière's address to the Congrès à Lyon des Sociétés de Photographie de France, 1 July 1895, quoted in Jacques and Marie André, *Une Saison Lumière à Montpellier* (Perpignan: Institut Jean Vigo, 1987), p. 64.
5. 'Effets de foule', André, *Une Saison Lumière*, p. 78.
6. Accounts of the filming of these films and their contradictions with the claims made by Louis Lumière and Doublier are covered in Bernard Chardère, *Le Roman des Lumière* (Paris: Gallimard, 1995), pp. 293–7, and in Vincent Pinel, *Louis Lumière inventeur et cinéaste* (Paris: Nathan, 1994), pp. 30–5.
7. Chardère points out that Doublier first made this claim in printed form, which he later repeated to Georges Sadoul, in the journal, *Pour le Victoire*, 3 March 1945. It is quoted in Chardère, *Le Roman des Lumière*, p. 293.
8. Chardère, *Le Roman des Lumière*, p. 297.
9. Hepworth and Co. advertisement of 1901. I am indebted to Simon Popple for supplying this information.
10. *Optical Magic Lantern Journal and Photographic Enlarger*, January 1901, vol. 12, no. 140, p. 2.
11. *The Showman*, December 1900.
12. Tom Gunning, 'The Cinema of Attractions', in Thomas Elsaesser and Adam Barker (eds), *Early Cinema: Space Frame Narrative* (London : BFI Publishing, 1990).
13. There are three titles in the Mitchell and Kenyon Collection filmed at Haslam's factory in Colne. Numbers 760 and 761 form a sequence dated to 1900/1 and Number 6, Haslam's Ltd was filmed 29 January 1900.
14. Robert Bresson, *Notes on Cinematography* (New York: Urizen Press, 1977), p. 53.
15. Many thanks to Vanessa Toulmin for supplying information relating to the identification of James Kenyon.
16. Information supplied by the Mitchell and Kenyon Project staff confirms that he was a showman and appears in M&K 812: *St George's Day Procession Massed Bands and Procession* (1901), overseeing the camera's sightline.
17. Information supplied by the Mitchell and Kenyon Project Staff at the University of Sheffield and the *bfi*, reveals that a further film in the Collection, M&K 670: *His Worship the Mayor Leaving the Town Hall* (1902), features the short man as a showman in his own right.
18. Vachel Lindsay, *The Art of the Moving Picture*, in *The Prose of Vachel Lindsay*, Volume I, ed. Denis Camp (Peoria, IL: Spoon River Poetry Press), p. 230.
19. Ibid., p. 234.

6 'We take them and make them': Mitchell and Kenyon and the Travelling Exhibition Showmen

Vanessa Toulmin

If you run a CINEMATOGRAPH SHOW
See our FILMS – Specially designed for Showmen
If you value your films, and want to give a perfect Show quickly and well, see our New Machine
for 1900. And if you want Attractions in the way of Special or Local Pictures consult us.
WE TAKE THEM AND MAKE THEM.[1]

One of the most neglected and forgotten components of the early film industry is that of the itinerant exhibitor and the part he played in the dissemination of the new medium of cinema. Although the role of the travelling showmen in the exhibition of early film has been examined by myself and others in the field in the past decade, particular emphasis has been devoted to the evolution of the cinematograph show and its importance as a performance venue.[2] The rise of the itinerant cinematograph exhibitor in Edwardian Britain is an area where further research is necessary. Pioneering research by Ivo Blom on the life and career of Desmet in the Netherlands, work on travelling film exhibitors in Italy[3] and Charles Musser's study of Lyman Howe are excellent examples of research in Europe and America.[4] Tony Fletcher's important publication on exhibition practices in London in the late Victorian period and Jon Burrows work on the penny showmen are two examples where the world of the itinerant exhibitor has been studied.[5]

The restoration of the Mitchell and Kenyon Collection by the *bfi* and the associated AHRB-funded research project with the National Fairground Archive finally brings together the world of the professional showman/exhibitor with the business practices of the film-makers in the regions outside the south east and London in the late Victorian, Edwardian period. For the first time in the United Kingdom a body of films can be researched in the context of local exhibition, demonstrating direct links between those who commissioned the films, the audiences and the development of the programme. Building on Alfred Bromhead's classic definition in 1933 of three main types of exhibitors in the early British film business: the music hall, the fairground and the town or public hall showmen,[6] Deac Rossell categorises travelling exhibitors into four main groups: fairground showmen who turned to moving pictures from already existing fairground shows; independent travelling showmen who presented short-term movie shows in public venues and rented spaces; the theatrical exhibitor, who used an agent to present a variety of music hall bookings in fixed theatrical venues; and finally the eager amateur or outsider with little experience of the entertainment industry. Rossell writes:

> For the most part, travelling exhibition has been treated by historians as a romantic interlude in the story of exhibition, a kind of sideshow on the way to real exhibition in the movie palaces built after the First World War.[7]

The exhibition showmen presented films in a variety of venues and to some extent the programme of material on display was dictated by the venue and the audience. As John A. Prestwich writes in *The Showman* in 1901, 'the film subjects are a matter of choice for the exhibitor himself and must depend on the class of exhibition.'[8] A film programme could consist of fifteen minutes on a fairground cinematograph show, a ten-minute presentation within a music hall setting or a two-hour, stand-alone cinema show in a town or civic hall. In 1900 for example, the largest percentage of Mitchell and Kenyon's customers were those associated with the fairground in particular the north-west based operators such as Sedgwick, George Green and Captain Thomas Payne. The films commissioned were largely of the factory gate variety and were filmed or purchased specifically for the purpose of showing the audience on the screen.[9] However, the stand-alone showmen, with their two-hour film programme, utilised the local film as a drawing card to maintain the audience on a daily or weekly basis and presented a set of material comprising fiction and non-fiction, with a daily change of actualities in the middle of the programme.[10] They arranged for Mitchell and Kenyon or their own film crew to film specific events in the locality, advertising widely and lavishly. They often paraded through the town in the days before the exhibition opened with a film crew to shoot local scenes or people on their way to a football match.[11] Music hall proprietors would use the cinematograph on a regular basis, occupying one part of the music hall programme with prominence depending on the nature of the material and the drawing power of the subject matter. For example, in February 1900, Thomas-Edison Animated Photos is just one of ten acts on at the Argyle Theatre of Varieties in Birkenhead, where they are showing a series of interesting and military pictures.[12]

Part of a surviving fragment from an Thomas-Edison show in Halifax advertising Halifax v Salford Northern Union Football in March 1901.

However, the arrival of Lord Buller warrants a different approach and the subsequent films are given prominent billing on the poster and within the programme.[13]

Over thirty-eight individual companies or exhibitors have been identified with the Collection and they represent all types of travelling cinematograph companies and shows active in the Edwardian period with the exception of the eager amateur, the last of Rossell's categories.[14] This article will present a case study of the three types of commissions received by Mitchell and Kenyon: films solely or principally for the fairground; stand-alone or town hall showmen exhibiting in civic or other centres; exhibition which used principally film and material commissioned by an independent proprietor as part of a variety bill in a music hall. These categories have proved useful when examining exhibition practices through the Mitchell and Kenyon Project and are recognised as providing a basis for preliminary analysis. The categories do not take account of whether the commissioners may have been doing their own filming and using Mitchell and Kenyon's technical services to develop and print the material.[15]

FAIRGROUND SHOWMEN

Mitchell and Kenyon's association with travelling fairground showmen may have started through James Kenyon's penny-in-the-slot machine business, which he still advertised in *The Showman's Year Book* until 1902.[16] A number of fairground showmen are associated with the Collection, including G. T. Tuby from Doncaster, Colonel Clark and Professor Wall.

The best-known of these connected with Mitchell and Kenyon is George Green who became one of the most successful cinema proprietors before World War I. Other striking films connected with the fairground cinema shows include M&K 181–2: *Opening of Accrington Electric Trams* (1907) with wonderful footage of the manager for Relph and Pedley positioning himself in front of the camera with his advertising board on five occasions. However, the films that demonstrate showmanship and reveal the close working relationship between Mitchell and Kenyon and the fairground fraternity are those commissioned by Sedgwick.

James Sedgwick was a member of a fairground family which had success for many years with a travelling menagerie. He had a travelling ghost show, turning to film exhibition from 1900. There is a remarkable series of three films which represent without doubt the most accurate record of how a fairground showman would have used the product offered by Mitchell and Kenyon. M&K 58: *Pendlebury Colliery*, (1901), M&K 61: *Pendlebury Spinning Co.*, (1901) and M&K 772: *Sedgwick's Bioscope Showfront and Stage Show* (1901), are three separate reels shot for Pendlebury Wakes held in Manchester August 1901. They comprise an exit from the pit-head at Pendlebury Colliery where Sedgwick himself is seen directing the movements of the workers; a classic factory gate exit from the Pendlebury Spinning Company where James Kenyon is observed interacting with the crowds of mill workers and displaying obvious familiarity. Similarly the last film (numerically at least) in the series takes place on the front of the bioscope show itself and features both Sedgwick and Kenyon working together both controlling and animating the unfolding scene which was clearly carefully planned and executed to a tight schedule. The showman and the film-maker are in this instance working in parallel. The three films together give us the first real glimpse of how individual reels may have been strung together on a bioscope show to make the most of a potential audience. M&K 772: *Sedgwick's Bioscope Showfront and Stage Show*, in particular, was probably filmed immediately prior to the opening of the fair and may record one of the shows which many successful showmen ran for free for poor children or as a ruse to overcome limitations on showing films on Sundays. In this context it is noted that Sedwick advertises the passion play in M&K 58: *Pendlebury Colliery*. The workers from a given area, the showmen themselves, the showfront and happy

M&K 772: *Sedgwick's Bioscope Showfront and Stage Show* (1901) with James Kenyon of Mitchell and Kenyon standing to the left of the poster advertising Sedgwick's Exhibition at Pendlebury Wakes.

crowds form a complex programme which was repeated upwards of fifteen to twenty times a day. Mitchell and Kenyon had clearly formed a productive and reciprocal relationship with the bioscope showmen which was to provide the basis for much of their future success.

MUSIC HALL PROPRIETOR

Thomas Barrasford was born in Newcastle and became associated with film exhibition through his ownership and management of a string of music halls in the early 1900s. Unlike his contemporary, Signor Rino Pepi who performed as protean fabulum or 'Italy's Greatest Quick change Artist' and who also commissioned Mitchell and Kenyon to make films,[17] Barrasford was not formally connected to the entertainment world in any other capacity than as manager and proprietor. In 1895 Barrasford, in partnership with a man named Varah, took over a wooden circus building on the Ormond Street pit-heap in Jarrow and turned it into a music hall called the Jarrow Palace of Varieties. In 1899 he expanded his operations and purchased the ailing Leeds Tivoli Music Hall and transformed it into a 'little gold-mine' by presenting twice-nightly performances. He began presenting film shows in the music hall in 1900 and is credited with patenting the 'Barrascope' with Leeds cinematographer Owen Brooks, who, with assistance from engineer Borland, put the machine on the market.[18]

His involvement with Mitchell and Kenyon dates from 1902 when he used their services to prepare films of Leeds Athletic and Cycling Club[19] and the Leeds Lifeboat Procession together with the ensuing water sports at Roundhay Park.[20] These were advertised as showing on the 'Viagraph'.[21]

Barrasford clearly found the arrangement with Mitchell and Kenyon to his satisfaction. Why he chose to use their services is not clear as we have seen he is credited with having his own 'Barrascope'. It may have been the pressure on local cinematographers due to the large number of films made of the lifeboat procession which encouraged Barrasford to turn to Mitchell and Kenyon. In 1903 he again used Mitchell and Kenyon's services to film the opening of the new electric trams from Lytham.[22] These were shown at the Alhambra[23] along with films of the North Pier Steamships.[24] As an example of the importance of the interrelationships between the various film exhibitors it is noted that Barrasford advertised in the weeks preceding the showing of the Lytham tram and North Pier films that films were shown by 'Vernon's Imperial Bioscope'[25] who are also connected with Mitchell and Kenyon films through their appearance in association with a 1902 A. D. Thomas show at Lancaster.[26]

In the Mitchell and Kenyon film *Mr Moon* (1901), the Variety stage provided the context for an individual showman to display his particular skills. In some ways this film, despite being fictional and clearly narrative, is related to the broader Collection of non-fiction films in the sense that it was brought about by the initiative of a showman himself. Perci Honri, a music hall performer wrote the scenario himself [27] and Mitchell and Kenyon produced the film which was projected onto a screen set up behind Honri as he performed his famous song 'Oh! Mr Moon'. While not wishing to dwell on an aspect of the Mitchell and Kenyon Collection already well known, it is valuable to note that this is a further example of showmanship leading the company in a particular direction.[28]

STAND-ALONE SHOWMEN

The major commissioners of the films outside the travelling fairground fraternity presented films under the banner of the Thomas-Edison Animated Photo Co., Ralph Pringle's North American Animated Photo Company, Tweedale's Bio-Motograph or Edison and Tweedale, and Sydney Carter with his New Century Pictures operation.[29] However, the career of Ralph Pringle is particular interesting due to his involvement with Moss, Stoll and Thornton, the music hall proprietors and his relationship with Mitchell and Kenyon.

Unlike his one-time associate A. D. Thomas, Ralph Pringle was largely forgotten both by his contemporaries in the early film trade and by later historians. He is chiefly remembered on a more local level for his successful cinemas in Scotland, Huddersfield and Bristol for example, rather than for his contribution to cinema exhibition.[30] Ralph Pringle was the proprietor of the North American Animated Photo Company, a travelling exhibition company which from early 1901 presented film shows in town halls and theatres throughout the United Kingdom.[31] Pringle's involvement with Mitchell and Kenyon was not only extensive but lasted longer than any of his contemporaries. Between 1901 and 1907 he commissioned a range of non-fiction films of local scenes that were shown whenever possible the same evening.[32] Of the 800 films in the Mitchell and Kenyon Collection, approximately 170 titles were commissioned by Pringle, making his associated material the largest related to one individual company within the Collection.[33] The company presented film shows throughout the United Kingdom and Ireland including, Belfast, Liverpool, Edinburgh, Newcastle, Sunderland, Leeds, Northampton, Bristol, Rotherham, Sheffield and Chester. Pringle originally acted as a lecturer/manager for A. D. Thomas of the Thomas-Edison Animated Photo Co. and presented shows in Huddersfield in November and Newcastle in December 1900.[34] By March 1901, he became involved with the North American Animated Photo Company as the show is advertised in Newcastle as solely under the direction and management of Mr Ralph Pringle.[35]

Pringle became associated with Mitchell and Kenyon when working with A. D. Thomas in Huddersfield in October 1900. He is seen in M&K 28: *Messrs Lumb and Co Leaving the Works*

Scene of one of the numerous sporting occasions commissioned by Ralph Pringle shown at the Circus Hull during the successful 1902 season. M&K 660: *Hull F.C. v. Hull Kingston Rovers* (1902).

(1900), directing the movement of the crowds of workers as they come down the hill and over the bridge. In the review of the showing of the film we hear that 'Mr Pringle shared the duty of making references to the pictures'.[36] His competence in the organisation of the filming is clear and he next appears in December 1900 as the manager of the Thomas-Edison show in Newcastle,[37] commissioning titles from them directly but on behalf of A. D. Thomas's company.[38] In January 1901, the North American Animated Photo Company makes an appearance at the Corn Exchange, Doncaster where the show was managed by Mr Henry N. Phillips.[39] As we know, Pringle was the director of the North American Animated Photo Company and interestingly his manager here is the same individual who later manages shows for both A. D. Thomas and Walter Gibbons Royal Animated Photo Company.[40] The complexities of Edwardian showmanship are hinted at in details like this, but it is clear that Pringle was heavily involved in a complex series of professional relationships some of which are not clearly documented. A further example of this is to be found in Pringle's advert for the North American Animated Photo Company's show in Chester and Bolton in January 1901, where the adverts lead with the same text used by A. D. Thomas : 'WAR IN CHESTER/BOLTON'.[41] From 1901, he extended his touring operations to Edinburgh, Glasgow, Sunderland, Newcastle, Bristol, Huddersfield, Liverpool, Birmingham and Dublin. The relationship between Pringle and Mitchell and Kenyon is demonstrated by the account in *The Showman* of the filming of the arrival of the Liverpool Volunteers in May 1901, by Mitchell and Kenyon:

A record in photography or rather cinematography was achieved by Messrs Mitchell and Kenyon of Blackburn, on Saturday last, on the occasion of the homecoming of the Liverpool Volunteers. An animated picture of the arrival of the troops was taken by Messrs Mitchell and Kenyon a few minutes before 6 o'clock p.m. and was developed and ready for exhibition between 9 and 10 o'clock the same evening. It was shown to a crowded audience at Hengler's Circus by the North American Animated Photo Co.[42]

Pringle would hire Mitchell and Kenyon to film a series of local views or scenes pertaining to the town where he was exhibiting. This kind of business arrangement is revealed in the memo to New Century Pictures from Mitchell and Kenyon, in which they discuss the costs for a day's filming of local subjects.[43]

The Pringle films reveal another aspect of the showman's/or exhibitor's relationship to the work of Mitchell and Kenyon. There is a large preponderance of football and rugby films in the material attributed to Pringle and this was a distinctive feature of his commissioning. Pringle's Hull films from the 1902 season at the Circus, show the activities of one of Pringle's collaborators directing the players onto the pitch.[44] The same season sees Pringle involved in a local battle for audiences with Sheffield's Jasper Redfern, where both exhibitors shot and displayed a similar series of films recounting the homecoming of the Boer War veteran, Clive Wilson.[45] Pringle is typical of the stand-alone showman in that he used the material commissioned from Mitchell and Kenyon to construct a film programme that was built around the advertisement and promotion of local scenes. As mentioned above, his relationship with Mitchell and Kenyon is one the longest lasting (with the possible exception of George Green) with M&K 118–19, 142, 147: *Sunderland v Leicester Fosse* filmed in January 1907.[46]

CONCLUSIONS

One of the immediate repercussions of the initial Mitchell and Kenyon Project is the indication not only of the variety of exhibitors, but their profound interrelationship. The Collection confirms that the film exhibitor drew on a vocabulary derived from previous entertainments but that they not only shared a common language of spectacle but also personnel. The geographical breadth of the Collection is a result not only of the successful business practices of Mitchell and Kenyon but of the network of connections between the showmen. Initially built on the itineraries of the fairground bioscopes, this web of contacts spread to include the burgeoning practices of the stand-alone/town hall showman. Independent film exhibitors such as Vernon's grew out of these networks establishing their own circuits as a result and variety proprietors such as Barrasford had access to Mitchell and Kenyon's expertise as a direct result of the wide dissemination of their products. Bromhead's categories have proven relevance for the study of film exhibition but the complexity of the relationships in the Collection make it vital not to ignore the individual, the exception. The current interest in non-fiction film should not be limited to attempts to categorise but acknowledge that local films were made for local purposes as well as being part of national and regional complexes of exhibition.

This is only a brief introduction to the showmen in the Mitchell and Kenyon Collection and several of the other essays in this volume deal with aspects of showmanship as the two are unavoidably intertwined. The showmen led Mitchell and Kenyon literally in particular directions and provided them with the web of connections which were to give them growing success throughout the early years of the 1900s. Subsequent developments in film exhibition, culminating in the classic trajectory of the early cinemas, were profoundly influenced by the dynamics of the showmen's circuits and the Mitchell and Kenyon Collection not only helps reinstate the importance of non-fiction film but emphasises above all the influence of the exhibitors.

As John Bird wrote in *Cinema Parade*:

Hundreds of those early picture shows excited crowds on fairground, in empty shop, in town hall, temperance room and music hall. And when the cinema came, the manager was often a blend of the fairground showman, the travelling theatre proprietor and the panorama lecturer.[47]

NOTES

1. Advert for Mitchell and Kenyon, *The Showman's Year Book*, edited by Reverend Thomas Horne (Manchester: UKSVDPA, 1900).
2. Nicholas Hiley '"At the Picture Palace": The British Cinema Audience, 1895–1920', in John Fullerton (ed.), *Celebrating 1895: The Centenary of Cinema* (London: John Libbey, 1998), pp. 96–106 and 'Early Cinema Audiences', *Iris: A Journal of Theory on Image and Sound*, no. 11 (Summer 1990). Vanessa Toulmin, 'Telling the Tale: The History of the Fairground Bioscope Shows and the Showmen Who Operated Them', *Film History*, vol. 6, no. 2 (Summer 1994), pp. 219–37 and Mervyn Heard, '"Come in please, Come out Pleased": The Development of British Fairground Bioscope Presentation and Performance', in Linda Fitzsimmons and Sarah Street (eds), *Moving Performance: British Stage and Screen, 1890s–1920s* (Trowbridge: Flicks Books, 2000), pp. 101–11.
3. Aldo Bernardini, *Cinema italiano delle origini: gli ambulanti* (Urdine: Cineteca del Friuli, 2001).
4. Ivo Blom, *Jean Desmet and the Early Dutch Film* (Amsterdam: Amsterdam University Press, 2003); Charles Musser and Carol Nelson, *High-Class Moving Pictures: Lyman H. Howe and the Forgotten Era of Traveling Exhibition, 188–1920* (Princeton, NJ: University of Princeton Press, 1991).
5. Tony Fletcher, 'The London County Council and the Cinematograph, 1896–1900', *Living Pictures: The Journal of the Popular and Projected Image before 1914*, vol. 1, no. 2 (2001), pp. 69–83. See Jon Burrows Penny Pleasures: Film Exhibition in London during the Nickelodeon Era, 1906–1914', *Film History*, vol. 16, no. 1 (2004), pp. 60–91.
6. *Proceedings of the British Cinematography Society*, no. 21 (1933), p. 4.
7. Deac Rossell, 'A Slippery Job: Travelling Exhibitors in Early Cinema', in Simon Popple and Vanessa Toulmin (eds), *Visual Delights. Essays. On the Popular and Projected Image in the 19th Century* (Trowbridge: Flicks Books, 2000), pp. 50–60 (51).
8. John A. Prestwich, 'How to Give a Good Cinematograph Show', *The Showman*, 6 September 1901, p. 571.
9. For a breakdown of the ratio of exhibitor types to material commissioned within the Mitchell and Kenyon Collection, see Vanessa Toulmin, Patrick Russell and Tim Neal, 'The Mitchell and Kenyon Collection: Rewriting Film History', *The Moving Image: The Journal of the Association of Moving Image Archivists*, vol. 3, no. 2 (Fall 2003), pp. 1–18.
10. For further information on a stand-alone film programme of this type see Vanessa Toulmin, 'The Importance of the Programme in Early Film Presentation', *KINtop*, vol. 11 (2002), pp. 19–33.
11. Numerous examples of this kind of advertising or product placement can be found in the Collection, for example see M&K 527: *West Bromich – Comic Pictures in the High Street* (1902), where Tweedale's advertising boards can clearly be seen on the horse and cart advertising and M&K 184: *Tram Ride through Halifax* (1902), where Tweedale prominently displays a hoarding board announcing that films will be taken today and shown in the Victoria Hall on Monday.
12. Poster for the Argyle Theatre of Varieties, Birkenhead, Monday 5 February 1900, National Fairground Archive Poster Collection. The cinematograph was competing against the McConnell Family, the Lancashire Quartette and the Three Albions Comedy Musical Act, among others.

13. Poster for the Argyle Theatre of Varieties, Birkenhead, Monday 19 November 1900, National Fairground Archive Poster Collection. Films of return to England of General Buller and the CIV produced by the Royal Bioscope share top billing with the Brothers Luck.

14. See Rossell, 'A Slippery Job'.

15. This is certainly true in the case of A. D. Thomas in Ireland. A memo in the notebook of Louis De Clercq notes 'Tram Fair (sic) to Kingstown 7d. – Film from M. & K. 4d'. Kingstown was the port just outside Dublin where the mail boat from Holyhead docked and the note implies that Mitchell and Kenyon were developing and printing films for Thomas-Edison that De Clercq was shooting.

16. Advertisements for Kenyon's penny-in-the-slot business and Automatic Machines appeared in *The Showman's Year Book*, 1900, 1901 and 1902 where it states that 'the well-known Kenyon's penny-in-the-slot business will from 1 January 1902 be carried out by us and exhibition proprietors may look out for some new money-making ideas. Mitchell and Kenyon.'

17. See: M&K 225–7: *Royal Visit to Barrow and Launch of HMS Dominion* (1903).

18. For information on Barrasford, see G. J Mellors, The *Northern Music Halls* (Newcastle upon Tyne: Frank Graham, 1970) and for information on Tom Barrasford's music halls, see http://pages.britishlibrary.net/mikepymm/barrasfo.htm

19. See M&K 550–3: *Leeds Athletic and Cycling Club* (1902).

20. See M&K 558–62, 564, 808: *Leeds Lifeboat Procession and Sports at Roundhay on the Viagraph* (1902).

21. *Yorkshire Evening Post*, 10 July 1902, 'Viagraph: Lifeboat Procession etc.', p. 1.

22. M&K 185, 195–9: *Lytham Trams and the Views along the Route* (1903).

23. *Blackpool Herald*, 12 June 1903.

24. M&K 204–9: *Blackpool North Pier* (1903).

25. *Gazette & News For Blackpool, Fleetwood, Lytham, St Annes, and Flyde District*, 26 May 1903.

26. *Lancaster Guardian*, 12 April 1902, p. 1, advert for the Palace of Varieties with the Edison-Vernon animated pictures. Note that a similar show also appears at Carlisle, see *Carlisle Journal*, 20 December 1901, p. 4. Advert for Algies Circus with 'Vernon's Imperial Bioscope – First time' and later, *Carlisle Journal*, 18 February 1902, p. 2, advert for Algies Circus including Edison-Vernon's Bioscope.

27. See article in *Lancashire Evening Telegraph*, 16 December 1976. Report of the finding of the script for the Mr Moon film by Percy Honri.

28. A hitherto unseen version of this film has been identified in the Collection: M&K 780: *Mr Moon* (1901). For details of the showing of the film, see *The Era*, 14 December 1901, p. 35.

29. For further information on these travelling film exhibitors, see Geoff Mellor, *Movie Makers and Picture Palaces* (Bradford: Bradford Libraries, 1996). For additional information relating to A. D. Thomas, see Toulmin, 'The Importance of the Programme', pp. 19–34.

30. For details of Pringle's cinemas in Huddersfield, Bristol and Scotland, see Bruce Peter, *100 Years of Glasgow's Amazing Cinemas* (Edinburgh: Polygon, 1990). For details of Pringle's other cinemas in Edinburgh and Huddersfield, see Brendon Thomas, *The Last Picture Shows: Edinburgh. Ninety Years of Cinema Entertainment in Scotland's Capital City* (Edinburgh: Moorfoot Publishing, 1984) and Stanley Chadwick, *The Mighty Screen: The Rise of the Cinema in Huddersfield* (Huddersfield: Venture Press, 1953) and Charles Anderson, *A City and Its Cinemas* (Bristol: Redcliffe, 1983).

31. For information on Ralph Pringle, see Vanessa Toulmin, 'An Early Crime Film Rediscovered: Mitchell and Kenyon's *Arrest of Goudie* (1901)', *Film History*, vol. 16, no. 1 (2004), pp. 37–53.

32. For details of Mitchell and Kenyon's relationship with the travelling film exhibitors, see Vanessa Toulmin, '"Local Films for Local People": Travelling Showmen and the Commissioning of Local Films in Great Britain, 1900–1902', *Film History*, vol. 13, no. 2 (2001), pp. 118–37.

33. Toulmin, '"Local Films for Local People"'.

34. Pringle appears to have worked for Thomas on many occasions during the 1900 season. For two examples of the shows, see *Huddersfield Examiner*, 3 November 1900 and *Newcastle upon Tyne Evening Chronicle*, 3 December 1900, p. 1.

35. *Newcastle upon Tyne Evening Chronicle*, 4 March 1901, p. 1.

36. *Huddersfield Examiner*, 3 November 1900, p. 5.

37. *Newcastle upon Tyne Evening Chronicle*, 3 December 1900, p. 1

38. M&K 35: *20,000 Employees Entering Lord Armstrong's Elswick Works* (1900).

39. *Doncaster Chronicle*, 18 January 1901, p. 1.

40. For example, *Derby Daily Telegraph*, 7 January 1900, p. 1: 'DRILL HALL, DERBY. EDISON'S ANIMATED PICTURES OF THE CHINA AND BOER WARS. ... Manager: Mr Henry N. Phillips.' *Bristol Times and Mirror*, 27 May 1901, p. 1: 'VICTORIA ROOMS, CLIFTON. ... ROYAL ANIMATED PICTURE CO. AND GIBBONS' PHONO-BIO-TABLEAU ... Manager – Mr H. N. Phillips.'

41. *Chester Chronicle*, 19 January 1901, p. 1 col. 1. *Bolton Chronicle*, 26 January 1901, p. 1.

42. *The Showman*, 24 May 1901, p. 328.

43. Memo from Mitchell and Kenyon to Sydney Carter, February 1902, Sydney Carter Collection, West Yorkshire Archives Service.

44. M&K 131: *Pringle Football* (nd).

45. *Hull Daily Mail*, 7 April 1902. For Report of Clive Wilson's return from the war to Hull: 'During the proceedings, Mr Jasper Redfern and the NAAPCo secured some excellent cinematographic pictures, and they will be reproduced at the Assembly Rooms and the Circus during the week.'

46. *Sunderland Daily Echo*, 12 January 1907, p. 1.

47. John H. Bird, *Cinema Parade: Fifty Years of Film Shows* (Birmingham: Cornish Brothers Limited, 1947), pp. 21–2.

7 New Century Pictures: Regional Enterprise in Early British Film Exhibition

Richard Brown

Our first cinema show was in '96; the first full programme of nothing but animated pictures was in 1901, and soon after that we had frequently audiences of 2,000 to 3,000 in Bradford, Leeds, Hull, Halifax, Manchester and other places, whereas one often reads that the industry was started in this country years later in shops or small places seating about 200 people. Andin those days we had good programmes, good prices, (2s, 1s and 6d); we advertised well and generally had a band of twelve or fifteen.

Sydney Carter, 1916.[1]

In what has now become a classic definition, Alfred Bromhead, general manager and later managing director of the British Gaumont Company from 1898 to 1928, noted that there were three main types of exhibitors in the early British film business. These were the music hall, the fairground and the town or public hall showmen.[2] Of these three main categories, (there were several minor ones not mentioned by Bromhead), it is the public hall showman who is currently by far the least researched and least well understood. By 1900, two-hour, stand-alone public hall film shows, complete with live acts, singers, orchestra, sound effects, a 'lecturer' and specially taken 'local' films were being presented in the cities and towns of the north of England. Indeed, it is the regional location of companies such as New Century Pictures and Mitchell and Kenyon which is an important factor in encouraging a new and less metropolitan focus in the current re-assessment of early British film history.

Public hall shows have not received sufficient attention from film historians in the past, but it must be admitted that they represented a film exhibition 'dead-end'. They did not foreshadow later practice, and virtually no aspect of their 'individualised' form of presentation was carried into the later homogenised permanent cinema operation. Because they could not be neatly categorised as an early manifestation of what later became standard operational practice, they were isolated in a historical context. public hall shows were, in fact, an advanced form of early cinema which was incapable of further development, and whose basic economics were antipathic to later investors and unsuitable for incorporation into the pattern of the 'industrialisation' of film exhibition considered as a marketing process.

COMMERCIAL ASPECTS OF EARLY BRITISH FILM EXHIBITION

Music hall, fairground and public hall exhibitions were quite different in terms of their economic characteristics. There was for example, a firm correlation between seating capacity and the frequency of shows, and hence the profit potential available to each class of exhibitor. The smaller the size of the auditorium, the shorter the programme had to be in order that multiple showings could ensure viability. This was the reason for the adoption of a 'continuous-performance' schedule by both

An enterprising form of advertising the filming in process for Waller Jeffs New Century Picture show at the Curzon Hall in Birmingham on 15 July 1902. M&K 513: *The Champion Athletes at Birmingham* (1902).

fairground and later, permanent cinemas.[3] There was then the difficult question of customer perception of the exhibition and its relative value. Both music halls and fairgrounds presented films as only one part, and often a very small part, of a series of attractions available. In a music hall one higher price was charged for admission to the whole programme. On a fairground the total cost of a visit was an accumulation of many individually smaller amounts paid separately to gain access to separate attractions. The music hall therefore promoted one integrated entertainment experience which included a film performance, while the fairground stressed the diversity of entertainment available. Fairground exhibition presented film as a separate entertainment, and thus differentiated it both physically and thematically from an integrated programme. Consequently, viewing experience was closely linked to venue, and individually distinct.

For film exhibitors the risk/reward ratio differed substantially in each case. The fairground film exhibitor had an initial capital outlay for his showfront and tent, but thereafter virtually no fixed costs; only variable ones. The music hall exhibitor avoided both fixed and variable costs since both the building he used and the staff he required were provided for him; but his profit potential was severely reduced since he was paid a previously negotiated flat rate fee. His position, as just one attraction out of many, resulted in a loss of negotiating power and however successful, he was unlikely to be able to obtain sharing terms from the hall. The public hall film showman was faced with yet another set of conditions. In sociological terms, he was a 'hunter–gatherer' descending on an area, usually for six to eight weeks, exploiting its resources intensively for this period and then moving on to fresh territory. Halls where the show had been well received could be revisited, and other locations avoided. This made it possible for the public hall showman to identify business potential while reducing speculative risk and giving minimal commitment. If the public hall showman opted for, or could only obtain, a small hall, his money-taking capacity was restricted, but his rent for the hall and his variable costs would only be modest. However, if he chose a large hall the rent went up, but potential profit was increased enormously, providing that he could fill the hall. To gain such a mass audience required mass advertising and in a large urban area, this could not be achieved by word of mouth. This was why, as New Century's general manager later noted, 'advertising was on a big scale, as much as 5,000 sheets of posting being put out before the opening day'.[4] Similarly Cecil Hepworth noted of the leading public hall showman A. D. Thomas, that 'He plastered the whole town wherever he went, and he went nearly everywhere, with tremendous posters in brilliant colours describing his wonderful shows and his still more wonderful self'.[5] Because of the size of public halls, elaborate presentations could be mounted and sufficient profits obtained from one evening show in a small town; or a matinee and an evening performance in a large one, usually held at 2pm and 8pm.

But suitable large halls were in very short supply – one of Sydney Carter's main advantages was that he had immediate and uncontrolled access to one at all times. Consequently public hall showmen resorted to extraordinary lengths to attempt to 'freeze-out' the opposition.

> There was great rivalry between the various proprietors to get hold of the best halls in the country, one man going so far as to wire a substantial deposit to almost every town to secure their first vacant dates.[6]

In these circumstances it is not surprising that obtaining an unopposed run once a hall had been located was regarded as of vital importance. A printed letter circulated by the West Country public hall exhibitor Albany Ward (1879–1961) asks the owners of halls for a detailed list of marketing information, and ends with stating: 'If I book with you, it must be on the distinct understanding that no similar show is booked in before me.'[7] When the 'Thomas-Edison Animated Photo Co.' hired the Ancient Concert Rooms in Dublin for a seven-week run in August–September 1901, one of the clauses in the agreement specifically noted that; 'no other animated picture company is to be allowed to show previous to the fulfilment of this agreement.' A contravention of this condition by the hall led to a court case which the hall lost.[8] 'Locking-up' a hall was not simply selfish – it had the benefit of avoiding a potentially ruinous conflict

Letterhead for Thomas-Edison Animated Photo Co. (National Fairground Archive).

between rival exhibitors, which ultimately would have damaged the film exhibition business as a whole. A self-regulatory input into a new market was beneficial to its long-term prospects. Information on the cost of hiring public halls at this period is sparse, and can only be relied on when the details emerged as the result of a legal dispute. The New Brighton Tower Company, a very large leisure centre near Liverpool, asked the Veriscope company for a deposit of £125 and £100 a week for a thirteen-week run of the great *Corbett v Fitzsimmons* prize fight film in 1898.[9] At the other extreme, the Ancient Concert Rooms in Dublin only wanted £100 for a seven-week booking in 1901, despite this being the school holiday period.[10] Many public hall film show arrangements probably involved sharing terms, especially when the showman was already known to the hall manager. It was an arrangement which benefited both parties. The exhibitor's initial outlay was reduced, and the hall was likely to receive more than it would have done from a flat rate fee. Most importantly, sharing terms encouraged both parties to work together, for both would share increased rewards if the show was a success.

It is nonetheless clear that hall costs varied widely according to the size and importance of the venue. Significantly, hall rent does not appear to have been reduced over the period of the rental. Thus the cost/profit ratio would inevitably become less favourable over time, and it is very probably this equation, rather than any lack of 'faith' in the commercial potential of early film, that was a key factor in limiting the length of run recorded for public hall shows at this period.

NEW CENTURY'S MANAGERS AND SHOWMEN

Sydney Carter had been intended from an early age to be his father's successor as manager and lessee of St George's Hall, Bradford and, 'in a great school of experience … passed through every grade from bill distributing and programme selling to playing a more or less important part on the stage'.[11] But for Sydney Carter, even more than for his father, the growing professionalism of leisure management at the turn of the century demanded organising ability to a greater extent than entrepreneurship. Unlike the various showmen who used the hall and exploited a cult of personality, Carter remained in the background, facilitating and controlling, but not overwhelming – a business-like and impersonal style of management very similar to that pioneered by major figures such as Oswald Stoll or Edward Moss.[12] Occasional film shows had been given at the hall in the 1890s and Sydney Carter later recalled that he had, on his own initiative, booked the 'American Biograph' in October 1899 at £30 per week, a considerable sum for a film performance at that date, but that although both the programme and the picture quality were excellent, business was poor.[13] Not until the appearance of the master showman A. D. Thomas, was he able to claim that film show takings now exceeded those of the opera company, despite the much higher seat prices charged for the opera.

Arthur Duncan Thomas (aka Arthur Dewdney) or 'Edison-Thomas' as he sometimes billed himself, was an erratic and unreliable personality with an unfortunate habit of leaving town before paying his bills. But he was also a film exhibitor of considerable experience, recognised as such by his contemporaries. His important catalytic effect on other public hall film exhibitors and their style of presentation has been noted in a recent study of Thomas's Manchester shows of 1900–1.[14] There can be no doubt that it was Thomas's presentational style that Sydney Carter adopted for the New Century operation, and retained after Thomas had ceased to be connected with the show. Thomas's flamboyant public persona resembled that associated with some Victorian music hall entrepreneurs, and was no doubt based to a great degree on their approach. Their image was that of the big man with the big heart doing things in a big way, representing himself as both larger than life and as humanity itself.[15]

The Scottish film pioneer, James Joseph Bennell, who worked for both Thomas and for New Century Pictures had this to say about him:

> He was a man of wonderful ability, energy and resource … His plan was to take the largest hall in a city or town, bill and boom the show very extensively, and give away great numbers of passes, entitling the holder to admission for one penny. He also engaged popular local bands for parading the streets, and for playing in the hall. He often succeeded in filling his halls to their utmost capacity, and at times he had twenty or thirty shows running at the same time.
>
> Sometimes they were a huge success, and he made big profits, at other times there were severe losses, and as he was anything but a skilful manager of finance, difficulties frequently arose. While in prosperous times he had abundance of money, in lean times he was penniless, and writs sometimes fell like leaves in Vallambrosia. Financial difficulties were often responsible for preventing him from keeping engagements to appear at certain halls on a given date.[16]

Although his fortunes were declining throughout 1901, Thomas was still very active in film exhibition, and gave a show at St George's Hall in March of that year. This must have favourably impressed Sydney Carter for in August, Thomas signed an agreement to present several further short seasons, with bookings extended to Easter 1902, including a show on Christmas Day. This contract, preserved in the Carter papers, gives a unique, hitherto unavailable, insight into the minutiae of mounting an early public hall film show in Britain.

> Memorandum of Agreement made this sixteenth day of August 1901 between S. H. Carter of St George's Hall, Bradford of the one part & A. D. Thomas of the Thomas Edison Animated Photo Co of the other part. Whereas the said S. H. Carter agrees to provide Hall, Light, Box Office charges money & check takers, advertisements in newspapers, billposting & distributing on the following dates viz August 29 to October 19 1901, (Except Oct 4th) December 25 1901, February 17 to March 8 1902, (except February 21 & March 7) March 24 to April 5 1902 and the week immediately succeeding the Coronation & undertakes that no similar exhibition be allowed to appear in the Hall during that period and whereas the said A. D. Thomas agrees to provide complete & high class entertainment including the Thomas Edison Animated pictures with all necessary apparatus, full company, full Military Band and undertakes to exhibit the latest and best subjects with a change of not less than one third of the programme each week including films of any great National event and one local picture specially taken for this exhibition each week and to provide all printing and whereas the said A. D. Thomas agrees to receive as his share 60 per cent of the gross takings including programmes and the said S. H. Carter agrees to receive as his share the remaining 40 per cent.
>
> In witness thereof the said S. H. Carter and A. D. Thomas have hereunto set their hands the day and year first hereinbefore written.
>
> A. D. Thomas
> S. H. Carter[17]

Thomas's projectors were seized by his creditors in April 1902 for non-payment of rent,[18] an event that was presumably foreseen, for a note in the Carter collection from Mitchell and Kenyon dated 17 February 1902, offers 'A projector with the best arc lamp as used by Mr Wilkinson' (Mitchell and Kenyon's cameraman). Carter's partner Frank Sunderland later recalled 'Buying New Century's first cinematograph projector in Blackburn' on Good Friday 1902. The machine caught fire at St George's Hall 'and only liberal supplies of buckets of water saved it.'[19] After finishing his season at

Wood engraving advertisement for New Century
Pictures show in York (Carter Collection, West Yorkshire
Archive Service).

Curzon Hall in Birmingham, Waller Jeffs, one
of Thomas's associate managers came to Bradford to run the first 1902 shows.

Osmund Waller Jeffs (1861–1941) is
unique in early British film history in being
both the subject of a biography published
shortly after his death, and a more recent
university thesis.[20] Jeffs was a very different
personality from Thomas. More conventional,
he lacked Thomas's directness in engaging
with film in a way that exploited its full
potential; something that is especially obvious
if a comparison is made between the way each
advertised and promoted their shows. In fact,
as Jeffs' history shows, he remained rather too
much attached to the travel and 'educational'
lecture. Jeffs' shows represented a step away,
not a break from the past … he simply made
the animated rather than the non-animated
the dominant element in a continuing tradition
of public hall screen spectacle.[21] According to
his biographer, Jeffs came from an educated,
upper middle-class background; both his father
and his grandfather being London surgeons.
He first became a journalist and then a
travelling lecturer, working with such shows as
Caygill's *Pictorial Tours* (1898) West's *Our
Navy* (1899) and Irving Bosco's *Briton or Boer*
(1900). In May 1901 he opened at the large
(3,500 capacity) Curzon Hall managing the
'Thomas-Edison Animated Photo Co.',
which, as already noted, was one of A. D.
Thomas's numerous ventures.[22]

Sydney Carter's business partner and the
general manager of New Century Pictures
was Francis ('Frank') Dargue Sunderland
(1875–1939) and documents in the Carter
collection reveal that their relationship was
far closer than merely commercial for both
Carter, Sunderland, and Richard Appleton
(another early Bradford-based film pioneer)
were all members of the same Masonic
Lodge.[23] The extent of Masonic involvement
in the early British film business is currently
unknown, as is their possible influence on
market entry. It is however interesting to

note that the British film industry's first historian Will Day ' … occupied a high position among the Freemasons', according to his obituary'.[24] Writing about early touring with New Century, Frank Sunderland gives an evocative picture of what was involved.

> The languid and aristocratic managers of the luxurious picture houses of today [1917] would have done well to have tasted of the joys of touring fourteen years ago, when after the Saturday night's show everything was to pull down and pack – machine, lamp, resistances, switches, band lights, screen, draperies, 'effects', advertising matter, and films. Next day the railway journey, and Monday morning very early, all to fit up again, disputes with the local electrical power company, difficulties with the police, and trouble with the local staff – it was a lucky day if the show got through the first day without serious mishap.[25]

'A HIGH CLASS ENTERTAINMENT COMPANY'

With Sunderland, Thomas and Jeffs, Carter had created an autonomously based structure, something between a holding company and a partnership, although lacking formal incorporation. In 'buying in' talent in this way, he was drawing on his knowledge of contemporary theatrical practice. As Tracy C. Davis has noted,

> Holding companies could be comprised of dozens of small, single-function sometimes family run enterprises. These were usually horizontally integrated; that is, all specializing in a single process … forming a circuit of separately owned but cooperating venues to facilitate the movement of whole programmes from place to place.[26] … Partnerships tended to develop around the need to consolidate resources and combine skills.[27]

Thus, by offering Thomas and Jeffs sharing terms rather than paying them a flat rate hire fee, Carter was able to lock them into the success of the new venture and encourage them to use their specialised skill to maximise its potential. This, in turn, made it possible for him to access, through them, a network of essential information and established suppliers. The value, in both the tangible and intangible sense, of networking in this way effectively reduced the true cost to Carter of his surrender of sixty per cent of the takings to Thomas. A letter from Jeffs to Carter written at this time of business establishment, offers a mixture of firm information and trade gossip.

> I went over to Leeds yesterday. The Coliseum is not booked for the Coronation. They would let it in July for £35 including light. They have 2 wks open September 1 to 13 @ £42.00. (Last week in Augt. could be had at July rate) and are also vacant Jany. 5 to 17 @ £63. Pringle is expected to book, but has not taken any date so far.
>
> Re Victoria Hall, Sunderland. I enclose copy of my last letter & of their reply to hand this morning. It looks as if they meant to 'stick us' I do not admit any 'contract' as they did not reply promptly & definitely to our wire & letter – offering to book 4 weeks if we could open for the 30th – I thought of telling them so. After talking the matter over with Sunderland, we decided not to reply until we had placed the matter before you. I hope we shall be able to run B'ham for the Bank Holiday; on the other hand, if we postponed visiting Sunderland too long, we may have another Co. in before us. *I should prefer to see one Co on its feet before launching another*, but as we are certain to want this town some day, it would be unwise to have a rupture with the people at the outset, which might prejudice us at another time.
>
> The question of the risk of running a third Coronation show depends to some extent on the actual outlay you would be obliged to incur. It would mean £200 for a *complete* outfit. If you borrowed a machine from Wray & had sufficient ordinary films, with changes from B'ham & Bradford you would only have Coronation films to consider. The other preliminaries would run into £70.

Rent deposit	£20
Printing, advertising	£40
Outfit, sheet, box sundries	£10

Your brother has, of course, a good knowledge of the town. What do you think about it?

Thomas. I have a letter from Paul [R. W. Paul, film-maker] wanting all kinds of information. Let the O. R. [Old rogue?] find all that out. He is paid for it. I have had enough worry and anxiety to banish A. D. T. from my mind, & shall have quite enough to think about & work for in running our show and making it 'hum'. I presume Paul thought I knew Thomas's 'secret' etc. but he never confided it to me.[28]

Ten days after Jeffs had written to him, Carter received a letter from Cecil Wray offering his services as an agent. Wray was a highly experienced maker of film projectors and accessories and had been associated with film from the time of the Edison Kinetoscope. His letter sheds new light on early film business practices.

I have seen Mr Sunderland to day re another projector, & I enclose you Messrs Prestwich's invoice to me, so that you will see Hepworth is listing the outfit at the nett cost price … I have however agreed to get you the other outfit you require at Hepworth's prices & if I can squeeze any more out of Prestwich, I shall of course share it with you as agreed. We have also had here today Messrs Pathé Frères traveller [i.e. salesman] with their latest film subjects. I have arranged to let you have their films at 6d per foot, less 12½% dis., but you must keep this secret as their prices are strictly agreed. If you call in Paris whatever you require you can get & have it invoiced on to me & I will allow this discount. There is not much variety however in their new subjects, we ran about 30 or 40 through your machine, so that Sunderland has a good idea of what they have.[29]

PRESENTING THE SHOW

Aspects of the programming devised by Thomas and Jeffs throughout this period are particularly interesting. While film historians are agreed on the creative role played by the exhibitor in the programming and the presentation of early film, there is still some doubt about the importance of single films in the programme before 1904. Programming sometimes tends to be solely linked to its film content and its important strategic and marketing purpose ignored. Certainly an examination of the public hall shows run at the turn of the century by such showmen as Thomas, Jeffs and Pringle does not support the idea that the constituent parts of the programme were unimportant.[30] Indeed, in the case of New Century, the promotion of individual subjects is frequently headlined. This is especially the case with 'local' films. In the Bradford 1902 performances local films were not simply used to please audiences, but fulfilled a public relations role to support the company's intangible assets of 'respectability branding' and approval by local politicians. A review from early in the season emphasises this, and gives a good impression of the total impact of such a show, which is lost if film titles are extracted in isolation. It represents a surprisingly complex interaction of themes, with dependent relationships existing between film-maker, commissioner/exhibitor, 'patron' and paying audience.

ST GEORGE'S HALL VISIT BY THE MAYOR, CORPORATION OFFICIALS, VOLUNTEERS AND ARMY VETERANS.

A large audience greeted the New Century Animated Picture Company's second week sojourn at St George's Hall last night, and testified their appreciation of the quality of the display. Included in the audience last night was the Mayor (Mr W. C. Lupton), Coronation procession officials, the returned Active Service Volunteers, and Bradford's veteran soldiers. The first picture put on the screen was portrait of the Mayor (Mr W. C. Lupton), which received tremendous applause, and the next instant the audience broke into 'For he's a jolly good fellow'. The next film showed a number of amusing and curious incidents, which the audience did not fail to show their delight in. Miss May Fallowfield appeared on the stage and sang 'On the Banks of Allan Water' and 'The Boys of the Old Brigade' and was received with warm demonstrations of approval. The Mayor and Corporation of Bradford on their way to the thanksgiving service at the Parish Church on Peace Sunday, June 8th, formed a very good picture. The views of the procession were splendidly developed and most satisfactorily shown. The pictures of the scenes in which the audience had taken part were received with wild enthusiasm. 'Palmer's Cycling Sensation on the Tea Cup Track' owing to its success last week is being repeated. The Bradford Volunteers in camp at Aldershot, and return from South Africa, were received with huge delight. Another very interesting item was the review of the Colonial and Indian Troops by Her Majesty the Queen and the Prince of Wales. The West Riding Military Band played selections of music.[31]

There are innumerable examples of single 'local' films being individually promoted during the 1902 season and indeed by July it was noted in a review that the show 'is proving exceedingly popular on account of the great local interest [contained] in the pictures'.[32] Examples range from shots of the Bradford Grammar School sports, (always a reliable subject to bring in parents and relatives),[33] to film of a local fire – 'first time a living photograph of an actual fire has been taken in the city'.[34] There was even an example of a 'crossover' film appearing from an associated show when M&K 531–4: *Lady Godiva Procession* (1902), 'The exclusive property of the New Century Animated Picture Company', was screened.[35] This subject had been originally commissioned from Mitchell and Kenyon by Waller Jeffs for his Birmingham show and was shot by M & K's cameraman Mr Wilkinson.[36]

More ambitious still was the 'Magnificent series taken with the Bradford Volunteers at Aldershot'[37], a series of short films combined together in a narrative structure reminiscent of Robert Paul's *Army Life – Or How Soldiers Are Made* (1900). The arrangement of the shots offered viewers a simple time progression framework, 'The regiment leaving Belle Vue Barracks', 'In Camp', 'Under Canvas', 'On Outpost Duty', 'The Return', 'Arrival at the Midland Station'. The presentation was supported by the 'special engagement of the splendid Band of the West Yorkshire Regiment'. Drawing together information preserved by Jeffs' biographer, and material from the Carter collection, it is now possible to demonstrate in one unique case exactly how early British public hall showmen developed and 'built up' a special film feature. This consisted in using one outstanding film as an 'anchor' and constructing a narrative around it supported by a lecturer's commentary and sound effects.

On a visit to the Warwick Trading Company in London, Thomas had been shown a 'rough-sea' subject that he particularly liked. He telegraphed St George's Hall on 20 December 1901.

You can bill in addition to locals a voyage to New York during the great gale. Magnificent rough seas. The Kronprinz Wilhelm cutting through the Atlantic rollers. One of the finest scenes ever depicted as shewn before the German Emperor. Grand series of pictures appropriate to the season. Have cable laid ready. Sending screen.[38]

When Jeffs received the film he provided an elaborate scenario clearly based on the 'travel' panorama format he was familiar with.

Pictures:	Music:	Effects:
Panorama of Southampton	'Life on Ocean Wave'	Steam Whistle
Leaving Port	'Anchors Are Weighed'	
Down Channel:		
Warships and Torpedo		
Boat Destroyers	'Heart of Oak'	Foam Effect
View to the Kronprinz Wilhelm	Tacit	Foam Effect
On Board:		
Fine Weather	Hornpipe	
Captain on the Bridge	'Hornpipe'	(Lecturer's Note:)
		(Observe the Captain has
		got his sea legs on!)
Man Overboard		Bosun's Whistle
		cries : Man Overboard –
		Man the Boats.
SONG : : :	The Little Hero : : :	Vocalist
Pictures	Music:	Effects:
Rough Weather	Storm Movement	Sandpaper, Rain box and
		muffled drum roll for waves
		breaking over bows.
Statue of Liberty		
(Slide)	'Yankee Doodle'	
New York harbour	Sousa March	
	(Liberty Bell or some other)[39]	

On 1 April 1902, the film was advertised in the *Bradford Daily Argus* as:

MAGNIFICENT SERIES TAKEN DURING A VOYAGE TO NEW YORK
Scenes on board an Atlantic Greyhound.
Realistic Picture of a gale in mid-ocean.
Panorama of New York harbour and docks.
Ride Down on Broadway on a Cable Car.[40]

Two weeks later it was claimed that the film was 'admitted to be the most interesting and realistic picture ever exhibited in Bradford'.[41] And two days after, the advertising noted that 'Notwithstanding the numerous additions to this week's programme, the unique series, A Voyage to New York, which has become the talk of Bradford, will, by special request, be shown each evening.'[42] That this was not mere advertising hype is suggested by the fact that the film was brought back to St George's Hall for inclusion in the 1903 season. The 1902 Bradford season was clearly very successful. By the end of May the company was claiming that 50,000 people had seen it, and that it 'had established a reputation as the finest entertainment of its kind ever seen.'[43] Jeffs later claimed that £51 was taken in a single day at a matinee and £115 paid for a single night.[44] When A. D. Thomas showed Robert Paul's 'pathetic' title, *Ora Pro Nobis* (1902) later in the year at Durham the build up was, if anything, even greater than for *The Voyage to New York*. Thomas presented it 'with organ and dioramic effect' and a choir and, just in case there were still any dry eyes in the house, gave the audience the whole presentation again as a finale to the show! That was 'showmanship'!

THE AUDIENCE

Discovering what was shown at early film performances is fairly straightforward and completeness is only prevented by the availability of information preserved in entertainment journals and local newspapers. But determining *who* watched early film is a considerably more difficult task. How can the public hall audience of a century ago be identified? And more specifically, to what extent did New Century seek to define and influence the social demography of its audiences? The company's interest in promoting its respectability by cultivating an association with civic leaders has already been noted. Advertising stressed the same theme. New Century was a 'High Class Entertainment Company'.[45] It was 'under the patronage of the worshipful Mayor of Bradford'[46] and its pro- grammes were 'entirely free from anything to offend the most fastidious'.[47] A leaflet printed at the end of 1902 for Waller Jeffs, and now in the Carter collection, promoted *his* propriety as much as that of his shows. His learning ('has edited a number of scientific works') and his philanthropic work on behalf of hospitals and other charities, are mentioned. The list of his 'distinguished patron- age' is given; and this includes a bishop, a judge, a duke, several Mayors and politicians including Joseph Chamberlain. The history of his activities in Birmingham provides many more examples of his 'educational and entertaining' shows.[48] The hint of self-improvement and 'rational recreation', present in both the Bradford and Birmingham advertising, suggests that it is being directed at an aspirational middle- and lower middle-class audience.

But access to respectability at a New Century show came at a price. There are two notable aspects of New Century's seat prices in 1902 – their level, and the uniformity with which they were applied. Irrespective of the location, the hall, the programme, or even the time of year, they were always the same – 2s, 1s and 6d; with 'early doors' (i.e., the opportunity to obtain the best seats by being in first) an extra 3d.[49] These were high prices – there were many film shows at this date that were far cheaper – and they parallel instead large panoramic entertainments such as Hamilton's Excursions. Prices so consistently applied were as much a part of New Century's 'brand' as its name. The price level informed potential customers in advance that this was a superior show and certainly not a cheap form of entertainment. The high cost of a seat also acted as a discriminatory tactic to exclude the poor and confirms that a middle-class audience was being sought. Advertising may have given the impression that all were welcome, but in reality, this was far from being true. But perhaps the most persuasive evidence of deliberate demographic profiling by New Century is to be found in the interesting case of 'factory gate' films. This subgenre of local films showed large numbers of workers leaving places of mass employment such as factories and mills. Clearly the people most interested in watching factory gate films were those who had been filmed and their immediate family and work colleagues. And indeed this was the way these subjects were promoted; with exhor- tations to 'Come and see yourself on the screen'. This highly specialised category of early British film is therefore unique in offering historians a high level of specificity and very precise geo-demo- graphic profiling. The Mitchell and Kenyon Collection includes ninety-nine examples taken between 1900 and 1902. Although the names of the commissioners are not known, it has been possible to show that several were exhibited on fairgrounds during the 'Wakes' or holiday weeks in the industrial towns in the north of England.[50]

Although Sydney Carter is known to have commissioned six 'local' films from Mitchell and Kenyon in 1902, none are factory gate films. Furthermore, no factory gate films are mentioned in any of New Century's Bradford newspaper advertisements in either 1902 or 1903. The cumulative evidence provided by programming, seat price levels, and the lack of factory gate films is entirely consistent – New Century's target audience was middle class. Working-class audiences in Bradford went to the fairground to experience film.

POSTSCRIPT

For the purpose of this study, this analysis of New Century Pictures has been limited to just one year, 1902, when the company was formed and gave its first shows under Sydney Carter's control. New Century developed into a highly successful company, which diversified into equipment manufacture, film rental, film production and permanent cinema exhibition. It survived for the whole of the silent period, and was sold to Gaumont in 1928.

NOTES

1. 'Great Britain's Leading Cinema Proprietors or Managers. Mr S. H. Carter', *The Cinegoer*, 26 February 1916, p. 15. Carter Collection. Bradford Archive Office. Scrapbooks compiled by Sydney Carter offer an important new primary resource which has been utilised in this account. The collection was donated to the West Yorkshire Archive service in Bradford in the 1990s. A selection of the letters and contractual agreements it contains is now published for the first time.
2. *Proceedings of the British Cinematography Society*, no. 21 (1933), p. 4.
3. Nicholas Hiley, '"At the Picture Palace": The British Cinema Audience 1895–1920', in John Fullerton (ed.), *Celebrating 1895: The Centenary of Cinema* (Sydney and London: John Libbey, 1998), pp. 98–9.
4. Frank Sunderland, 'How the Picture Show Evolved', *The Bioscope*, 4 February 1917, p. 28.
5. Cecil M. Hepworth, *Came the Dawn. Memories of a Film Pioneer* (London: Phoenix House Limited, 1951), p. 58.
6. Sunderland, 'How the Picture Show Evolved', p. 28.
7. This circular is reproduced in John Barnes, *The Beginnings of the Cinema in England 1894–1901*, vol. 4 (Exeter: Exeter University Press, 1996), p. 79.
8. 'Animated Pictures in the Courts', *The Showman*, 28 March 1902, pp. 93–4.
9. *The Era*, 14 January 1899, p. 18.
10. 'Animated Pictures in the Courts', *The Showman*, 28 March 1902, p. 93.
11. *The Cinegoer*, p. 15.
12. Andrew Crowhurst, '"Big Men and Big Business": The Transition from "Carters" to "Magnates" in British Music Hall Entrepreneurship 1850–1914', *Nineteenth Century Theatre*, vol. 25, no. 1 (1997), pp. 33–59. See also Michael R. Booth, '"Varieties of Life": The Making of the Edwardian Music Hall' in M. R. Booth and J. H. Kapland (eds), *The Edwardian Theatre* (Cambridge: Cambridge University Press, 1996), pp. 61–85.
13. 'The History of St George's Hall', *Yorkshire Observer* (supplement), 29 September 1953, p. 3. The original source of the Carter interview is not given but it probably dates from 1938, the seventy-fifth anniversary of the hall.
14. Vanessa Toulmin, 'The Importance of the Programme in Early Film Presentations', *KINtop*, vol. 11 (2002), pp. 19–33.
15. Peter Bailey, '"A Community of Friends": Business and Good Fellowship in London Music Hall Management c. 1860–1885' in Peter Bailey (ed.), *Music Hall– The Business of Pleasure* (Milton Keynes: Open University Press, 1986), p. 36.

16. J. J. Bennell, 'In the Days of the Pioneer Showman', *Cinematograph and Lantern Weekly*, 8 March 1917, p. 19.

17. Agreement. 16 August 1901. S. H. Carter and A. D. Thomas. Carter Collection. It is interesting to compare these terms with those that Carter was prepared to give to a local author for writing a Christmas pantomime for the 1901–2 season. If house receipts were below £200, the author received nothing; from £200 to £300 he got £10 to £15; and if they reached £300, he was paid £30. vide. Agreement 14 October 1901 between Sydney Carter and Percy Newstead. Carter Collection.

18. *Times*, 26 November 1902, p. 4, col. 5.

19. Sunderland, 'How the Picture Show Evolved'.

20. John H. Bird, *Cinema Parade. Fifty Years of Film Shows* (Birmingham: Cornish Brothers Limited, 1947); Christopher Dingley, 'Waller Jeffs at Curzon Hall. A Study in Early Film Showmanship 1901–1912', MA thesis, University of Derby 2000. (Copy in the local History Department, Central Reference Library, Birmingham). See also Waller Jeffs, *President's Address* at the Cinema Veterans' Reunion Dinner, December 1932, BFI library.

21. Dingley, 'Waller Jeffs at Curzon Hall', p. 11.

22. Bird, *Cinema Parade*, pp. 43–4. A close American parallel to Jeffs is Burton Holmes. See Charles Musser, *The Emergence of Cinema. The American Screen to 1907* (Oxford: Maxwell Macmillan International, 1990), pp. 221–3.

23. Carter Collection. Documents 46D 84/1.

24. *The Photographic Journal*, September 1936, p. 524.

25. Sunderland, 'How the Picture Show Evolved', p. 28.

26. Tracy C. Davis, *The Economics of the British Stage, 1800–1914* (Cambridge: Cambridge University Press, 2000), p. 177.

27. Davis, *The Economics of the British Stage*, p. 247. During 1903, New Century Pictures was advertised in the *Bradford Daily Argus* as an 'Amusement Combination'. New Century was formally incorporated as the 'New Century Animated Picture Company Limited' in 1908 (Pro.BT31/12390/97998). A public flotation with a nominal capital of £60,000 took place in November 1911 (Pro.BT31/42967/118640). 'Sydney Carter's New Century Pictures Scenic Entertainment' was entered for copyright protection in the 'Dramatic and Musical' class at Stationer's Hall on 28 November 1905. The date of the first performance is given as 27 March 1902.

28. Jeffs to Carter, 6 June 1902. Carter Collection.

29. Wray to Carter, 16 June 1902. Carter Collection, 46D 84/4/89. Cecil Wray was closely involved in the introduction of the Edison Kinetoscope in Yorkshire at the beginning of 1895. See Richard Brown, 'The Kinetoscope in Yorkshire. Exploitation and Innovation', in Simon Popple and Vanessa Toulmin (eds), *Visual Delights. Essays. On the Popular and Projected Image in the 19th Century*. (Trowbridge: Flicks Books, 2000), pp. 105–15. Further information on Wray's later film career can be found in G. J. Mellor, *Movie Makers and Picture Palaces – A Century of Cinema in Yorkshire 1896–1996* (Bradford: Bradford Libraries, 1996) and in volumes 1 and 2 of Barnes, *The Beginnings of the Cinema*.

30. Hiley suggests that 'marked as from 1895 to 1920, the individual film was of little significance. The basic unit of exhibition was not the individual film but the programme, and the commodity that most patrons wished to buy from the exhibitor was not access to an individual film, but time in the auditorium' (Hiley, '"At the Picture Palace"', p. 97).

31. *Bradford Daily Argus*, review, 22 February 1902.

32. *Bradford Daily Argus*, review, 29 July 1902.

33. *Bradford Daily Argus*, advertisement, 12 July 1902.

34. *Bradford Daily Argus*, advertisement, 26 April 1902.

35. M&K 531–4: *Lady Godiva Procession* (1902).

36. *Bradford Daily Argus*, advertisement, 30 October 1902. (Incorrectly stated by Bird, *Cinema Parade*, pp. 72–3 to have been shot by Waller Jeffs. But see *The Era*, 16 August 1902, p. 17, for a note of the filming by Wilkinson of Mitchell and Kenyon).

37. *Bradford Daily Argus*, advertisement, 27 May 1902, p. 1.

38. Telegram, Thomas to St George's Hall Bradford, 20 December 1901. Carter Collection.

39. Bird, *Cinema Parade*, p. 24. 'Details are taken for the original working plot given to me by Waller Jeffs'. The present location of this document is unknown.

40. *Bradford Daily Argus*, advertisement, 1 April 1902, p. 1.

41. *Bradford Daily Argus*, advertisement, 19 April 1902, p. 1.

42. *Bradford Daily Argus*, advertisement, 21 April 1902, p. 1.

43. *Bradford Daily Argus*, advertisement, 21 April 1902, p. 1.

44. Bird, *Cinema Parade*, p. 46. Bird incorrectly gives the year as 1901.

45. *Bradford Daily Argus*, advertisement, 1 April 1901, p. 1.

46. *Bradford Daily Argus*, advertisement, 11 August 1902, p. 1.

47. *Bradford Daily Argus*, advertisement, 22 May 1902, p. 1.

48. See Dingley, 'Walter Jeffs at Curzon Hall', for many more examples of this, and for the way in which Jeffs consolidated his 'image' over several years.

49. These admission prices have been documented for 1902 at St George's Hall, Bradford, St Andrew's Hall Glasgow, Curzon Hall, Birmingham and in Durham.

50. Vanessa Toulmin, '"Local Films for Local People": Travelling Showmen and the Commissioning of Local Films in Great Britain, 1900–1902', *Film History*, vol. 13, no. 12 (2001), pp. 118–37. See especially pp. 126–9.

8 Mitchell and Kenyon in the North East

David Williams

By the time the first showman-sponsored films by Mitchell and Kenyon were being projected in halls and marquees across the north east of England, audiences were well used to local scenes appearing in front of them. In 1896, R. W. Paul had filmed the Newcastle Fire Brigade and shown it to enthusiastic audiences in Newcastle, Sunderland and Durham.[1] These scenes did not, however, have the direct personal appeal of those the later showmen commissioned.

In the north east, there were three major promoters of the 'see yourself on the screen' films: A. D. Thomas (in a number of guises), New Century Pictures and Ralph Pringle.[2] The films themselves can be categorised as belonging to three distinctive genres: factory gate films, events and processions and panoramas. The specific nature of the films in most cases seems to have limited their showing to the particular locations, though, as will be shown, a number had a wider appeal.[3] At the end of December 1900, 'Edison's Animated Pictures' came to the Exchange Hall in Stockton-on-Tees, Co. Durham, with a Christmas season show. This was one of A. D. Thomas's travelling shows masquerading under that title. The *North Eastern Daily Gazette* of 29 December reported on the whole programme.[4] In the previous edition, there had been some local views including the Mayor of Stockton and '10,000 employees leaving the Stockton shipyards'.[5] The firm of Ropener and Co. was the largest ship-building employer in town and the film was taken in December 1900.[6]

The *Newcastle Evening Chronicle* of 3 December 1900 has an advertisement for the Thomas-Edison Animated Photo Co. season at the Olympia, Newcastle upon Tyne. The headline features Local Animated Pictures and lists them as

> A Gorgeous animated procession of the Mayor, Sheriffs, and Members of the Newcastle Corporation leaving the Town Hall on Sunday November 10th for St Nicholas Cathedral.
> 20,000 EMPLOYEES ENTERING LORD ARMSTRONG'S ELSWICK WORKS
> Mr Justice Grantham's arrival and departure from the Assize Court Newcastle accompanied by the Mayor, Sheriffs, Heralds and mounted escort. The Mayor (John Beattie Esq) and Sheriff (John Jas Gillespie) holding an arresting conversation.
> FIGHTING FIFTH (Northumberland Fusiliers) just returned from South Africa. Lieutenant Sturgess at their head (Bradford Barracks).[7]

This A. D. Thomas show was under the management of Ralph Pringle. M&K 35: *20,000 Employees Entering Lord Armstrong's Elswick Works* (1900), filmed in November, clearly shows workers coming down a slope towards the work's entrance. Given that one of the films in the show was shot on 10 November, it might be reasonable to assume that this was the film shown in the same programme. The angle and the length of the shadows suggest that the camera was placed on the south side of Scotswood Road looking up the hill. The horse buses and the draymen are busy on the road. There is evidence here that the cameraman was already using a two-times telescopic lens, since the foreground is much foreshortened, and the sudden appearance moving left to right of a horse bus surprises the viewer by occupying the space between the camera and the close appearance of the first line of workers. The heads of some pedestrians can be seen on the same side of the road as the camera. The sequence is two minutes thirty-four seconds long. There are eight distinct stops and starts for the camera. It has been possible to identify Ralph Pringle and his colleague Loder Lyons in the approaching crowd.[8]

The report in the *Newcastle Evening Chronicle* for 18 December 1900 from the description of other films in the show suggests a change of programme. It states that

> So great was the success of the animated pictures at Olympia Newcastle last week that the management made arrangements to stay over another week and thus gave many who could not get in before an opportunity of seeing pictures of great historical and some of local interest … Local scenes of interest are being added constantly lending a fresh attraction to the show.[9]

The film description here suggests that the workers at Elswick are leaving the factory. This cannot be a description of M&K 35: *20,000 Employees Entering Lord Armstrong's Elswick Works*, but could be another film taken of the same factory.

In March 1901, the North American Animated Photo Company, managed by Ralph Pringle, also showed a film of workers leaving Armstrong's shipyard. The *Newcastle Evening Chronicle* of 4 March had listed twelve items on the programme including local animated pictures of Newcastle, Boer and China War and Lord Armstrong's funeral. Besides the Elswick Works film, the local pictures are described as being M&K 678: *The Newcastle Fire Brigade* (1901*)*, and *Sunderland v Notts Forest*. The wording of the 'wonderfully reproduced scenes in the China and Boer Wars' would suggest that they are also the work of the Mitchell and Kenyon team dramatising and/or faking the material.[10] *Attack on a Mission Station* (1900) had been released in July, along with eight Boer War dramas.[11] Lord Armstrong died on 27 December 1900 and his funeral took place on 31 December 1900 at Rothbury. The event was highly publicised and there were special trains laid on between Newcastle and Rothbury. It is possible that, while the Mitchell and Kenyon cameramen were in Newcastle for the funeral, they re-filmed the Armstrong works at leaving time.

One of the other locally filmed events in this programme has also been preserved in the Collection. M&K 678: *The Newcastle Fire Brigade*, is a carefully arranged sequence of the turnout and the return of the fire brigade. It is clear from the gathered crowds that the event has been signalled widely beforehand and, from the actions of certain recurring individuals in both sequences, that it has been carefully stage-managed. Sequence one of the turnout runs for one minute and ten seconds and sequence two, the return, for fifty-two seconds. Once again showmen and the police are very much in evidence, signalling to the cameraman and directing the movement of the crowds. A large contingent of local dignitaries are also in both sequences. Although this would seem to signify that the filming was itself an event, no newspaper report has yet been discovered.

'Edison's Electric Animated Pictures' were at the town hall in Gateshead during the week of 4 March 1901 with A. D. Thomas's No. 2 show under the management of Isaac Thomas. Among the local films advertised were employees leaving John Abbot and Son's engine works and M&K 41: *Employees Leaving the North Eastern Engine Works in Gateshead* (1901). The film is taken from opposite the exit of the work's yard and opens with an empty frame. The following crowd of workers is then led into the frame by a moustachioed man in a bowler hat who would appear to be part of the showman's team. The lighting suggests early evening though it is a dull day and there are no shadows. One particular young man stands for a long time in the background, but his later conversation with a passing newsboy suggests that he is a local watching the proceedings. At one point, he waves at the camera and seems to recognise a group in the crowd who also wave. After two minutes of this shot, there is a camera break. The final shot lasts fifty seconds and closes as workers continue to stream past.

'Edison's World Famed Electric Animated Pictures' visited the Olympia in Newcastle from 4 to 9 November 1901 with a programme that included 'Newcastle United versus Notts County, General Buller, New Animated Pictures of the Fighting 5th and the Fleet in the Tyne'.[12] Although one of these was inscribed as the fleet in Sunderland, it has now been identified as M&K 683–4: *The Fleet in the Tyne* (1902). The advertisement in *Northern Gossip* for Saturday 23 November includes the information that 'Scenes in Blackpool, and Magnificent Animated pictures of the Visit of the CRUISERS AND TORPEDO FLOTILLA TO NEWCASTLE, THE FLEET IN THE TYNE' would be shown.[13] A *Newcastle Daily Journal* report of 24 October describes the visit of torpedo boat destroyers of the reserve fleet.[14] Three vessels are named: *HMS Spiteful* and *HMS Petrel* which were in collision in fog on the way from the Forth, and *HMS Electra* which was in collision with an unnamed steamer en route for the Tyne. The ships shown in the several sequences have been tentatively identified as *HMS Petrel*, a four-funnelled torpedo boat destroyer built on the Tyne in 1900, followed by a small torpedo gunboat of the sharpshooter class, probably *HMS Skipjack*, built in 1889. Next is *HMS Flirt*, a three-funnelled torpedo boat destroyer built at Palmer's yard in 1898. The distant cruiser is probably the Apollo class *HMS Andromache* since between 1901 and 1903 she was listed as being attached to North Shields Royal Naval Reserve.[15] The remaining footage features the showman and the crew of the boat from which they were filming. The showman is trying to provoke some movement and joviality in the men with little success. The presentation at the Olympia was again managed by Isaac Thomas.

There is a possible origin for the Sunderland title that is attached to it on the Mitchell and Kenyon negative: the *Sunderland Daily Echo* advertisement for the Thomas-Edison Animated Photo Co. show at the Victoria Hall, Sunderland for the week of 11 November 1901 includes 'Torpedo Flotilla and Fleet at Sunderland'.[16] When the Tyne fleet film was shown in Grimsby in late 1901, also in an A. D. Thomas programme, the advertising text said 'The Fleet in the Tyne. The Torpedo boat flotilla. The ill-fated Cobra and Viper'.[17] A. D. Thomas was erroneously trying to make his programme seem more topical by this reference to two Armstrong–Whitworth torpedo boat destroyers that met with accidents during the year. *HMS Viper* ran aground in the Channel Islands on the 3 August 1901 and *HMS Cobra* was wrecked on 19 September 1901 after striking shallow water near Cromer. At the time of the Tyne fleet showing in Newcastle, a fund had been created for some of the Tynesiders lost in the wreck. As we have seen, neither ship was included in the Mitchell and Kenyon film.

Also at the time of the Newcastle show, one of the worst gales of the time was raging along the eastern coastline, and there were reports of shipwrecks, harbour damage and tidal encroachments. A report in *The Showman* of 29 November 1901 describes how Mr Kenyon rushed to catch the train to Sunderland to capture the drama with his camera. He had already taken 300 ft of the crashing waves from the foot of the Roker Pier lighthouse when he decided to venture to the edge of the jetty for something even more dramatic. A huge wave engulfed him and the backwash dragged the camera and tripod from his grasp and into the sea. Grappling irons only managed to recover the leather camera case. Children were observed trailing ribbons of cinematograph film around the town the next day to the chagrin of Mr Kenyon.[18] A very placid reel of seawater at Sunderland has survived in the Collection.[19] The length of its undramatic content is difficult to justify. It is the least interesting of all the north eastern reels. Eddies lap against the base of a cliff and a slight tilt of the camera reveals the railings on the cliff top. During the minute of the film, there are several crashing waves but nothing else happens.

Two film sequences taken in Tynemouth were shown at the magnificent Tynemouth Palace managed by Linden Travers. The first, M&K 685: *Tynemouth Swimming Gala in the Haven* (1901), featured a comic event in the Annual Tynemouth Amateur Swimming Club's Gala which took place on 31 August. The film is advertised on 9 September in the *Shields Daily News* as being part of Payne's New Animated Pictures. 'Mr Walter Payne will show the Animated Photo of the Tynemouth Swimming Gala in the haven. Film 374 feet long. A Great Success.'[20] The given length would have produced a film of six minutes. The preserved footage is only two minutes and twenty-seven seconds long. Other events in the gala must have been filmed and only two have survived. The sixty yards comic obstacle race is shown first in all its hilarity. The camera, rather awkwardly, pans with the competitors as they swim from left to right wearing top hats and gloves. After a camera stoppage, it then follows them back to the start line.

On the opposite bank of the haven, some men are diving into the water from a wooden structure. The cameraman attempts to capture the dives themselves but is in something of a dilemma. If he catches the water entry he misses the dive from the steps. If he takes the leap from the ladder,

M&K 731: *North Sea Fisheries* (1901). A scene showing some of the workers cleaning the fish on the dockside, exhibited in September at the Tynemouth Palace in North Shields.

he misses the entry into the water. He begins in the latter mode, but changes his tilt after a number of attempts to catch the action. At one point, as the camera boat rocks to the divers' splashes, we see that there is an adjudicator in another boat signalling to the divers. What at first sight appeared to be a random series of dives now becomes a structured event. This sequence, while managing to include several hundred people in shot, really falls into the event category and would be valuable in a programme for its topicality and local interest as much as for its 'see yourself on the screen' exploitation.

M&K 731: *North Sea Fisheries* (1901) was taken contemporaneously with the swimming gala film and was advertised as a forthcoming programme at the Tynemouth Palace in the *Shields Daily News* for 23 September 1901.[21] On 24 September, the newspaper adds the information that it is included in a programme for Reed's American Bioscope.[22] The film is identified by the negative inscription as one commissioned by the showman Tweedale. The origin of Reed's American Bioscope has yet to be investigated. The content of the film is part document and part construction. It opens with a slow panorama of the fisherwomen filleting the fish. As the camera pans further, a showman in a white hat is seen playfully urging everyone to work faster. The film cuts to a panoramic shot of the fishing fleet tied up at the quayside as a basket is unloaded. There is then a cut to the showman on the quayside apparently making a deal with a fisherman. Everyone in the crowd is amused by his antics. A quick jump cut shows him, in fun, picking a fight with a man in the crowd.

On 16 November 1901, Lord Durham as representative of King Edward VII, presented medals to members of the Third Volunteer Battalion of the Durham Light Infantry at their drill hall ground at the top of High Street West in Sunderland.[23] This battalion of part-time soldiers was based in Sunderland. The bicycle company seen in the film was formed in 1899. The surviving films of the parade M&K 733–4: *Lord Durham at Sunderland* (1901) are technically exceptional; the shots in each reel building to the eventual inspection. The first reel opens with two takes of the parade turning and moving into position with arms at the port. Then there is a shot of soldiers going into the drill ground. The coach carrying Lord Durham can be seen in the background, and the flags and bunting. There is a cut to the military band playing and the reel ends.

The second reel begins with a brief shot by the ground entrance. The head of the coachman is just in view. This is followed by shots of the parade dressing from the right. They are standing on the opposite side of the road from the entrance. The flagpoles inside the ground can just be seen on the right of the picture. Some of the bicycle squad then cycle by on the diagonal. They appear to have been escorting Lord Durham's coach which comes into view at the end of the shot. In the background, the soldiers present arms. Lord Durham is then seen, already out of the coach. He shakes the hand of one of the officers. The three leading officers turn and exit on the left diagonal. The inspection group are then seen walking towards us on the front rank. They turn and walk down the front rank and the reel ends. The second reel is one minute and twenty-five seconds' long.

The newspaper report in the *Sunderland Daily Echo* of 18 November 1901 shows that twenty-five men were actually nominated for the awards, but since five had already returned to South Africa only twenty could actually be presented.[24] The medal presentation is not included in the film. It was first shown on 18 November 1901 at Ralph Pringle's show at the Victoria Hall, Sunderland in the last week of a three-week engagement.

Two church congregation sequences filmed in Middlesbrough in 1902 offer a variation on factory gate films. In the factory gate film, there was the clear prospect that the participants would want to see themselves on the screen and persuade their friends to come too.

Congregations leaving churches, however, might not want to see themselves on screen. The Anglican church was fairly ambivalent towards the film presentations of the showmen, though church halls were sometimes used as venues. The Free Churches were often scathing in their criticism of places of popular entertainment and the content of their programmes. It is possible that the inclusion of these films heralded an attempt to recruit a new audience, but from the discreet positioning of the camera, it would seem that no prior arrangement had been made with the establishments. The films were advertised in the *North Eastern Daily Gazette* of 23 December 1902 as being shown in a programme given by the North American Animated Photo Company, directed by Ralph Pringle.

A great deal of local content was presented under the title of 'Living Middlesbrough'. 'Scenes of Workmen leaving Sir Ralton Dixon and Co.'s Shipyard, a panoramic view of the River taken from Port Clarence, Tram ride, the Grand football match, Middlesbrough v Sunderland on December 20th, Congregations leaving St Hilda's Church, The Centenary Chapel and St Mary's Cathedral on December 21st'.[25] The proximity of each of the church establishments enabled the cameraman to film all three in one morning. The opening fifty-seven second shot of M&K 735: *Congregations Leaving St Hilda's Church* (1902), shows a rather dull December day. Several other non-continuous shots capture the departure of a hire coach and other parishioners. The total length of the sequence is one minute fifty-five seconds. The second Sunday sequence of Centenary

M&K 680: *Hollow Drift Children's Procession* (1902) shot at the top of the hill showing the Coronation celebrations in September 1902.

Methodist Wesleyan Chapel, M&K 736: *Congregations Leaving the Centenary Chapel* (1902), is taken from across the street in an extreme long shot. The opening forty-four-second series of shots shows a large number of men, women and children descending the steps from the building. The cameraman then fits an enlarging lens to complete the one-minute sequence. The third film of St Mary's Cathedral does not seem to have survived in the Collection.

New Century Pictures paid their first visit to Durham on Friday 5 September 1902. They had been in Sunderland at the Victoria Hall for the previous four weeks (28 July to 30 August). The company continued their policy of taking local pictures to encourage people to patronise their performances. In the Durham area, the cameraman had captured pictures of the inspection of the Sunderland Police and Fire Brigade by the former chief constable of the county, Lieutenant Colonel Eden, and the procession of the school children from Durham Market Place to Hollow Drift for the Coronation festivities of 3 September. The children's procession was of particular interest because it had only been filmed two days before the show and four reels of film were needed to capture the events. Developing and printing facilities must have been near at hand. The huge procession, a quarter of a mile in length, with 2,700 children was filmed with a two times telescopic lens from the pavement in front of Elvet station. The cameraman had still not quite mastered the restricted view of the new lens and most of the participants are only seen from the shoulders up. As can be discerned from existing Prestwich cameras, the side-mounted viewfinder had no facility for reframing the scene of the taking lens. The surviving title M&K 679–82: *Hollow Drift Children's Procession* (1902), is in four reels of about 120 ft each. At the weekend, the cameramen also filmed the congregation leaving the Sunday morning service at the cathedral.

The *Durham Chronicle* reporter gave a particularly detailed description of the content of the local films:

> In the first picture, which contained 100 ft of film, Dr Armes was most conspicuous standing on the platform in front of the Londonderry monument, and the conducting and singing of Mr B. Scott-Ellis's Coronation Ode, whilst the Mayor of Durham (Councillor R. T. Herring) could be seen ascending the platform in order to address the children. In the procession to Hollow Drift, many local ladies and gentlemen were easily recognised. Taken all round, it was a splendid reproduction and it has nightly been received with applause. Altogether the film is 500 feet in length and occupies about a quarter of an hour to reproduce. Fifteen pictures were taken in every foot of film and they were thrown onto the screen at about one foot per second.[26]

It would appear, from the timing given, that either the projectionist put each of the four reels on separately, or under-cranked a spliced-together series to lengthen the item. The significant thing about these reels, besides their survival, is that they played to packed houses again the next time New Century Pictures came to Durham. Their advertisement in the *Durham Chronicle* of 21 November 1902 declares 'The Hollow Drift procession especially taken by the New Century operators during their last visit', and the report says 'One can wish for nothing more remarkably distinct than this picture.'[27] Five months later, the initial advertisement for the commencement of the show on Monday 6 April 1903, makes no mention of the local film but the newspaper report indicates that the reels were being shown by special request, along with film taken of the First Volunteer Battalion D.L.I. returning from South Africa. There were full houses each night.[28]

The manager, H. G. Carter, had also proposed to the city authorities that he might put on a special sacred concert and cinematograph show on Good Friday, but permission had been refused. The New Century cameraman it seems then went on a tour of the city and obtained some 'splendid views of the river banks and the sports activities on the Sands.'[29] The advertisement for the final two days gave full details of the new and old local items.

> SCENERY OF THE RIVER WEAR – Framwellgate Bridge, The Banks, The Weir, Prebends Bridge, The Cathedral – A triumph of animated photography. The Most Beautiful Animated Pictures Ever Exhibited and DURHAM SANDS RACES on Good Friday – Specially taken by the New Century Company. Come and see yourselves as others see you. By special request the management will once more exhibit the recent successful picture "HOLLOW DRIFT PROCESSION". Matinee for Scholars on Saturday at 3.[30]

Ralph Pringle's North American Animated Photo Company commissioned M&K 170–1: *A Tram Ride through Sunderland* (1904), first shown at Victoria Hall on Monday 19 January.[31] A series of local films were taken during the four-week engagement between 26 December 1903 and 28 January 1904. The Sunderland 'Phantom' tram ride begins with a static shot of the Crawford Monument in Mowbray Park on Burdon Road. Another static shot follows of the impressive Museum and Winter Gardens on Borough Road. Opened in 1879, the glass Winter Gardens were destroyed by bombing in the 1940s; as indeed was Victoria Hall where the films were shown.

The Sunderland electric tram system was opened in 1900, so there was a certain newness in the experience of a view from the front of a tram. 'Phantom' railway films had been popular since the first years of the cinematograph, and their interest had clearly not entirely faded. The first tram scene is initially static. Townsfolk are crossing the road and a policeman stands on duty in the middle of the track! Approaching the camera with linked arms are three of the showmen and walking alongside them just to their left is a tramways inspector. The commissioners would have required permission to film from the vehicle and he is obviously there to observe that all is under control. The showmen come very close to the camera and their features are plainly recognisable. Presumably they get on the tram, because it moves off immediately after they go out of shot. An approaching tram turns to the left at the road junction with Brougham Street and as our tram gathers speed a double decker tram no. 33 passes by on the right, followed immediately by a single deck tram (no. 25) with a destination board 'HIGH STREET AND VILLETTE ROAD'. Our tram continues down Fawcett Street. After one minute, there is a camera pause, and a film join. The new scene is a hundred yards further down the road and a double decker tram with a single deck trailer attached (no. 57) is approaching. As the tram combination passes, there is another camera pause, and a further film join. The new shot starts about thirty yards on and shows another policeman on point duty at the road junction with High Street West. It is interesting that lots of pedestrians are crossing at this point, too. They are clearly using the policeman's control of the vehicles to assist them. The scene ends four seconds later.

A second reel now shows a single deck tram in front of the camera tram with the destination board 'VILLETE ROAD SOUTHWICK'. As this tram moves forward a double deck tram (no. 42) passes on the right (with a headboard that reads 'CIRCULAR'). The journey continues through the centre. Two of the showmen stand in front of the tram directing what appears to be a tramways inspection gantry vehicle passing by on the right. This looks like an arranged shot and may have been at the suggestion of the previously noted tramways inspector. After this brief shot, we are now shown the forecourt of the Roker Hotel on the seafront. A barrel organ operator is in the background with the tramways inspector standing close by. To the left of the barrel organ is a homburg-hatted showman and the other two showmen can be seen hamming it up by dancing to the barrel organ tune. Another tramways inspector walks diagonally across the scene. The film ends with the three showmen joined by a fourth individual, playfully lobbing seashore stones at each other on the beach at Roker.

CONCLUSION

The Mitchell and Kenyon films of the north east in the early part of the last century, reveal a region still prospering from the expansion of the Industrial Revolution. The factory gate films demonstrate the good-naturedness of urban, heavy-industrial workers. The cinematograph proved itself to be not just an instrument capable of recording major news events, but also as a tool for portraying ordinary people. As the showman's advertisement put it: 'See yourselves as others see you'. The camera is not a mirror; viz 'See yourself as you see yourself'. It shows all these people in their setting. In retrospect, there could be no greater memorial to them.

ACKNOWLEDGMENTS

I would like to thank Frank Manders of Sunderland for his expert research on the early film shows in Sunderland and Newcastle; Robert Kennedy for his assistance in locating various places in Sunderland; Mr Todd of the Greenwich Maritime Museum; and Steve Sutton of the D. L. I. Museum and Arts Centre, Durham.

NOTES

1. *Durham County Advertiser*, 27 November 1896, p. 4.
2. Arthur Duncan Thomas was one of the most colourful characters in early British film exhibition. For further details of his life and career see Stephen Herbert and Luke McKernan, *Who's Who in Victorian Cinema* (London: British Film Institute, 1996), pp. 140–1 and Vanessa Toulmin, 'The Importance of the Programme in Early Film Presentations', *KINtop*, vol. 11 (2002), pp. 19–33.
3. Vanessa Toulmin, '"Local Films for Local People": Travelling Showmen and the Commissioning of Local Films in Great Britain, 1900–1902', *Film History*, vol. 13, no. 2 (2001), pp. 118–37.
4. *North Eastern Daily Gazette*, 29 December 1900, p. 3.
5. *North Eastern Daily Gazette*, 24 December 1900, p. 1.
6. M&K 37: *Ropener & Co., Shipworks* (1900). The film is completed in two takes: the first section taking two minutes thirty-eight seconds and the second thirteen seconds. Approximately 750 workmen and boys are seen going from right to left on a diagonal. There is no distortion that can be observed and thus the camera would seem to have a standard taking lens. The film was shot on a Saturday, probably at lunchtime, or if the works had a six-and-half day week at going home time.
7. *Newcastle Evening Chronicle*, 3 December 1900, p. 1.
8. For further information relating to Ralph Pringle, see Vanessa Toulmin, 'An Early Crime Film Rediscovered: Mitchell and Kenyon's *Arrest of Goudie* (1901)', *Film History*, vol. 16, no.1 (2004), pp. 37–53.
9. *Newcastle Evening Chronicle*, 11 December 1900, p. 4 and 18 December 1900, p. 4.
10. *Newcastle Evening Chronicle*, 4 March 1901, p. 1; *The Showman*, 15 March 1901, p. 179.
11. Denis Gifford, *The British Film Catalogue 1895–1985*, (Newton Abbot and London: David and Charles, 1986), film 00309, July 1900.
12. *Newcastle Evening Chronicle*, 1 November 1901, p. 1.
13. *Northern Gossip*, 23 November 1901, p. 23.
14. *Newcastle Daily Journal*, 24 October 1901, p. 4.

15. Mr R. G. Todd, Head of Historic Photographs and Ship Plans, Greenwich Maritime Museum: 'It is possible to distinguish numerous funnel configuration and accessory details, and thus identify individual class characteristics and distinctive individual vessels. Collision enquiries in the Admiralty Archives and newspaper reports of the reserve fleet in the Firth of Forth at this time might further identify accompanying vessels.' As a measure of his accuracy, Mr Todd identified *HMS Petrel* before he had seen the report in the *Newcastle Daily Journal*.

16. *Sunderland Daily Echo*, 11 November 1901.

17. Programme for Thomas-Edison Animated Photo Co., Grimsby, 1901, pp. 2–3, for details of the full programme of events (Barnes Brothers Collection).

18. This showman report is quoted from Colin Harding and Simon Popple, *In the Kingdom of the Shadows* (London: Cygnus Arts Press, 1996), p. 165.

19. M&K 732: *Rough Sea Sunderland* (1902). The stylus title is 'Waves at Sunderland' and the running time sixty-seven seconds. In eight jump-cut shots, waves are seen breaking against the cliffs at Roker. *Rough Sea at Sunderland* was reported in the New Century show of 28 July 1902 (*Sunderland Daily Echo*, 29 July 1902, p. 5).

20. *Shields Daily News*, 9 September 1901.

21. *Shields Daily News*, 23 September 1901, p. 1.

22. *Shields Daily News*, 24 September 1901, p. 2.

23. Steve Shannon of the D. L. I. Museum and Archive confirms that the soldiers in M&K 733–4: *Lord Durham at Sunderland* (1901) are indeed the Third Volunteer Battalion of the Durham Light Infantry. Each local township had a regiment of volunteers. The Third Volunteer Battalion D. L. I. was assigned to Sunderland.

24. *Sunderland Daily Echo*, 18 November 1901, p. 3.

25. *North Eastern Daily Gazette*, 23 December 1902, p. 1.

26. *Durham Chronicle*, 12 September 1902, p. 2.

27. *Durham Chronicle*, 21 November 1902, pp. 4, 12.

28. *Durham Chronicle*, 10 April 1903, pp. 4, 8.

29. *Durham Chronicle*, 17 April 1903, p. 8.

30. *Durham County Advertiser*, 17 April 1903, p. 3.

31. *Sunderland Daily Echo*, 19 January 1904, p. 5.

9 The Irish Films in the Mitchell and Kenyon Collection

Robert Monks

INTRODUCTION

The Mitchell and Kenyon Collection contains thirty-three films made in Ireland between May 1901 and December 1902 of Dublin, Belfast, Cork, Curragh, Co Kildare and Wexford were made principally for exhibition in Ireland by three exhibitors, none of whom were Irish or based in Ireland. These were the North American Animated Photo Company, the Thomas-Edison Animated Photo Co. and George Green. In this period, of course, the United Kingdom of Great Britain and Ireland formed a single political entity, though Home Rule for Ireland (not separation from Great Britain) was the major political issue. The visiting film exhibitor could anticipate frequent, regular, cross-channel transportation without customs problems, an excellent rail service and audiences avid for film exhibitions.

Film companies had visited Ireland prior to 1900, including Professor Jolly (Joli) who shot scenes in Belfast and Dublin and Jean Alexandre Louis Promio of Lumière Frères in 1897 who also filmed panoramas from trains. These were followed by Robert Armstrong Mitchell's *Yacht Race off Bangor, Co. Down* (1898) and the Warwick Trading Company, British Mutoscope and Biograph Company and the Belfast branch of J. Lizars filmed *Launch of the Oceanic II* in Belfast, 1899. Cecil Hepworth, Warwick and Belfast-based J. Walker Hicks, alias Professor Kineto, assisted by J. Lizars, also filmed Queen Victoria's visit to Dublin in 1900. Warwick's series of tourist films *With the Bioscope through Ireland* (1900) were all films of locations or events.[1]

NORTH AMERICAN ANIMATED PHOTO COMPANY

The first of Mitchell and Kenyon's three arriving customers was the North American Animated Photo Company. The sole proprietors of this company were Thornton, Stone and Pringle and the exhibition was under the direction of Ralph Pringle. Pringle was associated with A. D. Thomas, the owner of the second company to visit Ireland, as a lecturer/manager from the 1900 season in England. By March 1901, Pringle formed his own company and exhibited under the banner of the North American Animated Photo Company. In that month the show was advertised in Newcastle as 'under the direction and management of Mr Ralph Pringle'. They also presented shows in Hengler's Circus, Liverpool for six weeks during April–May 1901 with, among other films, *Queen Victoria's Funeral* (1901) and *Attack on a Mission Station* (1900).[2] Pringle's show was given prominent coverage in the *Belfast News-Letter* and the *Irish News* on 25 May 1901 which carried an advertisement headed 'WAR IN BELFAST'.[3] The war was not, for once, in Belfast but consisted of an exhibition of 300 animated pictures of the Boer War and 200 of the China War. The latter was, of course, Mitchell and Kenyon's fictional *Attack on a Mission Station*. They also exhibited 'magnificent animated pictures of the Queen's funeral', *Queen Victoria's Funeral* (1901) and stated that 'as the coffin is carried into St George's Chapel', a 'surpliced choir of 30 voices will sing the beautiful hymn

"Lead Kindly Light".' The show was advertised as appearing for two weeks only at Ulster Hall from Monday 27 May.[4] A later review in the the *Belfast News-Letter* reported that local pictures exhibited included 'the workers on Queen's Island (Harland & Wolff's shipyard) leaving for home, Royal Avenue thronged with traffic and the launch of the Celtic'.[5] The *Irish News* report stated that 'a series of local animated pictures of Belfast is an enjoyable one'.[6] It wasn't until 5 June that there was a 'Grand Change of Animated Pictures' and the Irish items included *Irish Scenery, Life in Belfast* and M&K 724, 183: *Ride on a Tramcar through Belfast* (1901).[7]

Of the material filmed by Mitchell and Kenyon for Pringle during the May 1901 visit, two have survived – M&K 724, 183: *Ride on a Tramcar through Belfast*. This is one of the most interesting titles in the Collection. The camera and tripod were placed on the front of the upper deck of a horse tram. The filming, carried out while the tram was moving, is notably smooth and the camera aimed to the right favoured shops and pedestrians on that side. The summery scene depicted coincides with the date of Pringle's visit. The shooting date is unclear but it probably preceded the opening of the exhibition on 27 May.

The film begins with a static shot of Bedford Street with onlookers and includes shots of various streets in Belfast, including Donegall Place, past Castle Place junction on the right where three officials wave the tram through into Royal Avenue and then the camera stops, probably to reload film. The tram returns along Royal Avenue until eight men with large boards on wheels advertising the

M&K 183: *Ride on a Tramcar through Belfast*. (1901). Views of the hoarding boards advertising the North American Photo Company's show at the Ulster Hall, Belfast in May 1901

North American Animated Photo Company in Ulster Hall come into shot. Pringle was a consummate advertiser and never missed an opportunity to include shots of his own advertising posters and flyers in a film and similar examples can be found in the titles filmed in Nottingham.[8] The tram nears the High Street/Victoria Street junction where several trams are manoeuvring and filming finishes with a static shot of the driver, conductor and supervisor with horse and tram.

The North American Animated Photo Company returned to Ireland in 1902 when they exhibited in Dublin from 22 December 1902 to 10 January 1903. Pringle advertised this visit as 'The First Time to Ireland' thus placing Belfast in another country. The exhibition was held in the large concert hall of the Antient Concert Rooms in Great Brunswick (now Pearse) Street. Pringle selected a programme designed to appeal to the Roman Catholic population of Dublin. It included *Life at the Vatican*, *H. H. Pope Leo XIII in His State Chair*, *Wearing the Triple Crown*, *Blessing the People and Cardinal Logue*, *Primate of Ireland*. He also advertised *Living Dublin*, films of congregations leaving churches in the city and vicinity of which two are in the Mitchell and Kenyon Collection, M&K 729: *Congregation Leaving St. Mary's Pro-Cathedral* (1902) and M&K 730: *Congregation Leaving Jesuit Church of St Francis Xavier* (1902). M&K 729: *Congregation Leaving the Protestant Cathedral* was advertised by Pringle as being filmed on 14 December, with views of St Andrew's Church filmed the following Sunday.[9]

It is impossible to give as definitive a date for the filming of M&K 730: *Congregation Leaving Jesuit Church of St Francis Xavier*, but it would appear to have been shot when Pringle advertised that the congregations were filmed on either 14 or 21 December 1902. There is an interesting item in the film. On the right of the camera frame on the wall beside the door are two posters. One advertises an Irish concert and the other advises that the annual charity sermon in aid of the Convent of Our Lady of Charity, St Mary's Asylum, High Park, Drumcondra, will be preached in St Francis Xavier's Church by Revd. J. Conmee, S. J. on Sunday 11 January 1903. Revd. J. Conmee, S. J., makes an appearance in James Joyce's novel *Ulysses*, in a chapter describing his walk from the Presbytery to the Malahide Road and his thoughts during his walk. Joyce set the happenings described in his novel on 16 June 1904.

THOMAS-EDISON ANIMATED PHOTO CO.

A. D. Thomas trading as the Thomas-Edison Animated Photo Co. (original Irish company), with Arthur Rosebery as general manager, commenced film exhibitions in the Round Room of the Rotunda Rooms and Gardens, Dublin, on 2 December 1901 and continued until 17 January 1902 when they toured, visiting Wexford, Waterford and Belfast, filming local scenes as they went.[10] They returned to the Round Room on 24 March and remained there until 3 May. They were in Cork until mid-June and were touring Ireland until the end of 1902. The energetic Arthur Rosebery, by shrewd selection of the items filmed and programmed, persuaded H. E the Lord Lieutenant (the Royal Representative), HRH General the Duke of Connaught, Commander-in-Chief of the Forces in Ireland, (Edward VII's brother), various Lords Mayor and Mayors and many other prominent citizens to attend their exhibitions thus making them socially acceptable to all classes. The Round Room, located at the top of Sackville (now O'Connell) Street, was Dublin's premier concert hall.

During December, the company exhibited programmes including several films of Dublin people and events specially filmed by their operators. One of the operators, Louis de Clercq, born in Ghent, Belgium on 3 October 1871, arrived in Dublin to join the company on 8 January 1902. He was partly educated in England and was a keen stills photographer. On leaving school he trained as a horticulturalist and then as a watchmaker. He worked in film exhibitions and family lore has it that he worked on the Walter Gibbons' film *Tally-Ho!* (1901). He worked on film exhibitions in

Stockton-on-Tees before arriving in Dublin to operate projectors and photograph scenes for the company's local films with another employee named Wilkinson. Wilkinson also acted as a cameraman for Mitchell and Kenyon and exhibited films under his own name in the early 1900s. De Clercq settled in Ireland and remained connected with films all his life. He died aged 95 in 1966.[11] A record of his movements for Thomas-Edison in 1902 is recorded in his diary, now in the Liam O'Leary Collection in the National Library of Ireland:

> *15th Jan 1902* (Wednesday) Went to Eysfield (Eyrefield) Lodge to take Ambush. Good. Rosebery came to.
> *17 Jan 1902* Took Panorama of College Green, Left for Wexford.
> *18 Jan 1902* Wexford pictures taken in very poor light. Stayed in White's Hotel. Good.
> *19 Jan 1902* Left Wexford for Dublin arrived 12.40. Clarence Hotel. Good. 3/6d Bed and Breakfast.
> *20 Jan 1902* Left for Newbridge 10.30. Stayed at Ford's (?) Hotel. Dear but Good.
> *21 Jan 1902* Took another picture of Ambush II. Wilkinson came out two late. Left for Belfast.

De Clercq also left an entry in the 'Cash Mems' section of the diary which notes 'Tram Fair (sic) to Kingstown 7d – Film from M. & K. 4d'. Kingstown (now Dunlaoghaire) was the port just outside Dublin where the mail boat from Holyhead docked and the note implies that Mitchell and Kenyon were developing and printing films for Thomas-Edison. These were then shipped back in time for the exhibition, usually three to four days later. Although this is the only reference to Mitchell and Kenyon in the diary, it provides strong circumstantial evidence that Mitchell and Kenyon offered a developing and printing service to exhibition companies at this time, as well as taking commissioned work. The tantalising reference to Wilkinson also suggests a level of co-operation between Mitchell and Kenyon and A. D. Thomas.

There are two titles in the Collection which relate to the filming of King Edward's horse Ambush II, M&K 5 and 795: *Ambush II* (1902). These were filmed on 15 January and the later portion on 21 January by De Clercq. Ambush II won the 1900 Grand National in the Prince of Wales' colours. The horse did not race in 1901, possibly due to the extended period of court mourning after the death of Queen Victoria. However, Edward VII decided to race his horse in the Coronation Grand National of 1902 and the considerable interest this aroused at the time probably accounts for the filming.

The Thomas-Edison film unit travelled by train to Newbridge station and then by hackney car to Eyrefield Lodge where the horse was stabled. However, on their first visit they were unable to film the horse and contented themselves with filming the hackney car and party walking towards the camera. The party (left to right) are possibly: with bowler hat, jockey, A. Anthony or trainer; on car, Jarvey; carrying camera case labelled 'Edison', manager Arthur Rosebery; with top hat, possibly Thomas Lushington, who supervised the horse's training. De Clercq then filmed a scene with workers from the stables jumping fences and some falling in the ditch, apparently imitating horses in a steeplechase. Ambush II was not filmed on this occasion possibly because he had been exercised. In order to include actual footage of the horse, it was necessary to return and de Clercq travelled to Newbridge on 20 January and stayed overnight. However, he notes in his diary for 21 January that 'Wilkinson arrived too late' for filming. This day proved to be more fruitful and de Clercq filmed various shots of Ambush II and his trainer. Ironically, the film was not exhibited in Dublin nor probably elsewhere. A week before the race, Ambush II split a pastern pulling up after a gallop and was withdrawn. He ran in 1903 and 1904 but fell.[12]

In his diary entry for 17 January, de Clercq notes that he 'Took Panorama of College Green Left for Wexford'. This corresponds to M&K 728: *Panorama of College Green* (1902) and is a

Scenes from M&K 726–7: *Wexford Bull Ring* (1902) filmed by Louis de Clercq in January 1901.

series of static shots of statues located in College Green, Dublin and Foster's Place, including the west side of the Bank of Ireland, once the Irish Parliament House. After filming in Dublin, de Clercq left for Wexford and three of the films taken on the 18 January 1902 now survive in the Mitchell and Kenyon Collection: M&K 725: *Wexford Railway Station* (1902) and M&K 726–7: *Wexford Bull Ring* (1902). The Wexford railway title was filmed in the Wexford terminus of the Dublin, Wicklow and Wexford Railway Co. looking along the length of the platform with the engine sheds on the right. The individual dressed in a morning suit, is, I believe, Hugh McCarthy, manager of White's Hotel, where Louis de Clercq stayed, and who appears to be advisor, official or not, of the filming as towards the end of the film he is seen urging people towards the camera. M&K 726-7: *Wexford Bull Ring* was taken in the Bull Ring in the town square, a location confirmed by the background shop façade. Some shop frontages are visible in the footage including 'Richards & Walsh, Watch Manufacturers', who were located in the Bull Ring at the time.[13] Filming took place on Saturday and since fish, fruit and vegetables were on sale from the stalls it was possibly a regular Saturday market. In the second title, members of the Royal Irish Constabulary can be seen and the Mayor of Wexford with mace, chain and daughters. The films would have formed part of Thomas-Edison's Wexford Exhibition and be advertised in similar fashion to the Dublin and Cork titles, as 'Life in Wexford'.

The visit of the Thomas-Edison Animated Picture Co. in 1901–2 had consequences for film-making in Ireland. Their operator and cameraman Louis de Clercq remained in the country after their departure and joined the company set up in the autumn by the Irish journalist and printing works proprietor, James T. Jameson. In imitation of A. D. Thomas's exhibition techniques, Jameson styled himself as Edison's Electric Animated Pictures and there is a belief that he purchased the company from A. D. Thomas himself. However, in July 1903, Thomas Alva Edison's London representative obtained an injunction preventing Jameson incorporating Edison's name for exhibition purposes.

GEORGE GREEN

By far the most impressive films relating to Ireland in the Mitchell and Kenyon Collection are those pertaining to the Cork International Exhibition of 1902–3. Twenty-two titles have survived from two different film companies: George Green and possibly Thomas-Edison. George Green was one of the most influential fairground showmen of the late Victorian era. Although synonymous with Glasgow, he was originally based in Preston where he travelled a variety of fairground rides, especially in the north of England, with his brother John. He installed a cinematograph show on the fairground in 1898 and was one of the first exhibitors to commission Mitchell and Kenyon to film events for his shows.

In 1902 the Cork International Exhibition was held and described as 'an honest effort for the benefit and improvement of the country'. The Cork International Exhibition Committee offered sole rights to provide for the cinematograph and entertainment attractions at the Exhibition. On 21 February 1902, George Green advertised in *The Showman* that he had secured the sole rights for the exhibiting of the cinematograph at the forthcoming event.[14] An advert in the same issue reveals that Green required 'a large quantity of Local Films taken, and also Films of the Official Ceremonies connected with the Exhibition, for which I have Sole Rights'.[15] Green appears to have hired one Thomas Moore to manage the cinematograph shows at the exhibition as his name also appears on the negatives of some of the films.

The exhibition opened on Thursday 1 May 1902 with a grand procession through Cork and the official opening by the Lord Mayor and the Earl of Bandon before an exalted company in the concert hall. Various events at the exhibition between May and July were filmed, including comprehensive coverage of the opening. However, two of the titles in the Mitchell and Kenyon Collection predate this opening, M&K 785: *Preparation of the Exhibition Grounds and Erection of Buildings* (1902) and M&K 703: *Panorama of Exhibition Grounds* (1902). These titles have been attributed to Edison, who operated a rival cinematograph show in the nearby Cork Assembly Rooms at the same time. 'Edison's Electric Animated Pictures' showed a series of pictures of Cork and the exhibition specially taken for the occasion in the Round Room, Rotunda, Dublin in aid of the Women's Section of the exhibition, on Saturday afternoon, 24 April 1902. This was under the patronage of their Excellencies, the Lord Lieutenant and Countess Cadogan.[16] From the unfinished state of the buildings, this film was probably made in early April. It may have been filmed by de Clercq, but who owned Edison's Electric Animated Pictures at the time is not certain, and it is possible that Thomas was no longer connected with the company, which was sold in August 1902 to James T. Jameson. M&K 703: *Panorama of Exhibition Grounds* was taken a day or two before the opening. Shot from the top of the water chute (about fifty or sixty feet high), it shows the domed entrance of the industrial hall, the machinery hall, the concert hall (with square towers), the band stand, a tea house and restaurant.

The titles associated with George Green commence with M&K 704–5 and 712: *The Grand Procession* (1902) and include the procession passing along the Western Road to the exhibition grounds with trade unions, national bodies, city bands, and country contingent identifiable by the banners they are carrying.[17] The banners were made for use in the annual processions held on St Patrick's Day, 17 March, in Cork.[18] The first banner on show is that of the Irish National Foresters

Views of the procession to mark the opening of the Cork International Exhibition on 1 May 1902. M&K 704:
The Grand Procession (1902).

(a benevolent society), escorted by members in full regalia, a uniform based on the Irish patriot
Robert Emmet's when he led his abortive rebellion in 1803. Then follow upholsterers, typographers,
solderers and preserve purveyors, a lorry with a tableau of Adam and Eve (both male), preceded by
a band. Another group in the procession is led by a uniformed horse rider carrying a banner in the
Irish language, followed by young people who are probably members of an Irish language class.

It was arranged that when the VIPs in their carriages arrived on the Western Road, the
procession would move to the right-hand side of the road (camera left) to provide free passage.
An Irish National Forester in regalia and on horseback cleared the way. The Lord Mayor of
Cork and the Lord Lieutenant of County Cork occupy one landau with the city mace bearer on
the box. The two state coaches, specially transported from Dublin, carry the Lord Mayor of
Dublin and his party of aldermen and councillors. Other landaux carry the Mayors of Derry,
Galway, Limerick and Waterford, the Cork city recorder and city registrar.

Within the Mitchell and Kenyon Collection there are two filmed sequences, M&K: 702, 717:
Opening of Cork Exhibition (1902), of the carriages arriving at the exhibition grounds, including
footage of the Lord Mayor of Cork.[19] The first scene, of the arrival of the dignitaries' carriages and
the two Dublin coaches, is chaotic. It is just possible to discern the Lord Mayor of Cork with a
mounted escort provided by the Irish National Foresters in regalia, including lances. The second title
in this sequence features the Lord Mayor of Cork arriving in state and a detachment of the Royal Irish
Constabulary who present arms and lower the flag in salute.[20] Between the official opening in May

and throughout June and July, other films were exhibited by Moore on behalf of George Green. One such title, M&K 715, 716: *Visit of the Duke of Connnaught C. I. C Forces in Ireland and Prince Henry of Prussia* (1902), was filmed on 8 May. Prince Henry, then on a cruise around Scotland and Ireland, was Commander of the First Division of the German Naval Squadron and accompanied the duke with military and naval staff to the exhibition a week after it officially opened. The royal party are seen passing through the grounds and climbing to the top of the water chute erected by the committee at a cost of £3,000. Unfortunately the chute was not ready in time for the official opening.

Other local films commissioned in Cork from this period include local city views, views of the quayside, M&K 708: *Albert Quay* (1902), and two titles relating to boat races, M&K 706: *Boat Race Cork Exhibition* (1902) and M&K 707–8: *Oar Boat Race* (1902). Two different boat races took place in Cork during this period, the first International Gig Races at Cork International Regatta held on 21, 22 and 23 July 1902 and exhibited on 25 July and secondly the Final of International Cup at Cork Regatta on 23 July, and exhibited on 1 August. Unfortunately, the cameraman was in a hopeless position and it is impossible to see who is racing.[21] Views taken of the city range from the standard factory gate type as in M&K 711: *Lee Boot Factory – Dwyer & Co. Ltd* (1902) to the illustrated tram ride sequence M&K 709–10: *Illustrated Tram Ride over Patrick's Bridge and Grand Parade* (1902).

As two showmen can be seen organising participants in several of these films, it is probable that the unit was filming some days before the official opening. One of the showmen, medium height, with beard, and usually wearing a long overcoat and a white Stetson-type hat, behaves like a film director and seems to know how to make the scene interesting. The other is tall, conventionally dressed and his height the principal means of identification. The films are listed in the probable order of filming and commence with M&K 709–10: *Illustrated Tram Ride over Patrick's Bridge and Grand Parade*. The tram travels through the city centre, beginning in King (now MacCurtain) Street, stopping at the junction with Coburg Street, restarting when turning left into Bridge Street, crossing Patrick's Bridge over the River Lee, into Patrick Street, the main street, where the shot ends. In the second part the camera is static and facing in the opposite direction, showing the street and the activity with Patrick's Bridge and Hill in the background. In the following sequence, the camera is set up on the left of Grand Parade, and footage of a steamroller, street sweepers and various carriages form part of the traffic scenes. Shots of the quayside formed part of M&K 708: *Albert Quay*, where the absence of activity suggests it was shot on a Sunday morning. The showman from M&K 709–10 can be seen walking along a ship's deck up the gangplank to the quay where he tries to persuade some onlookers to walk through the shot.

Local films of the kind shot by Mitchell and Kenyon in Great Britain consisted of factory gates, local sporting events, and processions and parades.[22] Sporting titles in the Cork material include M&K 714: *Sports Day at Queen's College* (1902), shot on 7 June 1902 on the college's sports ground, adjacent to the exhibition grounds.[23] However, the shots of congregations leaving their local churches on a Sunday morning appear to be more popular in the Irish films than in the British material. Films were made of church congregations in Cork, as they were in Dublin, and two titles can be found in the Collection: M&K 721: *Congregation Leaving St Patrick's Roman Catholic Church* (1902) and M&K 722: *Congregation Leaving St Mary's Dominican Church* (1902).[24] Both films comprise scenes of various members of the congregation entering and leaving the buildings and reflect a similar style to those commissioned by Ralph Pringle in Belfast where church sequences from different denominations were shot. Boer War-related titles were also filmed in Cork with M&K 713: *Regiment Returned from Boer War to Victoria Barracks, Cork* (1902) the only remaining example. The air of informality in the march sequence would suggest that the battalion was returning from the Boer War to spend a night in Cork barracks before moving onto their home barracks and furlough.

Another popular genre among non-fiction films from this time is that relating to turnouts of local fire brigades, of which many different examples for various towns in the United Kingdom can be found in the Mitchell and Kenyon Collection. An example of this was also filmed in Cork, M&K 718–20: *Cork Fire Brigade Turning Out* (1902). The *Cork Examiner* described it as 'a series of the Cork Fire Brigade turning out to a big fire and their work thereat'.[25] The film is a staged re-enactment of a fire rescue and consists of three main sequences. It begins with the escape ladder being pushed into position in the middle of the road and out of camera view. An organiser signals the brigade to move and the escape ladder, pushed by the firemen, leads the way, followed by two appliances each drawn by a single horse racing from the station. The following sequence shows a small fire in a gateway. Firemen, with hose, run into shot and douse it with a water jet. A fireman then emerges from the gate with a rescued woman, carried in a fireman's lift to safety.[26] The final sequence appears to be a repeat of the action from the previous scene but filmed somewhat closer.[27]

The final sequence of Cork films consists of M&K 243 and 723: *Train Drive from Blarney* (1902). The films are taken on the narrow-gauge Cork & Muskerry Light Railway, which ran from 1897 to 1934 between the terminus on the Western Road in Cork to Blarney, Donoughmore and Coachford. M&K 723 forms the first part of the sequence, consisting of a panorama from the Colthurst Family Mansion in Blarney over the grounds to an end shot of Blarney Castle seen through trees in the foreground. This is followed by a brief shot of Blarney station. Throughout filming, the camera is mounted in the second to last wagon of a company train only seen momentarily. The film shows the view behind the train throughout. M&K 243 begins with the train leaving Leemount station three miles from the city terminus, from where the single-line track occupied one side of the public road, sharing it with the usual traffic and pedestrians. It then passes through Carrigrohane station, two and a half miles from Cork, where a 'passing loop', which is visible, was provided. As the train travels along its side of the road on the outskirts of the city, an electric tram on its way to Sunday's Well is shown, as are horse-drawn carts and pedestrians. Coming into the city terminus, the train crosses a bridge over the River Lee, South Channel. As the train enters Cork terminus at an acute bend, the side of the last wagon comes briefly into shot and the shot ends.[28]

CONCLUSION

Before the discovery of the Irish material in the Mitchell and Kenyon Collection, subjects relating to Ireland were mainly tourist views, royal visits or spectacular events such as the launch of the Oceanic II (1899). The Mitchell and Kenyon Irish films show a dramatic change in the subjects filmed. Of the thirty-three Irish films, only about five are without numbers of people and provide us with a window through which to see aspects of everyday life in Ireland in the early 1900s. Panoramas were no longer buildings or scenery from passing trains but people in the streets filmed from trams, unaware that they were being filmed. The films justify the exhibitor's 'Come and see yourselves'. The viewers became the subjects, the ordinary everyday people walking in streets, in processions, leaving factories and churches, at sporting events, in street markets, or exiting trains or trams, were for a short period of history the featured attraction.

NOTES

1. For further details on early film in Ireland, see Robert Monks, *Cinema Ireland: A Database of Irish Films and Filmmakers, 1896–1986* (Dublin: National Library of Ireland, 1996).
2. For further information on Ralph Pringle, see Vanessa Toulmin, 'An Early Crime Film Rediscovered: Mitchell and Kenyon's *Arrest of Goudie* (1901)', *Film History*, vol. 16, no. 1 (2004), pp. 37–53.
3. *Belfast News-Letter* and *Irish News*, 25 May 1901.

4. *Belfast News-Letter* and *Irish News*, 25 May 1901

5. *Belfast News-Letter*, 28 May 1901.

6. *Irish News*, 28 May 1901.

7. *Belfast News-Letter*, 5 June 1901 and *Irish News*, 25 and 28 June 1901.

8. See M&K 163–5: *Tram Rides through Nottingham* (1902), for an example of where the tram stops to film the advertising boards for the North American Animated Photo Company.

9. NAAPC poster and brochure in Liam O'Leary Archive, National Library of Ireland; Dublin newspapers, 20 December 1902.

10. There is uncertainty about the ownership of the company at this time. Arthur Duncan Thomas, who regularly styled himself 'Thomas-Edison' and claimed to have had twenty-one shows under managers travelling England in 1898, founded the company. By 1901, he was in financial difficulties and declared bankrupt. For more information relating to A. D. Thomas, see Vanessa Toulmin, 'The Importance of the Programme in Early Film Presentation', *KINtop*, vol. 11 (2002), pp. 19–33.

11. Louis de Clercq's *Letts Pocket Diary for 1902* is in the Liam O'Leary Archive, National Library of Ireland.

12. Edward Spencer, *The King's Race horses: A History of the Connection of His Majesty King Edward VII with the National Sport* (London: John Long, 1902).

13. Advertisement in Dublin, Wicklow and Wexford Railway Co.'s. Tourist Guide, *c.* 1900.

14. *The Showman*, 21 February 1902, p. 7.

15. *The Showman*, 21 February 1902, p. 30

16. From a Dublin newspaper, 23 April 1902.

17. *Cork Examiner*, 1 and 8 May 1902.

18. Seamus Murphy, *Stone Mad* (London: Routledge and Kegan Paul, 1966).

19. M&K 702 starts with a sequence that is described as VIPs arriving at the entrance to the exhibition grounds, to distinguish it from M&K 717, featuring the Lord Mayor of Cork arriving at the exhibition grounds. In the forthcoming Filmography these titles will be listed under M&K 702, 717: *Opening of Cork Exhibition* (1902).

20. The Royal Irish Constabulary, founded in 1867, operated in all Ireland except the Dublin Metropolitan area and was a paramilitary force, equipped to deal with violence. Consequently, they were able to perform an arms drill at the opening ceremony.

21. Information on the boat films is taken from *Cork Examiner*, July to 1 August 1902.

22. For listing of types of local films shot by Mitchell and Kenyon in 1902 in the UK, see Vanessa Toulmin, '"Local Films for Local People": Travelling Showmen and the Commissioning of Local Films in Great Britain, 1900–1902', *Film History*, vol. 13, no. 2 (2001), pp. 118–37.

23. Advertisements for this film are found in *Cork Examiner*, 7, 11 and 16 June 1902.

24. The exhibition of the film of St Patrick's Church, Cork was not advertised. However, films of St Peter's and St Paul's Church and St Mary's Church were made on 18 May 1902 and were advertised in *Cork Examiner*, 22 and 23 May 1902. It is probable that St Patrick's Church was filmed on the same date.

25. *Cork Examiner*, 22 May 1902.

26. M&K 719.

27. M&K 720.

28. Sources of information: *Cork Examiner*, 1 May 1902; J. C Coleman, *Journeys into Muskerry* (Dundalk: Dundalgan Press Ltd, 1961); Stanley C. Jenkins, *The Cork & Muskerry Light Railway* (Oxford: Oakwood Press, 1992).

Acknowledgements: Liam O'Leary (1910–1992), the staff of the National Library of Ireland, Tony Fletcher, Vanessa Toulmin, Patrick Russell, Rebecca Vick.

10 Mitchell and Kenyon in Wales

Dave Berry

The relative abundance of extant north Wales moving images from the first ten to fifteen years of cinema seems surprising and ironic to those familiar with Welsh social and religious history immediately prior to World War I. This irony stems from the realisation that the period 1896 to 1910 embraced a tumultuous religious revival in Wales. Bible-punching Nonconformists, led by the charismatic Evan Roberts and steeped in chapel Puritanism, inveighed against all forms of popular entertainment and took their toll on theatre and local eisteddfodau, competitive poetry and choral events. The movement originated in rural west Wales and soon swept the entire country.[1]

Just as surprising is the disparity between the comparative richness of footage representing north Wales, now augmented by rediscovered material from the Mitchell and Kenyon Collection, and the relative paucity of surviving footage from the much more heavily populated south Wales, then an industrial maelstrom.[2] The first surviving films shot by a Welsh-based film-maker, Arthur Cheetham of Rhyl, date from 1898 and were taken in north and mid-Wales.[3] Mitchell and Kenyon's Welsh films, with one or two exceptions, were made no later than 1902 and pre-date the oldest extant film from south or southwest Wales, William Haggar's now celebrated chase film, *A Desperate Poaching Affray* (1903).[4] The Blackburn company's cornucopia of films includes possibly the oldest surviving international soccer match, M&K 153–4: *Football in Wrexham: Ireland v Wales* (1906) footage of royal visits to Rhyl and Bangor, and animated title lettering which just might be the earliest extant in Britain. These shorts cover a diverse and distinctive range of material, including steamship footage between Liverpool and north Wales and a Llandudno May Day fancy dress procession which provides tantalising clues about early cinema exhibition. The volatile industrial period immediately prior to 1914 saw turmoil in the south Wales coalfields on an unprecedented scale, yet this was almost completely neglected by film-makers.

The foundation of 'The Fed', the south Wales Miners Federation in 1898 and management intractability helped spark industrial action and incidents such as the so-called 1910 Tonypandy Riots. During this period of intense human drama, fewer films, extant *or* lost were made in south Wales than in north Wales. Short silent films, allowing scope for few intertitles, were hardly an ideal medium in which to represent these disputes, even before movie censorship in Britain imposed its own restrictions on the representation of trade unionism. Photogenic landscapes were obviously a key feature in establishing north Wales as a location, with Hepworth, Heron, Urban and Warwick all visiting to make actuality or travelogue films well before 1910. In contrast, south Wales yields the most interesting extant early cinema material in narrative fiction – and this is almost entirely due to the prolific showman film pioneer, William Haggar.[5] In the years before 1910, films shot in south Wales only significantly outnumbered the north Wales total in 1903 and 1905, the key years of Haggar productions. The lack of films representing the south is exacerbated by the loss of the first films from Wales, taken by Birt Acres and then R. W. Paul's

M&K 154: *Wales v Ireland at Wrexham* (1906), filmed 2 April 1906 showing the Welsh International team leaving the dressing room at the racecourse, Wrexham.

company in 1896, and by the later footage of the Senghenydd, Glamorgan mining disaster of 1913.[6] Few extant early actuality films set in Wales add more to British early cinema history than the rediscovered Mitchell and Kenyon films. The most entertaining footage is probably that of the picturesque M&K 223–4: *Llandudno May Day* (1907). It presents an assertive business community at leisure, wearing very diverse fancy dress and parading in floats touting individual companies and concerns. Most of these attractions finally play second fiddle in the film to humorous images of aggressive placard advertising for the upcoming screening at the town's Prince's Theatre of that very May Day parade by the 'Parisian Animated Picture Co'.

In contrast to the cheerful eclecticism of this Llandudno film, the other procession films fit relatively seamlessly into the usual, more formal style for high-profile parades, with processions captured with generally static cameras as they move sedately towards the camera or diagonally across the screen. Yet, in M&K 737: *Royal Visit to Rhyl* (1902), of the Prince and Princess of Wales in May, there is a pleasing chaos and informality, with city centre streets bedecked with a surfeit of bunting and uniformed soldiers and firemen featuring strongly among the marchers. Two hundred police lined the streets but crowd regimentation appears minimal as the people spill across the street and the wide sweep of a bend in the wake of the royal carriage. Elegant women with babies and youths walking briskly alongside the uniformed marchers compete for our attention. They all attest to the humanity of a scene at least partially untrammelled by protocol. Surviving material of the procession, which featured the royal couple in a carriage with the Lord Lieutenant of Flintshire (H. R.

Hughes of Kinmel), appears incomplete. It captures only part of the parade through streets in Rhyl's centre, showing Stead and Simpson's prominent shopfront and dozens of firemen. The parade, en route to the royal opening of the Royal Alexandra Hospital, included soldiers from the Burma and Boer War campaigns, and was headed by Flintshire's chief constable and a cavalry troop of the Denbighshire Imperial Yeomanry.[7] The Rhyl movie can now be seen as complementary to Arthur Cheetham's short of the royal visit to Conway in 1899.

M&K 495: *Royal Visit to Bangor* (1902) suggests in its opening footage little of the affable untidiness of the Rhyl scenes. The crowd are marshalled by police and line the exterior walls of what seem to be public grounds. The passing parade, moving from left to right diagonally, include six or seven carriages which pass out of shot in the foreground, accompanied by military officers. Spectators seem fascinated by one carriage with four white horses, apparently the royal conveyance. In the other shot, in what appears to be a park, men and women mill around a little aimlessly, many in close up, peering towards the camera. The film leaders indicate that it was made for the Sedgwicks, a show family based in the north of England. It seems most likely to have been taken in 1902, during the same north Wales royal trip, as the next such visit to Bangor was 1907 by Edward VII, and in 1906 Sedgwick's advertised the sale of their cinematograph equipment, following a fire at their show.[8]

Arthur Cheetham, the film-maker identified with M&K 737: *Royal Visit to Rhyl*, also shot the earliest surviving football footage anywhere, *Blackburn Rovers v. West Bromwich Albion* (1898),

M&K 223: *Llandudno May Day* (1907), filmed 1 May 1907, shows the screening by the 'Parisian Animated Picture Co' to be held at Prince's Theatre cart with the theatre manager Mr J. Ritson in the foreground.

in what became, of course, Mitchell and Kenyon territory.[9] The extant Blackburn images, consisting of long shots of indeterminate action, could or might just as well be out-takes. These few wan images are eclipsed spectacularly by surely Mitchell and Kenyon's most significant contribution to Welsh football history, M&K 153–4: *Wales v Ireland in Wrexham*, of the international football match held at the racecourse in Wrexham. The north Wales game, attracting a then record Wrexham crowd of 5–6,000, contains remarkable close-ups of the action and, despite obvious limitations, imposed by frequent camera roll change necessities, no fewer than four goals in a 4–4 draw, a significant achievement. Arguably the most arresting of the films is M&K 214–22: *A Trip to North Wales on the St Elvies* (1902). The steamship, under Captain John Young, sailed between Liverpool, the Menai Straits and Llandudno, during the peak years of the Liverpool and North Wales Steamship Company. The *St Tudno*, the biggest and fastest in the company's steamship fleet is glimpsed here, and valuable images of the *St Tudno* and a sister paddle steamer, *The Snowdon*, are in a separate film, held at London's Cinema Museum.[10] The trip, from Liverpool to the Menai Straits, offers a compelling, intriguing blend of animation and live action and was advertised as a 'splendid subject' and single film, by Norden films (Mitchell and Kenyon's trade name), in *The Era* in November 1902.[11] The animation of titles, at this early date, is a highly unusual feature, though the presence of splices before and after the animated material suggests the titles were added later, perhaps for a re-issue. This actuality or travelogue live-action footage is interesting enough *per se*, with views from pier and ship constituting an impressive social/historical document. The segment titled 'St Elvies steamship', contains effective shots of passengers waving handkerchiefs at the ship's rail, captured in a slow pan right.[12] Footage of the ship leaving Liverpool is particularly appealing.[13] Crew and passengers crowd in the foreground, other spectators feature in mid-shot and the eye is directed, amid all the dark clothing, to a man carrying a baby in a white shawl, moving from right to left at the top of the frame, with the vessel looming above them. These shots convey the enthusiasm generated in the first decade of the twentieth century, the peak popularity years of the steamship company (1891–1962) and of the *St Elvies* itself built (like the *Tudno*) by the Fairfield company of Glasgow, and launched in 1896.[14] The panning shots of congested decks in the sections titled 'Panorama of the Wake' and 'Panorama of the Bows' might suggest that some footage at least was shot on one of the last excursions of a season, probably 1902.[15] These late trips were the most successful judging by extant season ticket sale details for that year and 1903. The *St Elvies*, with a passenger capacity of 991, was crammed 'from bow to stern' in its last trip on 29 September 1902.[16] Totally different in atmosphere are the shots following one intertitle 'Arrival at Menai' with tranquil travelling shots of apparently sumptuous mansions and halls dotted in rolling hillside, contrasting interestingly with signs of dereliction or embryo building development defacing the shoreline.[17] Sailings by the *St Elvies*, to Llandudno and back, from the company's Liverpool base were priced at 4s 6d (or 5s) and 3s 6d, and enabled city dwellers to enjoy the delights of north Wales scenery, returning early enough in the morning for businessmen to reach their jobs at the Liverpool Stock Exchange or elsewhere.[18] In 1902, sailings to Liverpool would also have enabled rural dwellers to sample the talents of artists such as Dan Leno, Marie Lloyd, Vesta Victoria, Hetty King, Lillie Langtry, the Brothers Egbert, Wilkie Bard and George Robey.[19] The detailed steamship footage, particularly on-deck shots, has intrinsic historical value but modern early cinema screen historians and academics, sometimes too preoccupied with historic 'firsts', are more likely to seduced by the floating, animated letters. Those of the main title metamorphose, to form the words 'Leaving Liverpool'. Other intertitles include 'Panorama of the Menai Straits' and 'Arrival at Menai' but some are not animated.

Animation was also used for titling in several Mitchell and Kenyon films including the fictional comedy *Diving Lucy* (1903), in the Cinema Museum collection.[20] Certainly these two Mitchell and Kenyon films invite speculation about the identity of the unknown animator. The animation titling appearing on the 1902 film, if taken at face value, pre-dates by some distance English-born, US-based lightning cartoon specialist (and later the Vitagraph company's co-founder), J. Stuart Blackton's *Humorous Phases of Funny Faces* (1906) where letters of the title formed themselves from moving bits of paper.[21] Animation writer and academic Donald Crafton has stressed that certain Edison company films from 1905 used animated title cards, including *How Jones Lost His Roll* (1905). Before 1902, little if any animation had emerged and much doubt has been cast in recent years on the provisional 1899 dating of Britain's Arthur Melbourne Cooper's extant war propaganda film, *Matches: An Appeal.* It uses animated Bryant and May matchsticks to spell out that, for one guinea, the company would 'forward a case containing sufficient to supply a box of matches to each man in a battalion, with the name of the sender inside'. It is now thought that this surviving film, originally supposed to date from the Boer War, might have been made in World War I.[22] Another contender as first to use animated titles may be Georges Méliès, said by a modern source, Bendazzi, to have used animated alphabet letters in advertising films as early as 1898.[23]

The suggestion that *A Trip to North Wales on the St Elvies*, is a compilation of recent and older material might be given some guarded credence. However, it is difficult to ascertain if the editing slices in the negatives were contemporary or slightly later. There are certainly films of the Liverpool and north Wales steamships the *St Tudno* and *St Elvies* in the Warwick catalogue as early as 1900.[24] I have so far failed to unearth a screening of the entire 700 ft of Elvies material, under the advertised title in north Wales in 1902 or 1903, although there is evidence that a title, containing some footage from this film, was screened in Leeds in April 1902. It certainly seems safe to assume that the most recent footage was taken no later than 29 September 1902, when the steamship company's sailings ceased for the season.[25] Mitchell and Kenyon could have been commissioned by Warwick to shoot at least some steamship images earlier. It must also be possible that the animation titles were the *raison d'être* for assembling the compilation. The separate reel, *Paddle Steamers – 'St Tudno' and 'Snowdon'* (1902) held at the Cinema Museum, contains mostly footage of the *St Tudno*, apparently taken at Bangor. The *St Tudno* was the biggest and fastest member of the Liverpool and North Wales fleet, at 794 gross tons and nineteen knots (compared to the *St Elvies'* 567 gross tons). The 265-foot company founder vessel, launched in 1891 and taking a maximum 1,061 passengers, was given the same name as the vessel it replaced and therefore known as *Tudno II*. It generally ran from Liverpool to Menai Bridge every day except Fridays, from May to September. This film contains high-angle shots of the deck of its sibling minnow, the 175-foot Snowdon, a mere 338 gross tons, with a passenger capacity of 462 and fourteen knots maximum speed.[26] *The Snowdon*, specially built for excursions, plied its trade for Liverpool and North Wales for more than thirty years, sailing in its early period regularly between Llandudno and the Menai Straits and Caernarvon, calling at Beaumaris, Bangor and Menai Bridge.[27] In these images of the vessel, built by Laing Bros of Birkenhead in 1892 and in service for the Liverpool and North Wales in 1899, any formality is offset by hirsute sailors sporting jerseys with the 'Snowdon' logo on the breast and musicians unselfconsciously entertaining passengers and crew with violin and harmonium.[28]

The 1907 title, M&K: 223–4 *Llandudno May Day*, featuring what the local press called 'A Great Trades Procession', contains constant surprises.[29] The ingenuity of the cart and float owners and forthright lapel-grabbing finale, offer more felicities than we might have expected.

The clarity of the close-ups impresses, together with the confident selection of images worth holding on screen. The long take of May Queen Doris Ward, centre frame and half in shadow in an artificial bower aboard her float is pleasing and eloquent, implying her reticence.[30] It forms a neat contrast with the aggressive advertising ploy at the film's climax – an expedient image of three men in large masks, holding up a board advertising showings of the forthcoming procession film on 'Fri. Sat next. May 3rd and fourth and throughout following week', adding 'Don't fail to come and see yourself as others see you.' The screening, the board informs us, is by the 'Parisian Animated Picture Co.' and the prepossessing moustached figure prominent in this footage of the Prince's Theatre cart and its advertising is probably the theatre's manager Mr J. Ritson. The film, the first of several extant Llandudno procession shorts, conveys a heady air of celebration.[31] The carnival mood infected the *Llandudno Advertiser* of 4 May. One reporter wrote of 'the ancient time honoured and joyous customs of the first of May which for nearly a thousand years made that day one of mirth and gladness throughout "'Merrie England'" – then (as if by afterthought) 'which includes Wales'. For the first time children had chosen the Llandudno May Queen. Doris, seemingly, duly inspired the paper's 11 May poem in dialect (veering from northern English, Irish and Scots) which began:

> I went to see the May Queen,
> Tho' on a cowld May-Day
> Well I am plaz'd, bekase I've seen
> A mighty fine display.

The May Day parade attractions caught on film included an incongruous array of chimney sweeps, funeral businesses, farmers, joiners and builders, with many of their logos and names legible on floats and carts. The Prince's Theatre advertising cart brought up the rear. More than one float simulates a fully furnished business interior. A half-masked clown on a bicycle and a black minstrel are seen, together with various slightly sinister-looking masked marchers. A band from the *CLIO* training ship at Bangor and members of the Llandudno fire brigade are also prominent in a parade travelling from Gloddaeth Street, via the Promenade and Chapel Street, to South Parade where prizes were distributed for the best displays.[32] The procession film was virtually the only movie screened that year at the Prince's, a leading Llandudno theatre venue, and earned praise in the local press as excellent entertainment satisfying large crowds.[33] The show presenters were advertised under slightly different names at various times including the 'Original Parisian Animated Pictures'. *Llandudno Advertiser* issues of 27 April, 4 and 11 May advertised the May Day short, but Royal Parisian Co. films, with no specified titles, appeared in the same paper on 30 March and 18 May.[34] On 27 July at the Prince's, the Parisian outfit screened a series of films, billed as *Lovely Devon*.[35] In contrast to the Prince's apparent reluctance to screen films, three shorts (usually fictional) were advertised each week of the 1907 summer season at the less prepossessing Pier Theatre of Varieties. These were shown by the Royal American Bioscope company and on Saturday 4 May, the procession competed with a Pier Theatre screening of the FA Cup soccer final, Everton v Sheffield Wednesday.[36]

It is worth observing, especially given the peak years of the Welsh religious revival, that films set in or involving Wales did not increase in numbers between 1903 and 1910. Indeed 1898, thanks mainly to Cheetham's actualities output, remained, somewhat improbably, the most prolific year for 'Welsh' films in the entire pre-1910 period.[37] In 1902, the only two topical actualities, apart from the Rhyl hospital opening, given advertising prominence in north Wales newspapers were the delayed *Coronation Procession* movie and footage of *Kitchener's Return from the Boer War*. In 1903, the *Llandudno Advertiser* did not advertise or report on a single film.

M&K 494: *Royal Visit to Rhyl* (1902) in contrast, received massive press coverage in Wales and merited special supplements from two Rhyl weeklies.[38] The Prince and Princess, formerly the Duke and Duchess of York, were visiting Wales for the first time since succeeding to their titles. They were filmed at the end of a visit involving the laying of a Bangor University foundation stone, the Prince's installation in Caernarfon as Chancellor of the University of Wales, and a trip to the spectacular Llanberis Pass and to Dinorwic, then Wales's biggest quarry. The hospital, designed by architects A. Waterhouse and Son, was constructed on the site of a house, 'Plastirion', built by Queen Victoria's physician Dr Stephen Warren. The Alexandra, a former children's home, had initially been on another site, later found unsuitable, where the foundation stone was laid in 1894 before transfer to the new location in Coronation year. Much credit for help in raising the £60,000 needed to complete the re-sited hospital's 160-bed development in Marine Drive went to the late Duke of Westminster, who sponsored the appeal for a new site, donated £5,000 and added £10,000 when his legendary horse Flying Fox won a major race at Sandown.[39] We have been unable to trace any screenings of a Mitchell and Kenyon 1902 film of the *Rhyl Procession* either in 1902 or 1903, yet there is much evidence from contemporary reports, of Rhyl's film-maker *in situ*, Arthur Cheetham, shooting and showing such a film.

This was exhibited on Whit Monday on a bill he described in the *Rhyl Record and Advertiser* of 17 May as 'the most successful series of films' he had ever taken. Cheetham, a great self-publicist, explained how he'd even strapped his camera to the fishmonger's float of a Mr Boyle to provide moving pictures. This had enabled him, he claimed, to take a panoramic picture 'as the carriage moved along at a very rapid rate', which would show 'all the decorations along the route' and 'immense crowds in the High Street'. The film would also reveal movements of the carriage 'which will give the effect to the audience as if they were seated in it'. On 24 May, the paper reported that the film gave 'us a marvellously real idea of some leading incidents' from the occasion. A shot of the royal train departing in the distance was 'strikingly successful', the report added. Cheetham, who screened the film at his own regular Rhyl venue, regales us with details of several horses, captured by his camera, shying as they drew up at the hospital during filming. The *Rhyl Record and Advertiser* of 10 May claimed that the film-maker, through the kindness of the Lord Lieutenant, was given permission to take a cinematograph picture of the arrival and departure of the royal party from Rhyl station and planned to use two cameras to take both the view at the station and the procession's arrival at the hospital. The pictures would be shown for the first time in Rhyl 'by electric light'.[40]

On 1 December 1894 the same newspaper reported that Cheetham, a registered professional phrenologist, and an enthusiastic electric hygienist had installed the first electric light in Rhyl.[41] In view of Cheetham's own comments and adverts and the absence of any locally advertised specific Mitchell and Kenyon film of the Royal Alexandra opening, we should consider the possibility that they commissioned the film from the Rhyl pioneer. By 1902 Cheetham was, after all, an experienced film-maker, with more than twenty shorts behind him. Considering Mitchell and Kenyon's prolific work rate and the heavy commissioning demands on them, it would not be surprising if the two Blackburn-based stalwarts had to 'subcontract' work. It is logical to assume that they might rely on Cheetham who had already won his spurs making procession films such as the *Royal Visit of the Duke and Duchess of York to Conway* (1899), for example. He went on to film Buffalo Bill Cody in Rhyl in 1903.[42]

No such doubts exist about the provenance of the naturally truncated version of the 1906 Wales v Ireland football international held at Wrexham, a fixture noteworthy in retrospect, for the hat-trick scored by Arthur Green of Notts County (and late of Aberystwyth Town).[43] The game was also unusual for the absence (and reasons for non-appearance) of the greatest Welsh player of the day Billy Meredith, wing wizard of both Manchester City and Manchester United, who won a then-record, forty-eight Welsh international caps. Meredith was enduring a year-long expulsion from football, facing bribery and match-fixing allegations after offering £10 to a rival skipper to lose a match.[44] The M&K 153–4: *Wales v Ireland at Wrexham* footage, from the match on Monday 2 April, boasts no players of a similarly enduring reputation. The Welsh side did, however, include Wrexham's Horace Blew (later the town's mayor) and Bob Evans of Aston Villa and formerly of Wrexham. Evans gained notoriety when, after winning ten Welsh caps, he was found to have been born in Chester, just over the border (Meredith was born 300 yards the other side). The Football Association disqualified Evans from playing for Wales and he later gained four England caps.[45] This title containing the oldest known images of soccer in Wales is fascinating enough, for both layman and soccer and film historian. Match officials are seen in peaked caps and players clamber over a bench on their way from dressing rooms to pitch. Despite this small inconvenience the ground seems impressive enough for the period, especially for a non-league club, although Wrexham, after all, had won the Welsh Cup in 1904–5, for the fifth time! In 1905–6 they were minnows playing, curiously enough, in the Birmingham and District League. Wrexham finally gained league status with the launch of the Third Division (North) in 1921. The dressing rooms seen in the film behind the players entering the field were demolished in 1998 to be replaced by the Pryce Griffiths stand along Mold Road. One open side of the ground now houses the Yale/Sainsbury Stand.[46] There is also possibly the first football injury captured on film as an Irish scorer, after slotting the ball past the still-renowned Welsh goalkeeper, L. R. Roose (then of Stoke), immediately collapses, apparently with a groin injury, sustained, it seems when colliding with a post. The match result was hugely disappointing for Welsh supporters, with Wales surrendering a 4–2 lead in the last fifteen minutes. There was consolation enough when the Welsh, skippered by Meredith, won the Home International Championship for the first time the following season.[47] M&K 153–4: *Wales v Ireland at Wrexham* offers an unprecedented glimpse into Welsh football of this period and captures key players such as Blew and Roose not otherwise found on extant film. The 1906 football footage was screened locally by the showman Pat Collins, who was noted for his expensive Bioscope and resplendent fairground shows.[48]

Taken as a whole, the newly discovered Welsh titles in the Mitchell and Kenyon Collection add greatly to our knowledge of early cinema heritage in Wales. If one compares surviving titles from the period, Wales has a dearth of phantom ride material compared to many other areas of Britain. Haggar train and tram material supposedly made *c.* 1901–2 has disappeared, and the British Biograph *Conway Castle* is the only existing film shot and set in Wales which can be officially classified in this subgenre. Other travelogue titles similar to the Mitchell and Kenyon material include travelling locomotives from British Biograph, Cheetham's *Mailboat Munster Arriving at Holyhead* (1898) and the stunning Charles Urban film *North Wales, England: Land of Castles and Waterfalls* (1907). The Urban film includes delightfully varied footage of north Wales towns and beauty spots and contrives to show at least three trains steaming under, or adjacent to castle walls. The rediscovered films give north Wales a plenitude of turn-of-the-century material for historians and audiences in the principality to reflect on and savour when the Collection becomes more widely available.

NOTES

1. John Davies, *A History of Wales* (London: Penguin, 1994), pp. 505–6; Evan Roberts (1878–1951).

2. *Wales Film Chronology*, compiled by the author, at the National Screen and Sound Archive of Wales, Aberystwyth.

3. A 68mm hand-tinted British Biograph film of a phantom train ride film of Conway Castle from 1898 also survives. This was probably shot by Edison's former employee, French-born William Kennedy Laurie Dickson.

4. Richard Brown and Barry Anthony, *A Victorian Film Enterprise: The History of the British Biograph and Mutoscope Company* (Flicks Books: Trowbridge, 1999).

5. Only four of his documented thirty-five films are known to survive.

6. A tragedy with a death toll of 439, the worst in British mining history; *Wales Film Chronology*, Davies; *A History of Wales*. William Haggar made at least six films in 1903 and eleven in 1905.

7. *Rhyl Record and Advertiser –Special Royal Visit Edition Supplement*, 17 May 1902 and *Rhyl Journal Royal Visit Special Edition*, 12 May 1902.

8. Gwynedd Record Office note to cataloguer, National Screen and Sound Archive of Wales; Kevin Scrivens and Stephen Smith, *The Travelling Cinematograph Show* (Tweedale: New Era Publications, 1999), p. 141.

9. Philip Lloyd, 'Arthur Cheetham, Rhyl's Pioneer Filmmaker', *Rhyl Journal*, 19 January 1984.

10. *A Trip to North Wales on the St Elvies* is no. 02096, in November 1902 in Denis Gifford, *The British Film Catalogue Vol 2, Non-Fiction Film 1888–1994* (London and Chicago, IL: Fitzroy Dearborn, 2001), p. 90.

11. *The Era*, 8 November 1902.

12. M&K 220.

13. M&K 214.

14. John Cowell, *Liverpool to North Wales Pleasure Steamers: A Pictorial History 1821–1962* (Market Drayton: Sea Breezes Publications, 1990), pp. 7, 12, 39.

15. M&K 215.

16. *Llandudno Advertiser*, 3 October 1902.

17. M&K 219.

18. See adverts *Liverpool Echo*, 7 and 12 July 1902.

19. *Liverpool Echo*, various.

20. Tony Fletcher, 'The Evolution of the Story Film in Britain – Some Observations' in Alan Burton and Laraine Porter (eds), *Scene-Stealing: Sources for British Cinema before 1930* (Trowbridge: Flicks Books, 2003), pp. 29–35.

21. Donald Crafton, *Before Mickey, 1898–1928* (Chicago, IL: University of Chicago Press, 1993), p. 21.

22. See Denis Gifford, *British Animated Films, 1895–1985 – A Filmography* (Jefferson, NC and London: McFarland and Company, Inc., 1987), entry no. 6, p. 4.

23. Giannalberto Bendazzi, *100 Years of Cinema Animation* (London: John Libby, 1994), p. 7.

24. Warwick catalogue entries in Charles Urban material at the Science Museum, no. 3746b *SS Tudno Leaving Llandudno*, also shots of St Elvies 'approaching pier at full speed' – 5747b *Panoramic View of Menai Straits*. See also Gifford, *The British Film Catalogue,* for 1900 Warwick Films of the *St Tudno* and *St Elvies* in Liverpool and Wales nos 01440–01443. Toulmin, notes on Mitchell and Kenyon in catalogue of *22nd Pordenone Silent Film Festival*, Sacile, Italy, 11–18 October 2003.

25. At the Tivoli, Leeds: *Yorkshire Post*, 30 April 1902, p. 1. *Llandudno Advertiser*, 3 October 1902 and *Colwyn Bay Weekly News and Visitors Chronicle*, 3 October 1902, p. 8.

26. M&K 216.

27. Cowell, *Liverpool to North Wales Pleasure Steamers.*

28. Cowell, *Liverpool to North Wales Pleasure Steamers.*

29. *Llandudno Advertiser*, 4 May 1907.

30. Doris Ward identified in *Llandudno Advertiser*, 4 May 1907.

31. M&K 224: *Llandudno May Day* (1907) forms the additional part of the sequence filmed with the original negative inscriptions titling the individual film as Llandudno May Day no. 3 and no. 2.

32. Doris Ward identified in *Llandudno Advertiser*, 4 May 1907.

33. *Llandudno Advertiser*, 4 May 1907.

34. *Llandudno Advertiser*, 4 May 1907.

35. *Llandudno Advertiser*, 4 May 1907.

36. *Llandudno Advertiser*, 4 May 1907.

37. *Wales Film Chronology*. Cheetham made no fewer than seventeen of the twenty-four films set or shot in Wales in 1898. The figure is based on Philip Lloyd's original research.

38. *Rhyl Record and Advertiser – Special Royal Visit Edition Supplement*, 17 May 1902 and *Rhyl Journal Royal Visit Special Edition*, 12 May 1902. *The Story of the Royal Alexander Hospital* (booklet, undated) no. 83.48 in royal visit collection, Rhyl.

39. *The Story of the Royal Alexander Hospital*.

40. Philip Lloyd, Typed manuscript notes in Rhyl library, citing this issue.

41. Lloyd, Typed manuscript notes.

42. Philip Lloyd, 'Arthur Cheetham, Rhyl's Pioneer Filmmaker'.

43. *Western Mail*, 2 April 1906; *Wrexham Advertiser*, 7 April 1906, p. 3, col. 1, *Aberystwyth Observer, Cardiganshire and Montgomeryshire Advertiser and Merioneth News*, 5 April 1906; *Liverpool Daily Post and Mercury*, 2 and 3 April 1906; *Western Mail*, 3 April 1906. For other references, see cataloguer Mary Moylett, *What the Papers Said*, brochure of press cuttings of Wales v Ireland match, at National Screen and Sound Archive of Wales, Aberystwyth.

44. John Harding, 'Billy Meredith', in Peter Stead and Huw Richards (eds), *For Club and Country – Welsh Football Greats* (Cardiff: University of Wales Press, 2000), pp. 10–20. *Liverpool Daily Post and Mercury*, 31 March 1906, p. 5, col. 6.

45. Gareth M. Davies and Peter Jones, *Wrexham Football Club, 1872–1950* (Stroud: Tempus Publishing, 2000), pp. 14–16.

46. Davies and Jones, *Wrexham Football Club*, pp. 34–6.

47. Harding, 'Billy Meredith'.

48. *Wrexham Advertiser*, 4 April 1906. I'm grateful to Tim Neal of the National Fairground Archive, Sheffield for this information. Scrivens and Smith, *The Travelling Cinematograph Show*, for details of Pat Collins and Pat Ross Collins, his son, pp. 77 and 81.

11 Mitchell and Kenyon's Legacy in Scotland – The Inspiration for a Forgotten Film-making Genre

Janet McBain

There is a body of film evidence to suggest that the characteristics of 'local topicals' in the silent era and beyond were strongly influenced by the Mitchell and Kenyon style of film-making for the travelling showmen at the turn of the twentieth century. The archetypal local topical featured outdoor events that would attract the local populace. Most commonly represented were sporting occasions, social and commemorative events, celebrations of calendar customs and aspects of daily life. These films were on average under one reel (100 ft) in length, but were customarily longer than the standard national newsreel story of the period.[1] Exhibitors used these films to attract audiences into their cinemas with the prospect of seeing themselves, family and neighbours on the screen. They were often commissioned from professional film companies and occasionally produced by the cinema owners themselves.[2] These in-house productions were promoted as exclusive to the commissioning cinema and were intended for limited local exhibition. They would be silent (even well into the talkies era) and few, if any, would have explanatory intertitles, relying on audiences' local knowledge of the subject.

Evidence of the production of local topicals has been found across the UK, from the 1910s up until the 1950s.[3] The classic features of the local topical of the first half of the film century mirror many of the aspects of the earlier Mitchell and Kenyon productions and indeed those of other topical producers of the period such as Cecil Hepworth. Their characteristics are surprisingly similar and consistent, including the use of panning shots of spectators, exhibitors getting themselves and their cinemas in shot, close shots of faces in the crowd, establishing shots of local landmarks, factory gate films, parades and processions. Not every cinema exhibitor who included topicals in their programmes came from a fairground background but there is evidence of a direct link between the experiences of the first generation of film exhibitors on the fairground, and their successors in the picture palaces of the 1910s and 1920s. In Scotland, those who made most use of the topical as a publicity attraction had a family history in the industry dating back to the fairground era. This article will draw on film evidence in the Scottish Screen Archive and the history of two cinema families, Green and Kemp, to suggest that this neglected genre of film-making should be recognised as an enduring legacy of Mitchell and Kenyon's topical production.

The Greens were a large family of Lancashire showmen. The patriarch George Green and his brother moved to Glasgow to set up the hub of the family enterprise in 1894 and soon established a permanent site for their carnival in the east end of the city. George Green's entry into film exhibition came in the autumn of 1896 when, on a trip to London to seek out novelties for his show, he purchased Robert W. Paul's Theatrograph apparatus. His son Bert recalled he and his father testing it out, fitting the mechanism up with a carbon arc lamp in the animal house on the carnival site in the closed season. Bert and his brother, as schoolboys, were allowed to take turns at projecting *The Highland Dancers*.

an endless film, having been taken at 30 pictures per second the then American speed, instead of the British 16 pictures per second. We could not make them dance quickly enough. It was hard turning and made us perspire, and our arms ached.[4]

The first public performance of this apparatus was given at Christmas 1896 in a circus building on the carnival site.

George Green established his first travelling cinematograph show in 1898.[5] Bert recalled that his father's show went to Hyde and then on to Blackburn Easter Fair where there were about forty performances on the Easter Monday. George Green had commissioned Mitchell and Kenyon to make topicals for his show, which Bert remembered as containing scenes of the Blackburn mills closing on the Thursday before Good Friday and that these items served 'to help us to spin out the supply of films. We also had topicals at Barrow because people came again and again to see themselves or their friends.'[6] Green advertised these local topicals with the slogan 'See Yourself as Others See You'.[7] In common with his fellow showmen, Green commissioned films from Mitchell and Kenyon, of which thirty-five survive in the Mitchell and Kenyon Collection.[8]

In 1902, Green secured rights to the fairground and cinematograph concessions at the Cork International Exhibition and commissioned a series of local scenes to show in Ireland.[9] The Green collection contains films promoting his fairground attractions including the memorable panning shot in M&K 291: *Whitsuntide Fair at Preston* (1906), with the camera pausing on crowds in front of Green's cockerel ride and then continuing, ending on a static shot of patrons in front of the clearly visible cinematograph booth.

Green began to invest in permanent, fixed site cinemas as early as 1908 with the acquisition of Whitevale Theatre in Glasgow's overpopulated Gallowgate. The land around the theatre building was used as a park for showmen's caravans with Mrs Green exacting a shilling a week rent for each pitch. The whole family of three sons and four daughters moved into a flat above the Whitevale's box office and each had a job in the family business. The Whitevale was a success and encouraged George Green to expand his development of permanent sites. In the period up to World War I, he gradually built up a chain of halls (named Picturedromes) around the industrial central belt of Scotland. As the number of screens under his control grew, he determined that it would be more cost effective to buy the reels outright than rent increasing numbers of prints. So successful did his choice of purchases prove with the cinemagoing public that other showmen began to ask him to select and supply their programmes.[10] Thus was born the other major part of the family business: the renting and film production operation known as Green's Film Service (1915). After the premature death of his youngest son John in 1914, George sold off his travelling fairground assets and concentrated on his circuit of fixed sites.

By the time of George Green's death the following year the circuit stood at ten cinemas. Green's Film Service had offices in London and Glasgow. George had established himself and his family business in the cinema trade. He was a founder member of the Cinematograph Exhibitors Association and was president of the Roundabout Proprietors Association and Showmen's Union of Great Britain. After his death, his two surviving sons, Fred and Bert, took over the business, Bert on the cinema side, Fred concentrating on the renting, with their sisters managing halls.

Both Fred and Bert had been reared in the tradition of fairground showmanship and had witnessed the enormous growth in the public's appetite for cinema. Under their charge the business was set to expand on all fronts. By 1917, in addition to eleven cinemas, they had a department renting comedies, serials and dramas, a mechanical department selling projectors, a music department renting sheet music and their own printing facilities for programmes, tickets and posters. On the renting side, Fred had secured the sole Scottish agency for the catalogue of the American Triangle Company. Comments in the trade press of November 1917 suggest that Green's was becoming recognised as the largest cinema proprietor and film renter in Scotland, eclipsing former rival J. J. Bennell.[11] By 1916, the company had secured the Scottish agency for supplying Powers cinematograph apparatus, bought up Bradford-based Hibbert's Film Renters with their five offices countrywide and had reputedly lured 'Captain Kettle' of the Bradford Photoplay Producing Company to Glasgow to run the Whitevale.[12] Captain Kettle was a pseudonym for novelist C. J. Cutcliffe Hyne, who, along with Hibbert's Pictures of Bradford, had invested in the Captain Kettle Film Studios. The *Entertainer and Scottish Kinema Record*, 2 May 1914, carries a picture of the captain, promoting Green's 'Exclusives' with the legend 'If it's Good it's Green's', a slogan that was to be the hallmark of their exhibition business, even extending to specially woven carpets for their cinemas carrying the wording. At the beginning of 1917, Bert and Fred launched a trade magazine, *Green's Kinema Tatler* and in the spring they made their first cinema purchase outside the Scottish central belt with acquisition of La Scala Picture House in Aberdeen.

By now Fred Green was making weekly trips to his London office to buy films. Green's had also developed further interests in film production with a commercial investment in the Samson Film Company and had produced a two-reel comedy, *His Highness*.[13] It seems reasonable to suggest that the sons were inspired by their father's commercial success on the fairground with the Mitchell and Kenyon films to produce and exhibit local topical films beyond the era of the travelling shows. Mitchell and Kenyon had ceased film production by 1913. Green's had developed business connections with the Bradford studio-owning company, where topical films were made, and they had established their own in-house production facility to service their Scottish sites. In the 1910s, Green's Film Service was producing local topicals in the west of Scotland and, with the purchase of La Scala in 1917, they inherited Aberdeen's resident topical cameraman-cum-projectionist, Joe Gray.

In October 1917, Green's film production interest was further developed with the introduction of a regular Scottish topical. Unlike previous topicals, made erratically for individual customers, this new topical, the Scottish Moving Picture News would, it was promised, be available for purchase or hire to exhibitors across Scotland. The following month, Green's announced the buy-out of rival J. J. Bennell's producing plant, 'including cameras used by BB Film Service at Wellington Palace'.[14] It was reported that Green's were to make use of this plant for their extended topical. Early in 1918, the trade press offered very positive reviews of this new arrival on the topical scene. In January, the Scottish trade press reported on Green's scoop in covering the travels of Julian the Tank Bank around Scotland, with footage shot at 11.30am appearing on screen by 3pm the same day. Exhibitors who booked the reel 'all did excellent business'.[15]

By February 1918, Green's announced that cameramen representatives had been appointed across Scotland. In Glasgow, their staff cameraman was Alf Le Verne and in Aberdeen, they had the veteran Joe Gray, who had been making topical films in and around the city since the 1890s, initially for Walker's Royal Cinematograph and, after its demise in 1911, as a freelancer for city exhibitors. With this network of cameramen in place, Green's confidently predicted that the Scottish Moving Picture News would soon be going bi-weekly. Presumably in readiness for the move to two issues a week, in July Green's secured the services of Paul Robello, like Joe Gray in Aberdeen, a veteran from Walker's Royal Cinematograph and described in the trade press as Scotland's first cameraman. Robello was to run the production department under the supervision of Bert Green. The bi-weekly news began around the late autumn of 1918, a year after the launch of the newsreel itself.

In February 1919, the Scottish Moving Picture News began to appear in the listing in *Kinematograph Weekly* along with rivals Pathé Gazette, Gaumont Graphic and Topical Budget. Green's had been advertising all six of their trade departments heavily in the Scottish trade press for some time and now adverts for the newsreel also began to appear in the UK press. In May 1919, some six months into the new bi-weekly schedule, it was noted that the name of the newsreel was to change from 'Scottish' to 'British' Moving Picture News. 'This broadening out of the title will allow of a wider scope in treatment', reported *Kine Weekly*. In August 1921, and despite positive noises in the trade press about levels of subscription to the British Moving Picture News, there was word of another name change – back to 'Scottish'. A full-page advert in the *Kine Weekly* of 11 August 1921 for the Scottish Moving Picture News runs: 'General news in pictures is interesting but Scottish news in pictures for Scottish audiences is an absolute necessity. This can only be had in Scottish Moving Picture News – the Topical for Scotland.'

If the name change suggests some retrenchment in the face of strong competition for a national newsreel, Green's other exhibition-related business was still healthy. The cinema circuit was enlarging, they had their renting and printing departments and they had set up a cinema building company for the construction of halls for themselves and other exhibitors. They also had a branch selling cinema seating and furnishing and offered an equipment repair and servicing facility. The music department had been expanded under William Moore (formerly of the Empire Theatre) and supplied sheet music, touring sixtettes and pianists for performance.

The last issue of *Scottish Kinema Record* was December 1922. It carried a large back page advert for Scottish Moving Picture News but there is no information to suggest that the newsreel continued into 1923. Green's production department manager Paul Robello set up his own film company in September 1922 and was supplying stories to Topical Budget by spring 1923. Despite the demise of the Moving Picture News, Green's continued with the production of local topicals after 1922 under the name, Green's Topical Productions. Alf Le Verne stayed with the company as cameraman for the individually commissioned works for Green's halls and other exhibitors such as Harry Kemp and James Gillespie. However, by 1927, it would appear that Green's had largely pulled out of production and renting, to concentrate on exhibition and cinema construction in Scotland. The end of the local topical production wing of the business may have been anticipated by Bert Green. In a rather pessimistic address to cinema trade personnel in Glasgow in 1920, he bemoaned the lack of progress in the industry.

> I am young in years, but old in the trade. I remember seeing Green's pictures about that time (1896). One was a topical – 'The Gordon Highlanders Leaving Mary Hill Barracks'. There were no titles but we had a describer. The film broke and we had to hunt and grope for the ends in a basket … So you see films got into a bad condition even then; but our film stock is just the same today … Our topicals are still where they were 20 years ago … The way of the pioneer is hard, because there is little money in topicals and no profit in educational subjects – no one seems anxious to develop them … I am sanguine of the ultimate success of the topical and educational film.[16]

Only seventeen items from the five years' production of Scottish/British Moving Picture News are known to have survived.[17] A viewing of the remaining issues and surviving titles produced by Green's Topical Productions throws up similarities. Examples exist of different versions of the same story, one incorporated into a weekly issue of the newsreel with a longer version, presumably intended for use by the local exhibitor whose cinema was in the town or village where the filmed event took place. This suggests that there was a blurring in the editorial process as to what constituted a news item as opposed to a local interest topical. Green's British Moving Picture News covered Rothesay's peace celebrations in September 1919 in two stories in issue no. 165. A longer version, found in a local cinema, devotes more screen time to the parade, with close shots of spectators milling around, and with the local cinema proprietor visible in the crowd in much the same manner that the travelling exhibitors would appear in the Mitchell and Kenyon films. There is evidence in the Moving Picture News that footage was shot for dual distribution, one for the local market and a shorter 'newsier' version for the more widely distributed newsreel. The Greens were not the only travelling showmen who retained the Mitchell and Kenyon-style topical in the cinema programme of succeeding decades. Green's Film Service and their specialist production unit, Green's Topical Productions provided for themselves and fellow exhibitors a service that filled the vacuum left by the demise of Mitchell and Kenyon's company.

That there were other exhibitors in the market for such a service is clear. One of Green's most regular clients in the early 1920s were the Kemps. Related by marriage to the Greens, the Leicester-born family of George Kemp were contemporaries in fairground travelling shows. George 'President' Kemp introduced his first Bioscope show in 1901, followed in 1906 by the lavish and breathtaking Dreamland. His brother, Walter, enjoyed a reputation as a talented describer of silent films. In 1907, Kemp pioneered the use of the talkie system Gaumont's Chronomegaphone enjoying considerable success with Harry Lauder's 'singing pictures'. In 1908, President Kemp gave the Dreamland show to his son, Harry and Harry's bride, Susan Green, as a wedding present. Kemp ordered a replacement, the fabulous Theatre Unique, described in the World's Fair as eclipsing all other shows. Father and son were now in friendly competition on the road. A few years later, Harry built a wooden cinema, the Hippodrome, at Earlstown in Lancashire. About the same time, President Kemp came off the road and established in 1911 his first permanent cinema in Johnstone near Glasgow, with a flat above for his family. He kept the Theatre Unique show on the road, but toured it only sporadically, finally selling it to George Green in 1913. President Kemp had spotted a second potential permanent site in the seaside town of Saltcoats on the Ayrshire coast. He took his son to see it. The outcome was that they bought the site and built the 900-seater La Scala cinema in 1913. Harry gave up his wooden picture hall in Lancashire, sold his travelling show, and moved to Scotland to join his father in the new venture. Father and son were to build up a small but very successful circuit of cinemas on the Ayrshire coast.

President Kemp retired in 1925, leaving Harry to develop and expand the business with cine variety and concert parties in the summer tourist season. Harry was particularly successful with the Scotch Broth revues, bringing young stars such as Renee and Billie Houston to the fore. The Scotch Broth Entertainers toured Scotland to packed houses and enjoyed successful tours across England in the mid-1920s. The heart of the Kemp empire was Saltcoats where they had two cinemas facing each other across the street. La Scala was joined by Casino, rebuilt as the Regal in 1931.

President Kemp had commissioned Mitchell and Kenyon films for his Dreamland show in the early 1900s. Three films attributed to Kemp survive in the Collection. All were taken in 1904 when Kemp's Dreamland visited Buxton in Derbyshire for the annual well-dressing festival. A consummate showman and publicist, Kemp appears in all the films, at times discreetly in the crowd, on other occasions very visibly and pointedly on the steps of the Bioscope show or in the forefront of the crowd. In the third of the reels shot at Buxton, he figures centre stage, holding a baby in his arms and presenting her to the camera.[18] Son Harry reprised the success of these local films in his programming of the Saltcoats cinemas in the 1920s, commissioning Green's Film Service to make local topicals such as the local factory sports day and works outing and the departure of the Salt-coats pilgrimage to Lourdes. To promote his concert parties he also had topicals made of the cast

M&K 540: *Buxton Well Dressing* (1904), showing President Kemp on the front of his Dreamland Bioscope show with maypole dancers taken for the Buxton well-dressing celebrations, June 1904.

of the Scotch Broth revue relaxing, the celebrities enjoying a round of putting, with a shot of the cinema featuring the playbill for the show. Made by seasoned topical producers, these films echo many of the aspects of the Mitchell and Kenyon model. In the period after Green's ceased topical production, Harry engaged newsreel cameramen to make his topicals, emulating his father's self-publicity techniques at Buxton a quarter of a century earlier. There exists a short fragment of sound film of a 'piece to camera' with Harry standing outside the Regal bidding his patrons goodnight.[19] This valediction, screened in the Regal at the end of the last house of the night, was discovered on a reel of local topical made by Movietone's cameraman of the opening of the town's new esplanade in 1933.

The exhibitor enjoying a cameo role in 'his' topical is a feature of many of the Mitchell and Kenyon films made for the showmen. This is one aspect of the local topical that is reprised and retained through succeeding decades. Another recurring feature is a shot of the physical place of exhibition; typically the cameraman panning across the front of the cinema, or positioning the camera to film the parade as it passes with the cinema visible in the background. The use of the gag card, found in Green's showmens' films,[20] can also be found in topicals of the 1920s. James Gillespie, manager of the Palace Picture House on the island of Bute in the Clyde estuary, commissioned a film of Lady Lauder judging the final of the *Daily Mail* Sand Modelling Competition in 1922. Gillespie's daughter walks across the front of the assembled spectators leading a small seaside donkey with a placard on its side bearing the legend 'Everybody goes to the Palace but me'.[21]

The coming of the cinema newsreel in the years prior to World War I would appear to have filled in part of the production service vacuum left by the demise of Mitchell and Kenyon's business. Pathé and Gaumont were establishing networks of stringers (local cameramen representatives), who could be sent out to cover stories from all regions of the country for the national newsreels. Local exhibitors, it would seem from the evidence in film archives, were able to utilise the services of these professionals for the making of local films. Examples exist of local topicals made by Gaumont cameramen on commission for local exhibitors. The footage exhibits the classic local topical style, in the main longer than the edited and published newsreel story, and covering a subject unlikely to be classed as newsworthy for national audiences, for example the laying of the foundation stone of Kirkintilloch Parish Church in 1913 or the funeral of Stranraer's Provost Young in 1914. The inclusion of panning shots of faces, lengthy sequences of parades, faces of spectators in the crowd, suggests that the cameraman had his instructions from the commissioning exhibitor, in that he, the client, knew what he wanted from the footage.

Surviving copies of these films have formally styled Gaumont title cards, suggesting that they were made officially by Gaumont personnel and processed by Gaumont's laboratory. A review of Scottish film production in the trade press of 1918 refers to Gaumont's activities in local newsreel production, 'In short stuff there have been hundreds of films produced locally. The most important were the series of films taken by the Glasgow branch of Gaumont's some seven or eight years ago, under the auspices of the St Andrews Ambulance Association ... Following this, Gaumont's put out, and still put out, an enormous amount of topicals. The plant is as good as can be found anywhere.'[22] Just what financial arrangement was reached between cinema manager and cameraman on the ground remains to be researched. This form of 'local' was recognised officially by the newsreels in the post-war period. Gaumont British issue sheets in the mid-1930s distinguish stories shot for the 'super' (the general release reel) from 'locals' shot for news theatres and subjects 'covered for customer'. John Turner Gaumont British's news cameraman was engaged on these locals in the 1950s.

> A welcome diversion was when the reel was asked by a cinema, often one of our own, to cover a particular local event for showing only in that area. The story was usually a carnival or a bathing-beauty contest, the object being to film as many local dignitaries and crowds as possible in order to attract the people into the cinema to see themselves on the screen ... The cinema manager organised [camera] positions and obtained any necessary passes and often we would be taken to the town hall to meet the mayor and council and frequently be entertained to a buffet lunch. I usually filmed about 400 feet which would be edited, a commentary added and the story attached to the current issue of the general reel destined for that cinema.[23]

There are examples of showmen/exhibitors re-presenting topicals years after they were originally shot, harnessing the audiences' delight in recognising themselves as younger beings on the screen. Victor Biddall, of a family of touring showmen, had settled in Annan in Dumfriesshire, the family's wintering place and started showing moving pictures in the town in 1912. Biddall's travelling show finally came off the road in 1916 and the family concentrated on building up their cinema operation at Gracie's Banking. Victor Biddall commissioned Gaumont to film the town's Riding of the Marches parade in 1913, re-issuing it in 1925 as a coda to his topical of that year's Riding, with the on-screen invitation, 'We shall now take you back to 20th September, 1913 – to compare the event of 12 years ago'. George Kemp, Harry's son, interviewed in 1983, recalled that his father would get Green's to make films of local events for them. 'Even now, you know, we put them on occasionally and it's amazing the number of people that come in to see them, and they recognise certain people in them and things that happened in those days.'[24] The full history of the local topical in British

M&K 95: *Blackburn Rovers v Sheffield United* (1907), taken for George Green on 29 March 1907 and shown at the Easter Fair.

cinemas, as both a successor to the topical productions of Mitchell and Kenyon, and as a parallel or related genre to the newsreel, is yet to be recovered.

NOTES

1. For example, *Hampshire Boy Scouts Grand Rally at Southampton*, 2 October 1912. Wessex Film and Sound Archive, film ref AV548/1. Made for Southampton Picture Palace.
2. For example, *The Earl of Stamford Unveils the Chapel Street Roll of Honour Altrincham*, 5 April 1919. North West Film Archive, film ref 44. Produced by the Manchester Film Co for Altrincham Picture House.
3. From the evidence of examples that survive in the public film archives in the UK, the most prolific period for the local topical would appear to be from 1900 to the end of the 1930s. There exist fewer examples of local topicals from the 1940s and 1950s. These types of locally made films are not consistently identified in archival collections with the genre description 'local topical', they can be variously described as local newsreel, actuality, topical or as some early film historians have begun to class them, 'street films'. Titles noted on newsreel issue sheets appear to be classed variously as 'locals' or 'subjects covered for customer'. The Scottish Screen Archive, on whose collection this article is based, preserves about 400 local topicals dating from 1899–1963. Examples of this genre can also be found in the National Screen and Sound Archive of Wales and English regional film archives belonging to the UK Film Archive Forum. The *bfi* National Film and Television Archive also holds local topical material. Information on these archives can be found at *www.movinghistory.ac.uk*. An additional title is *The 'Powys' Cinema Presents Local Coronation Celebrations*, 1937 (National Screen and Sound Archive of Wales, film ref. 137), one of a collection of local

subjects including the Eisteddfod, the Welsh Show and demonstration of water pumping filmed by Arthur Prince, a projectionist at the Powys cinema in the 1930s to 50s.

4. Letter from Herbert J. Green to Henry Simpson, 8 January 1945, Scottish Screen Archive, ref 5/8/42.

5. Letter from Herbert Green to Henry Simpson.

6. Letter from Herbert Green to Henry Simpson.

7. T. A. Blake 'The Cinematograph Comes to Scotland', *Educational Film Bulletin*, no. 33, September 1946, p. 10.

8. M&K 50: *Coddington Ordnance St Mill, Blackburn* (1900); M&K 95: *Blackburn Rovers v Sheffield United* (1907); M&K 268: *Moss Street v St Phillips Football Blackburn* (1907); M&K 269: *Special March Past of St Joseph's Scholars & Special Parade of St Matthew's Pupils* (1905); M&K 271: *St Stephen's School Blackburn* (1904); M&K 277: *Blackburn Rifle Volunteers* (1900); M&K 288: *Preston Street Scene* (1904); M&K 290: *St Ignatius School* (1904); M&K 291: *Whitsuntide Fair at Preston* (1906); M&K 293: *Leyland May Festival* (1905); M&K 700: *Snowballs, Glasgow* (nd); M&K 702, 717: *Opening of Cork Exhibition* (1902); M&K 703: *Panorama of Exhibition Grounds* (1902); M&K 704–5, 712: *The Grand Procession* (1902); M&K 706–8: *Boat Race Cork Exhibition* (1902); M&K 709–10: *Tram Ride over Patrick's Bridge and Grand Parade* (1902); M&K 711: *Lee Boot Factory – Dwyer and Co. Ltd* (1902); M&K 713: *Regiment Returned from Boer War to Victoria Barracks* (1902); M&K 714: *Moore Cork* (1902); M&K 715–16: *Visit of General HRH Duke of Connaught and Prince Henry of Prussia* (1902); M&K 718–20: *Cork Fire Brigade Turn Out* (1902); M&K 721: *St Patrick's Church* (1902); M&K 722: *Congregation Leaving St Mary's Dominican Church* (1902); M&K 243 and 723: *Train Ride from Blarney* (1902); M&K 771: *Green's Bantam* (nd). List of films commissioned by George Kemp from Mitchell and Kenyon: M&K 540, 541 and 542: *Buxton Well Dressing* (1904).

9. *The Showman*, 21 February 1901, p. 7.

10. Obituary, George Green, *Bioscope*, 25 November 1915, p. 929.

11. *Entertainer and Scottish Kinema Record*, 27 October 1917.

12. *Entertainer and Scottish Kinema Record*, 30 June 1917.

13. *His Highness*: Club Comedies (Green), produced George Green, directed Mr Foote. Released 1916.

14. *Entertainer and Scottish Kinema Record*, 24 November 1917.

15. *Entertainer and Scottish Kinema Record*, 16 February 1918, p. 9.

16. 'The near future of our industry' *Entertainer and Scottish Kinema Record*, 1920.

17. For information on Scottish/British Moving Picture News issues, as listed in *Kine Weekly*, advertised in *Entertainer and Scottish Kinema Record* and catalogued in the Scottish Screen Archive, see British Universities Newsreels Database www.bufvc.ac.uk/databases/newsreels/.

18. M&K 540, 541 and 542: *Buxton Well Dressing*.

19. *Goodnight from Harry Kemp* (1933), Scottish Screen Archive, film ref 3658.

20. For examples of Green's usage of gag cards see M&K 95: *Blackburn Rovers v Sheffield United* and M&K 291: *Whitsuntide Fair at Preston*.

21. *Lady Lauder in Rothesay* (1922), Scottish Screen Archive, film ref 2339.

22. *The Cinema*, Scottish section.

23. John Turner, *Filming History: Memoirs of a Newsreel Cameraman* (London: BUFVC, 2001) p. 142.

24. Interview with the author, 28 June 1983, Scottish Screen Archive, ref 8/47.

III
The Films as Historical Evidence

12 'We had fine banners': Street Processions in the Mitchell and Kenyon Films

Andrew Prescott

'We had fine banners in those days', Mr Martin assured our representative. 'There weren't so many of them, but what there were were good. Old St Mary's had a banner which was the admiration of everybody that saw it. And a band: oh yes, we had a band, if we had to have two or three fast days every week, we were bound to have a band … '[1]

The Mitchell and Kenyon Collection provides rich new information about the way in which people used public space in the towns and cities of late Victorian and Edwardian England. Most striking are the energy and vibrancy of the street life the films record. The city streets depicted in the films are busy, jostling and full of a rough physicality which makes modern streets seem sanitised. This bustling street life concealed social tensions and anxieties. Jane Jacobs has observed that 'Sidewalks, their bordering uses, and their users, are active participants in the drama of civilization versus barbarism in the cities'.[2] While the streets were for the working classes a venue for gathering, celebration and recreation, the urban middle classes were anxious to impose civic virtues of order, rationality and mannered behaviour on the social fluidity of the streets.[3] The films reflect these tensions.

Many of the films record different types of street processions. The range of these parades was enormous. They included royal visits,[4] military parades[5] and processions by all sorts of local organisations, such as friendly societies,[6] churches,[7] schools,[8] temperance groups[9] and trade unions.[10] Street processions had been a feature of town life since the Middle Ages, but the late-Victorian and Edwardian city saw a vigorous late flowering of this English processional culture, which largely disappeared after World War II, the victim of increasingly heavy road traffic and competition from more glamorous leisure activities. It is difficult nowadays to imagine the Order of Ancient Foresters, a friendly society, bringing a city centre to a halt with a parade of members on horseback, dressed as medieval huntsmen and figures from Robin Hood, as regularly happened in towns such as Stafford at the beginning of the twentieth-century.[11] The Collection provides remarkable evidence of this exotic, largely forgotten, aspect of English urban history and the often equally forgotten organisations which staged such events.

The importance of processions in English town life at this time is apparent from browsing through local newspapers such as the *Coventry Herald* for 1901. At the end of April, a festival held by the temperance organisation, the Band of Hope began with a large parade headed by a drum and fife band.[12] The return of the City Volunteers from military service in South Africa was marked by a large parade.[13] When the Volunteers afterwards set off for summer training, the citizens of Coventry lined the streets to give them a hearty send-off.[14] Church parades with brass bands were a prominent feature of Hospital Sunday.[15] When the foundation stone of a new Salvation Army citadel was laid, a Salvation Army band marched through the city and streets near the citadel were decorated.[16] The biggest parade of the year was held in May, when almost all of Coventry's voluntary and philanthropic organisations joined a huge procession to raise money for lifeboats.[17] A similar event in Nuneaton in the summer also attracted substantial support from Coventry organisations, the climax of the day being the launch of a lifeboat on a local lake.[18] Even the local freemasons were involved. In September 1901, the Provincial Grand Lodge of Warwickshire met in Coventry. The freemasons attending the meeting paraded through the town in their regalia on their way to a service at St Mary's Church.[19]

These parades were the outward expression of the rich mix of voluntary organisations, clubs and societies forming the social cement of the English town.[20] Despite the importance of these parades in town life, their character makes them difficult to investigate. Roger Abrahams has commented that historians have been reluctant to use parades as evidence 'because of their perceived ephemeral character. These are events in which costumes and other devices of display are endowed with power and meaning for the day and then thrown away, or put back in the storeroom for use the next year ...'[21]

While local newspapers enthuse about the colourful and joyful nature of these parades, it is difficult to discover from written accounts how the components of the procession fitted together. Parades are street theatre, in which the setting of the streets, the interaction between marchers and onlookers, and even the weather, are key elements. Unless we can see these performances, it is difficult to interpret them. Mitchell and Kenyon's procession films are not only an eloquent – perhaps the single most eloquent – expression of the importance of these parades in the urban life of their time. They also provide the earliest evidence for parades as performances, enabling us to see how the different elements related to each other in a way that is not possible from written or even photographic evidence.

Film-makers quickly realised the interest of such events for local audiences, but filming street processions posed many difficulties. Some of these were discussed by G. Francis in an interview with the *Coventry Herald* in 1901.[22] Francis was described as the manager of Thomas-Edison Animated Photo Co. He claimed to have worked with the Lumière Brothers and to be the most experienced cinematographer in Britain. In discussing the cost of producing films, Francis noted that the organiser of the pictures took a good salary because his duties were very arduous: 'it is essential that before arranging a picture he should take into consideration the various possibilities of anything of a startling nature occurring during the time the picture is being taken.' These problems were even greater with parades since the route might cover more than one street:

> It therefore becomes necessary for [the filmmaker] to have his camera placed in such a position, especially in the case of a street scene, that will enable him to at once secure a side-street spectacle as well as that in the main thoroughfare in order to render his picture perfect and complete. This is exemplified in the picture that was taken of the Volunteer church parade a few Sundays ago. The organiser of the picture placed a lorry on which the instrument was resting at a corner which commanded a view of Broadgate, High Street, Smithford Street, and Hertford Street. By the adoption of this plan he was able to secure not only the picture of the Volunteers marching along Broadgate, but also the Royal Artillery coming up Smithford Street. Then by means of a turning tripod he secured a view over the four thoroughfares named ...[23]

When this film was shown in Coventry, the band of the Volunteers provided the music to add to the verisimilitude.[24] Although the ambitious film of the Coventry Volunteers has not apparently survived, some of the techniques described by Francis can be seen in the Mitchell and Kenyon Collection. In M&K 452–4, 797: *Manchester Catholic Whitsuntide Procession* (1904), multiple camera

M&K 531: *Lady Godiva Procession* (1902) featuring Vera Guedes, a London actress as Godiva. The Godiva Procession was held in Coventry as part of the city's Coronation celebrations on the afternoon of 9 August 1902.

positions were used to cover as much of the parade as possible. In all the Mitchell and Kenyon films of parades, great skill is shown in stopping and starting the film so as to show as much of the event as possible. Nevertheless, despite these techniques, the films still only give a brief glimpse of the parades. Even multiple rolls showing the Manchester Catholic procession or M&K 531–4: *Lady Godiva Procession* (1902), record just a few minutes from events which lasted two to three hours. As Francis's remarks suggest, the convergence of marchers, a common technique in these parades, posed particular difficulties for film-makers. As part of Coventry's Coronation celebrations in 1902, there was a parade of Sunday School children with nearly 20,000 participants. Thirty-five parades converged on Pool Meadow, where the children sang hymns. The appearance of the converging marchers, with their coloured sashes, was described as 'kaleidoscopic'.[25] Neither the convergence nor the subtle colour effects are evident from the film of this event, which simply shows one of the parades passing the camera.[26] Another major element of the parade not recorded in these films was music. Brass bands and singing were one of the major means by which the message of the parade was conveyed. Sometimes, there could be a mismatch between the music and parade. Complaints were made in 1904 about the lack of Irish music in the 1904 Manchester Catholic procession,[27] not surprising when the bands hired for the day included such non-Catholic groups as the Primitive Methodist Prize Band.[28] By 1912, the Catholic groups were hoping to improve matters by singing hymns en route.[29]

Despite these major limitations, the films nevertheless impart a powerful sense (not available elsewhere) of these parades as events. Using them, it is possible to explore for the first time such issues as the structure of parades, their use of costume and banners, and their relationship with their audience. They vividly convey how such processions were, in the words of the Welsh historian Andy Croll, 'a living, breathing, music-playing representation of the social order itself'.[30] It is impossible here to offer detailed analysis of all the films of processions in the Collection, so I will concentrate on the surviving films of five contrasting parades:

- M&K 256–60, 364: *Visit of HRH Princess Louise* (1905)
- M&K 594: *Miners Demonstration at Wakefield* (1908)
- M&K 452–4, 797: *Manchester Catholic Whitsuntide Procession* (1904)
- M&K 173, 441–2: *Manchester Band of Hope Procession* (1901)[31]
- M&K 531–4: *Lady Godiva Procession* (1902)[32]

These films emphasise the many features common to these varied events, reflecting the way in which they drew on long-standing traditions of street parading. Their family resemblance is apparent in the use of regalia and costume, the prominence of large banners, and the major role of music, chiefly provided by brass bands. The films provide fascinating insights into logistical details of the

M&K 452: *Manchester Catholic Whitsuntide Procession* (1904). This elaborate procession was part of the Whit-walks celebrations held on the 27 May 1904.

parades. For example, the large banners had to be kept under careful control during the march, and additional guide ropes were used to keep them steady, something not readily apparent from surviving examples of these banners in museum collections.[33] The parades were far from casual events. Each had a large number of marshals responsible for keeping them moving smoothly and ensuring the safety of participants and onlookers. These ranged from the large contingent of policemen guarding the royal party in Blackburn to the adults keeping a close eye on the children in the Manchester processions. A significant feature of the Godiva procession immediately evident in the film but not so readily apparent from newspaper reports is that most of the participants, unlike say the Manchester parades, were on horseback. This had major implications for the organisation of the procession. The need to provide a large number of horses made it more expensive to organise, helping to explain why at this time it was only an occasional event.[34] The horses also made the marshalling more complex, with the marshals also mounted on horseback and using a system of coloured pennants to direct the parade (the horse of one marshal alarmingly veers towards the camera at the end of one roll of film).[35]

While the films emphasise fundamental similarities between these events, they also highlight differences, which suggest a social hierarchy between processions. These differences are expressed in the relationship of the parades to the surrounding urban space: whether or not the streets are closed, the nature and size of the crowd of spectators, and the structure of the parade itself. At the top end of the hierarchy is M&K 256–60, 364: *Visit of HRH Princess Louise*.[36] The streets are completely dedicated to the procession. Shops are closed;[37] buildings are decorated with flags and bunting; large numbers of policemen keep crowds under control. Everybody on the street is connected with the procession, even the few people walking along the pavement seem to be following it. The community's participation in the parade is strictly controlled, and restricted to authority figures such as the police and military. The crowd's behaviour reflects the solemnity of the occasion. There is surprisingly little cheering and waving.

At the other end of the hierarchy is the Wakefield miners' demonstration, where the procession itself is completely informal, almost chaotic in character. The appearance of the miners is in some ways more reminiscent of factory gate films than the other procession films. Whereas in the Blackburn procession there is a strong line of demarcation between procession and onlookers, in the Wakefield demonstration there is virtually no gap between them, with some spectators joining the march. Not surprisingly, contemporary newspapers saw such a loosely organised demonstration as threatening. It was described as 'organised rowdyism' by the *Wakefield Express*.[38] But the film image also challenges such views. It shows that, although most of the participants were men, a significant number of women also joined the march, sometimes walking in prominent positions close to the banners. One miner is even carrying a baby in his arms. This demonstration was at one level a family day out, but one the local middle class found threatening.

The other parades in these films occupy intermediate positions in this hierarchy. The Catholic procession in Manchester is highly structured and organised, with streets closed for the parade and spectators kept at a safe distance. Despite the fact that participants were drawn from the poorest parts of Manchester's population, this was a high-status event, comparable to the royal procession in Blackburn. The Manchester Catholics were anxious to stress their respectability and distinguish themselves from the 'rowdy' Wakefield miners. The temperance procession is more spontaneous. Despite its large size, the streets have not been closed and marchers jostle with buses and cyclists. The onlookers are passersby, who grow in number as the parade passes along, and policing seems relatively casual. Within this hierarchy, the most puzzling is the Godiva procession. With its mounted marshals, elaborate floats and parade of cyclists, it is a highly organised piece of theatre. Yet the crowds seem relatively small and the sense of civic festivity surprisingly muted.

This sense of social hierarchy is evident in the cameramen's treatment of the different processions. The camera's view of the Blackburn procession and the Manchester Whit-walk is relatively distant and conveys a strong sense of the overall spectacle. In the other films, there is a more intimate relationship between camera and marchers. This was doubtless partly due to the way in which logistical requirements affected the positioning of the camera, but it also reflects the different social functions of the parades. The American parades' historian Susan Davis has described how 'People use street theatre, like other rituals, as tools for building, maintaining and confronting power relations ... Parades are public dramas of social relations ...'[39] The Mitchell and Kenyon films of parades not only document the power relations which shaped them, but also enter into and are affected by those power relations.

The use of processions during the nineteenth century by the middle classes to promote temperate and respectable forms of recreation is evident from the Whit-walks.[40] These were devised in the early nineteenth century as a more sober alternative to the boisterous recreations traditionally associated with that holiday, and were actively promoted by the churches. In south Wales, the Whit-walks became an expression of Nonconformist influence. In Manchester, from the mid-nineteenth century there were two processions, an Anglican one on Monday and a Catholic one on Friday: 'God Save the King Monday morning and God Save the Pope Friday afternoon'.[41] The rivalry was such that when, as in 1912,[42] there was good weather for the Anglicans and rain for the Catholics, it was taken almost as a judgment of God.[43] The two parades were, in the words of Steve Fielding, 'a ritual and largely pacific means for Anglicans on Whit Monday and Catholics on Whit Friday to express their respective sectarian identities'.[44]

For the largely Irish Catholic community in Manchester, the Whit procession was the chief vehicle by which they could affirm their importance and respectability. The means by which this was done are vividly illustrated in the Mitchell and Kenyon film. The sheer size of the procession forcibly expressed the importance of the Catholic population. Approximately 18,000 people representing twenty-two parishes took part in the 1904 parade, which lasted over two hours.[45] The great care which the local Catholic hierarchy took in organising the parade is evident at every point in the film. The marchers were assiduously supervised, marshalling being organised by the local clergy.[46] Although many of the children were from the poorest parts of Salford, parents scrimped and saved to ensure that each one was dressed in a special costume. Children whose dress was unsatisfactory were prohibited from joining the parade.[47] The children drilled for weeks beforehand,[48] and their impressive marching is apparent in the film. The large banners and brass bands were further items of major expenditure for poor parishes.

The Catholic hierarchy sought to avoid sectarian tensions in the parade. The only religious symbols permitted were banners and crosses, although as the film shows these could be very imposing. The only exception to this rule was the Italian community, which traditionally provided the most colourful display and carried a representation of the Madonna.[49] The prominence of Italians in the parade reflects the stress of the organisers on the international character of Catholicism.[50] Unlike the Anglican procession, the Catholic march included a significant number of adults since 'they gave an air of solidity to the faith'.[51] The emphasis on discipline was further expressed through indifference to the weather. As Fielding observes, 'It was rare for Catholic parents to rescue their children from a downpour once the walk had started as this would have destroyed the Church's famed discipline'.[52] In 1904, rain affected the end of the parade. While onlookers and some marshals took advantage of umbrellas, most of the children carried on marching without protection.

The film reinforces the social message of the procession by conveying a powerful sense of its size, while also ensuring that many participants could be seen in the short lengths of film available. The appearance of a child in the procession represented a considerable investment for many parents. It was said that many of the costumes were pawned as soon as the walk was over.[53] For those who had been stuck behind an umbrella trying to watch the parade and had barely glimpsed a daughter in her hard-won costume, the film provided an important record of a major family event which went beyond the simple pleasure of recognising a face on the screen. In this way, there was a symbiotic relationship between the film and the social message of the procession, which was to grow increasingly intimate. By 1913, a reporter commented that:

> To judge by the comments of some of the people one might have thought the whole pageant was arranged with a view to providing entertainment at the picture houses. 'Won't they look lovely photo-ed in the pictures' was the comment of a substantial lady …[54]

This complicity between film-maker and event is even more evident in the film of the Manchester temperance or Band of Hope procession. Susan Davis has stressed how American temperance processions sought to oppose traditional forms of street festivity by their orderly and rational character, making converging parades so vast that they seemed to take over the city.[55] A 1903 report of a children's temperance procession in Liverpool suggests that anti-alcohol campaigners in England sought to achieve a similar impact.[56] Seven thousand children converged onto three central points in front of St George's Hall, 'with banners flying, garlands waving, emblems aloft, and music resounding … The animation of the scene was equalled only by its prettiness. Many fond mothers had evidently bestowed the greatest pains upon the attire of their little ones … even the pale and poverty-stricken denizens of the slums were seen at their best'. Temperance campaigners were conscious that, if they were to protect the young from drink, they had to provide entertaining social events. Parades, with competitions for the best costumes and banners, were one means of doing this. The Mitchell and Kenyon film of the 1901 Manchester temperance procession with its lively display of banners and activities shows how enthusiastically children responded to this tactic. The film itself formed part of the message that temperance made for a healthy and enjoyable life. The children were probably on their way to a garden fete in aid of the Church of England Temperance Society, where a formidable array of entertainments was provided. Among the most popular booths was 'Edison's Animated Pictures', where this film was probably shown.[57]

At the fete, a local clergyman reminded temperance campaigners that they were guarding young people from the risk of contamination.[58] This stress on purity was also evident in the parade itself. Many of the participants are dressed in white and engage in activities expressing purity, such as dancing around a maypole or skipping. The preponderance of women and girls evident in the film of the Manchester procession was doubtless intended to reinforce this message, although it also raises the question of how far the temperance message was gender-oriented. The historian of the Victorian temperance movement, Lilian Shiman, argues that by 1901 the British temperance movement, having failed to vanquish alcohol by use of moral persuasion or statutory control, had become inward-looking and increasingly isolated.[59] This is not, however, the picture which emerges from the film, which shows an event closely engaged with the surrounding streets. It attracts a lively crowd growing in size as the parade makes its way along the streets. Of all the processions in the Collection, the temperance procession looks like fun! Many of the adult participants are smiling and laughing and enjoying the event. The joyfulness of the Manchester procession challenges preconceptions of the temperance movement as dour, and suggests that it did not necessarily feel itself in the cul-de-sac described by Lilian Shiman.

These Manchester processions illustrate how processional activity in the late-Victorian and Edwardian city reflected middle-class enthusiasm for parades as a respectable form of recreation and a means of promoting order. However, the roots of this processional activity lay deeper and it was inevitable that there should be tension between older forms of street festivity and the middle-class adoption of processions as a vehicle for promoting respectability. These problems are evident in the Coventry Godiva procession. The legend that the Anglo-Saxon noblewoman, Godgifu, rode naked through the streets of Coventry to save it from 'an oppressive and shameful servitude' first appeared in the twelfth century.[60] The appearance of a representation of Godiva in the mayor's inaugural procession at the Great Show Fair, Coventry is first recorded in 1678, but probably began some time before. Daniel Donoghue suggests that the mock procession began as a parody of the Corpus Christi procession and play cycle shortly after the suppression of the Coventry Corpus Christi plays in 1579.[61] The Godiva procession is thus a much older form of street festivity than the other examples considered. The Mitchell and Kenyon film of the 1902 procession is the first known film of a Godiva procession.

In 1678, Godiva was played by a boy, but thereafter the part was usually played by an actress who gave the semblance of nakedness by appearing in a flesh-coloured costume with chiffon drapes. In the 1820s, the procession was still relatively small,[62] but during the nineteenth century was made more elaborate, in the hope of increasing its educational content and discouraging prurient interest in the heroine. In the process, the procession became a social battleground. Among the first groups to develop parading as an improving recreational activity were friendly societies, and by 1842 they had become a prominent feature of Godiva processions.[63] The *Coventry Herald* commented approvingly on the colourful contribution of the friendly societies to the 1842 parade, but was scathing in its description of Godiva: 'a most humiliating evidence of what woman otherwise lovely may be reduced and degraded to'. In 1848, the *Coventry Standard* expressed its disapproval of the portrayal of Godiva by simply reprinting Tennyson's poem on Godiva with the words 'clothed on with chastity' in italics.[64] In 1877, the revival of the procession prompted a petition to the town council complaining that it encouraged 'the licence and saturnalia in which riff-raff invariably indulge'.[65]

To discourage boisterous behaviour, the 1883 procession was held separately from the fair and, to demonstrate Coventry's modernity, additional floats were provided by local manufacturers.[66] Four years later, the organising committee of the procession held to mark Queen Victoria's Golden Jubilee proposed 'a modification of or improvement upon the time-honoured Godiva procession'.[67] They promised an occasion 'which for historical truthfulness, correct taste and propriety will commend itself to the great majority of citizens'. An attempt was made to turn the procession into a historical pageant. The parade of historical figures was considerably extended, and Godiva herself appeared 'fully clothed as a Saxon Countess of the eleventh century'. Nevertheless, many still felt that Godiva was not the best way to celebrate Coventry's civic achievements. In 1887, the Godiva procession was preceded in the morning by a huge parade of Sunday School children. This proved popular, and was repeated for the Coronation celebrations in 1902 and 1911.[68] Godiva herself continued to create unease. She appeared again in her flesh-coloured costume in 1892, prompting a correspondent to describe her in the *Coventry Herald* as 'the incarnation of vulgarity'.[69] News in 1907 that Godiva would be represented by Pansy Montagu, 'La Milo', whose 'living statuary' had recently been banned in the London music halls, ignited another ferocious controversy, with angry protests from the local clergy.[70]

The 1902 film of the procession shows how these controversies had turned the event into a mish-mash of low-level historical pageantry, civic display and trade exhibition. The parade was dominated by a long cavalcade of historical figures, whose identity is by no means obvious. The determination to emphasise Coventry's commercial achievements meant that prominence was given to the floats of the city's ancient trading companies and modern firms, culminating in a display of veteran bicycles. The atmosphere seems surprisingly muted and the crowds relatively small, barely two or three people deep. This reflects the way in which the local press and dignitaries sought to marginalise the event as part of Coventry's Coronation festivities, instead promoting the morning Sunday School procession as the focal point. While the *Coventry Herald* described with breathless enthusiasm the 'strikingly picturesque' Sunday School parade with its 'wonderful display of colour', it reported the Godiva procession with a distinctly jaded air, suggesting that spectators felt much the same: 'though they were not particularly enthusiastic, they seemed delighted with the revival'.[71] Local clergy also damned Godiva with faint praise. One declared of the procession: 'Of this I had heard so much that I must confess to being rather disappointed. I admired our Chief Constable, his uniform, and his seat on horseback … Some of the trade exhibitions were interesting'.[72]

The maker of the 1902 film seems to have shared these uncertainties and to be unclear as to what would interest his audience. Most of the long cavalcade of historical figures is omitted. Much of the surviving coverage consists of the trade floats with their child followers, suggesting that he thought that these would be of most interest. Godiva was played on this occasion by Vera Guedes, a London actress.[73] The film is prefaced by a lingering portrayal of Godiva and her horse, taken before the beginning of the procession at the local barracks which served as changing rooms. While this recognises that Godiva was the centre of attention, it paradoxically displaces her from the procession. Her appearance in the procession is not to be found in the surviving Mitchell and Kenyon films. Curiously the city banner, behind which she was supposed to appear, is shown. Perhaps she may yet emerge, or perhaps the cameraman simply decided not to film her twice. Whatever the explanation, the central point is that at the beginning of the film Godiva is shown separately to us. This prefigures modern film treatment of Godiva, in which, as Donoghue points out, the audience become unwitting voyeurs: 'The film viewers, not the Saxons or Normans, are the only ones to see the naked Godiva'.[74]

The complexity of the interaction between film and procession, already evident in the Mitchell and Kenyon Collection, was to become greater. While processions provided a staple local subject for early film-makers, cinema was eventually to help kill off the street procession. Already by 1912, the popularity of the Whit-walks in south Wales was suffering from competition from the cinemas which attracted crowded houses.[75] Cinema was to prove one of the most popular of the new forms of commercial entertainment which by World War II had largely brought to an end the urban culture of parades and processions so lovingly documented in the Mitchell and Kenyon Collection.

NOTES

1. Reminiscence of Catholic Whit-walks in Manchester, *Manchester Catholic Herald*, 27 May 1904, p. 4. I am very grateful to my colleagues, Dr Vanessa Toulmin and Timothy Neal for their assistance in preparing this paper.

2. Jane Jacobs, *The Life and Death of Great American Cities* (New York: Vintage Books, 1961), p. 30.

3. A stimulating introduction to these issues is Andy Croll, *Civilizing the Urban: Popular Culture and Public Space in Merthyr, c. 1870–1914* (Cardiff: University of Wales Press, 2000).

4. For example, M&K 256–60, 364: *Visit of HRH Princess Louise* (1905); M&K 410: *Princess Louise at Liverpool* (1906); M&K 411: *Prince of Siam Aboard the New Ferry* (1901); M&K 435–6: *Royal Visit to Manchester, Owen's College* (1902).

5. For example, M&K 431–3: *Return of the Brave Manchester Volunteers* (1901); M&K 481: *Bolton Artillery Volunteers* (1901); and M&K 671: *The Return of the Lancaster Volunteers* (1901).

6. For example, a film of the St Helen's Oddfellows. Unfortunately, the film of a demonstration of friendly societies and athletic festival held in May 1904 on the Manchester Athlethic Club grounds at Fallowfield in connection with the meeting at Manchester of the Annual Movable Committee of the Independent Order of Oddfellows (Manchester Unity) and advertised in the *Manchester Evening News*, has not survived: *Manchester Evening News*, 23 May 1904, p. 5; 28 May 1904, p. 1.

7. For example, M&K 313–16: *Accrington Catholic Procession* (1912); M&K 376–80: *Warrington Protestants, Walking Day* (1902); M&K 375: *Warrington Catholics, Walking Day* (1902); and M&K 449–51. *Manchester Spirits* (1901).

8. M&K 530: *March Past of 20,000 Coventry Schoolchildren* (1902).

9. M&K 173, 441–2: *Manchester Band of Hope Procession* (1901).

10. M&K 393–6: *Bootle May Day Procession* (1903); M&K 594: *Miners Demonstration at Wakefield* (1908).

11. Staffordshire Arts and Museum Service, acc. no. P80.17.4. A copy of this photograph is available on the 'Staffordshire Past-Track' website: www.staffspasttrack.org.uk.

12. *Coventry Herald*, 26 April 1901, p. 8.

13. *Coventry Herald*, 3 May 1901, p. 8.

14. *Coventry Herald*, 9 August 1901, p. 5.

15. *Coventry Herald*, 3 May 1901, p. 8.

16. *Coventry Herald*, 13 September 1901, p. 6.

17. *Coventry Herald*, 10 May 1901, p. 8. The Collection includes films of a similar event in Leeds, M&K 554–6, 558–69: *Leeds Lifeboat Procession* (1902).

18. *Coventry Herald*, 2 August 1901, p. 8.

19. *Coventry Herald*, 27 September 1901, p. 5.

20. On the importance of voluntary organisations in English town life at this time, see Stephen Yeo, *Religion and Voluntary Organisations in Crisis* (London: Croom Helm, 1976).

21. Roger D. Abrahams, 'Introduction: A Folklore Perspective', in William Pencak, Matthew Dennis and Simon P. Newman (eds), *Riots and Revelry in Early America* (University Park, PA: Pennsylvania State University Press, 2002), p. 27.

22. *Coventry Herald*, 4 October 1901, p. 5.

23. *Coventry Herald*, 4 October 1901, p. 5.

24. *Coventry Herald*, 20 September 1901, p. 8; 27 September 1901, p. 8.

25. *Coventry Herald*, 15 August 1902, p. 6.

26. M&K 530: *March Past of 20,000 Coventry Schoolchildren* (1902).

27. *Manchester Catholic Herald*, 3 June 1904, p. 4.

28. *Manchester Catholic Herald*, 27 May 1904, p. 4.

29. *Manchester Evening News*, 27 May 1912, p. 6.

30. Croll, *Civilizing the Urban*, p. 206.

31. This probably took place before a temperance fete at the Botanical Gardens on 22 June 1901, the attractions at which included the showing of films by the 'Edison's animated pictures'.

32. The Godiva procession was held in Coventry as part of the city's Coronation celebrations on the afternoon of 9 August 1902.

33. Nick Mansfield, *Radical Rhymes and Union Jacks: A Search for Evidence in the Symbolism of 19th Century Banners,* working papers in economic and social history, 45 (Manchester: Department of History, University of Manchester, 2000). The National Banner Survey is available online at the website of the People's History Museum: www.peopleshistorymuseum.org.uk.

34. In 1907, the procession was thrown into crisis when only £250 had been collected towards its costs: *Coventry Herald*, 24 May 1907, p. 5.

35. Military riders were used to organise the marshalling. In 1883, the procession was superintended by Captain Fitzgerald of the Royal Military Riding School, Hyde Park, who had marshalled the Lord Mayor's Show in London: *Coventry Herald*, 2 August 1883, p. 3.

36. For details of this event, see *Northern Daily Telegraph*, 29 September 1905, p. 2 and 30 September 1905, p. 4.

37. The Blackburn Tradesmen's Association placed an advertisement in the local press respectfully requesting local tradesmen to close their shops between 10.30am and 2pm: *Blackburn Advertiser*, 30 September 1905, p. 2. The closure is apparent in the film from the lack of shop blinds.

38. *Wakefield Express*, 18 July 1908.

39. Susan G. Davis, *Parades and Power: Street Theatre in Nineteenth-Century Philadelphia* (Berkeley: University of California Press, 1986), pp. 5–6.

40. Steven Fielding, 'The Catholic Whit-walk in Manchester and Salford 1890–1939', *Manchester Region History Review*, vol. 1, no. 1 (Spring 1987), pp. 3–10; Steven Fielding, *Class and Ethnicity: Irish Catholics in England 1880–1930* (Buckingham: Open University Press, 1993), pp. 74–7; Croll, *Civilizing the Urban*, pp. 200–8.

41. Fielding, 'Catholic Whit-walk', p. 9.

42. The Anglican Whit-walk was held in brilliant sunshine; torrential rain meant that the Catholic procession could not take place, but one parish nevertheless walked the route so as to preserve the record that no parade had ever been cancelled: *Manchester Evening News*, 27 May 1912, p. 6; 31 May 1912, p. 2.

43. Fielding, *Class and Ethnicity*, pp. 75–7.

44. Fielding, *Class and Ethnicity*, p. 74.

45. Fielding, *Class and Ethnicity*, p. 75. For the most detailed report of the parade, see *Manchester Catholic Herald*, 3 June 1904, p. 4.

46. The marshalling of the 1904 procession was supervised by Canon Richardson, who had undertaken this duty for the previous nine years: *Manchester Evening News*, 16 June 1905, p. 2.

47. Fielding, 'Catholic Whit-walk', p. 6.

48. Fielding, *Class and Ethnicity*, p. 75.

49. *Manchester Evening News*, 16 June 1905, p. 2.

50. Cf. Fielding, *Class and Ethnicity*, p. 76.

51. Fielding, *Class and Ethnicity*, p. 74.

52. Fielding, *Class and Ethnicity*, p. 75.

53. Fielding, 'Catholic Whit-walk', pp. 3, 6.

54. *Manchester Evening News*, 16 May 1913, p. 5.

55. Davis, *Parades and Power*, pp. 148–9.

56. *Temperance Chronicle*, 3 July 1903, p. 329.

57. *Manchester Courier*, 24 June 1901; *Temperance Chronicle*, 28 June 1901, p. 320. Moving pictures had been taken up with enthusiasm by temperance campaigners. In June 1901, a living picture show was set up at Wigan Fair to encourage spectators to sign up for abstinence: *British Temperance Advocate*, June 1901.

58. *Temperance Chronicle*, 28 June 1901, p. 320.

59. Lilian Lewis Shiman, *Crusade against Drink in Victorian England* (New York: St Martin's Press, 1988), pp. 4–5, 221–48.

60. Daniel Donoghue, *Lady Godiva: A Literary History of the Legend* (Oxford: Blackwell, 2003), pp. 26–46.

61. Donoghue, *Lady Godiva*, pp. 47–57.

62. Donoghue, *Lady Godiva*, p. 68.

63. *Coventry Herald*, 3 June 1842.

64. *Coventry Standard*, 9 June 1848, p. 3.

65. *Coventry Herald*, 25 May 1877, p. 3.

66. *Coventry Herald*, 2 August 1883, p. 3.

67. *Coventry Herald*, 10 June 1887, p. 8; 17 June 1887, p. 2.

68. *Coventry Herald*, 15 August 1902, p. 5; 23 June 1911, p. 7.

69. *Coventry Herald*, 5 August 1892, p. 5.

70. *Coventry Herald*, 7 June 1907, p. 5; 14 June 1907, p. 5; 28 June 1907, p. 5; 2 August 1907, p. 5; 9 August 1907, pp. 4–5.

71. *Coventry Herald*, 15 August 1902, p. 6.

72. *Coventry Herald*, 15 August 1902, p. 5.

73. *Coventry Herald*, 15 August 1902, pp. 5–6: Miss Guedes was currently appearing at the London Hippodrome. There had been great concern up to the last minute whether Miss Guedes would be able to get back to London in time for her evening performance at the Hippodrome. She afterwards wrote that 'she will not forget the warm welcome and it made ample amends for the indisposition, including a bad headache, from which she was suffering when she joined the cavalcade'.

74. Donoghue, *Lady Godiva*, p. 122.

75. Croll, *Civilizing the Urban*, p. 211.

13 Mitchell and Kenyon: Ceremonial Processions and Folk Traditions

John Widdowson

The myriad customs practised both locally and nationally across the country at specific times of the year are a perennially fascinating aspect of English cultural tradition. Typically both singular and picturesque, these calendar customs lie at the heart of our sense of local, regional and national identity and allegiance. The principal celebrations tend to cluster at certain times of the year – springtime and early summer, autumn, and again around Christmas and the New Year. Many of them had their origins in the Christian calendar, which in turn often took over from earlier pre-Christian traditions. The historical accounts of these customs from the Middle Ages onwards focus primarily on their ecclesiastical significance and performance. Later descriptions, and especially those from the nineteenth and twentieth centuries, increasingly reflect the gradual secularisation of many of the celebrations.

As interest in them grew among historians and others investigating the nature, origins and development of English culture and tradition, the observation and chronicling of the events became more accurate and detailed. Older accounts of so-called 'popular antiquities' gave way in the mid-nineteenth century to more serious study by folklorists, and calendar customs come under scrutiny as an important and enduring aspect of the traditional heritage of England. Eyewitness accounts of the customs as actually practised in a specific locality began to appear regularly, both in academic books and journals and in popular magazines, newspapers and other publications.[1] Each of these contributions helped to build up a picture of the various events across the country, revealing typical general features which they shared, and also a wealth of local variation which indicated their root-edness within a given community. The accounts themselves were largely descriptive, and tended to paint a fairly generalised picture of the events, homing in on the broad outline, and ignoring minor characteristics or variations.

The accumulated knowledge in the late nineteenth- and early twentieth-century accounts led to the publication of the information in designated sections of compendia on English folklore,[2] and later to books devoted largely or entirely to calendar customs.[3] Initially, these publications tended to rely on previous accounts, and often not only successively repeated each other but also perpetuated earlier inaccuracies and misconceptions. They commonly failed to recognise one of the most fundamental traits of customs, and indeed of tradition in general: while the overall structure remains essentially the same, each performance is unique, and certain features of the enactment change subtly over time. Even the overall structure itself may be seen to alter over the years, accommodating to new situations and developments, and to an infinite number of other influences – personal, social, cultural, ecclesiastical, political, environmental, and so on. Despite efforts to maintain a given custom 'as it used to be', in response to the perceived need to continue or preserve the event in its 'normal' or 'accepted' form, tradition never stands still as long as it remains within a living culture. For example, just a brief glance at old photographs of a wedding or other occasion in the history of our own family shows us immediately that much has changed since those days – the way people dressed for the wedding, the accessories, the vehicles, the reception, even the way the photographs were taken – yet the event itself remains much the same today.

Undoubtedly the best source of information on continuity and change in calendar customs is to be found in local newspapers and magazines. The essential framework and structural pillars of a tradition change only very slowly, if at all, but each year there are bound to be differences – different participants, venues, costumes, and specific additions to or omissions from the enactment, as well as changes in theme, planning and organisation. As most calendar customs take place mainly or wholly out of doors, the weather may have a significant impact. In spite of claims that a custom has been celebrated continuously in a given locality for many years, it is inevitable that for various reasons the celebrations may not take place in a particular year. If the lapses become extended the custom may decline or even disappear. Local reporters familiar with the celebrations are best equipped to comment on new developments and on the significance of the occasion for the community. Collating such information over a period of time provides a clear and detailed picture of the custom as practised in the locality, including named personalities among the participants and references to streets, parks, buildings and other landmarks, thus sketching in the physical context of the event.

However, these perspectives tended to be lost when commentators in the late nineteenth and early twentieth century attempted to synthesise a number of local reports to create some kind of overview of the customs across the country. The tendency for the essentials of these generalised accounts to be borrowed and repeated by later writers often leads to the stereotyping of individual customs. Unfortunately, these early descriptions were increasingly regarded as in some way definitive, and may influence, guide or even dictate, the way in which a custom is enacted subsequently. The danger here is that they may cramp ensuing performances by encouraging conformity with a stereotype. Such pressure is particularly strong when a custom is revived after a temporary lapse and earlier descriptions are used as a blueprint for the revival.

The few existing early accounts of English calendar customs are mostly brief and unidimensional. Nineteenth-century descriptions were often written by antiquarians, ministers of religion, and other members of the educated middle and upper classes. It is therefore hardly surprising that their accounts tend to be somewhat detached and at times condescending, or even disapproving. Nevertheless, these descriptions not only provide important information on the customs as formerly practised, but also a baseline against which to measure subsequent change and development. With hindsight, it is easy to criticise these earlier efforts for their generalisations, their air of studied detachment and their lack of context and interpretation. Even so, they were merely following the conventions of their own time and, without them later scholars would be deprived of crucial historical information from those periods when many of the established customs were practised by a much larger proportion of the population than is the case today.

The older accounts inevitably lack another dimension which features increasingly prominently in later descriptions, from the 1930s onwards: photographs, initially black and white and eventually, of course, in colour. Apart from a few line drawings and occasional photographs, which began to appear in late nineteenth-century published accounts, we had very little visual information concerning calendar customs. In the early twentieth century one or two still photographs appear in publications on English folklore. Revealing though these are,[4] they tantalisingly capture only a single moment, and from one particular camera angle, of what was in fact an extended, vibrant celebration which still photography could not hope to represent in full. These early images usually lack context, both topographical and human, and can offer no more than a unidimensional snapshot of a tiny fragment of the event, frozen in time. The paucity of such visual images in published accounts of calendar customs by folklorists and others is all the more regrettable when it is found that far-sighted individual photographers were already documenting such events on a much larger scale.[5]

However, even with these endeavours, visual images of such events are rare, and consequently provide vital evidence to illustrate and augment the often sketchy published accounts. In these early years, even the local and regional newspapers which regularly covered the annual events only very occasionally included illustrations in their reports. The scarcity of visual evidence hampers the work of later chroniclers of calendar customs who are obliged to fall back on inadequate written accounts in attempting to reconstruct past events.[6] The few available still photographs are unable to convey any real sense of the liveliness, the activity, the exuberance and the hustle and bustle of the occasion as people gather together to enjoy a communal celebration.

It was therefore extremely fortuitous that pioneering efforts were made at the beginning of the twentieth century to capture some of these events on film. Travelling showmen had already taken the lead in recognising the growing public interest in moving pictures,[7] and picture shows quickly took a prominent place among fairground attractions. Shows also toured the country, presenting the latest films to audiences who had never seen the wonders of the new technology before. Among these early attempts to document English life and tradition using the movie camera, the work of Mitchell and Kenyon is remarkable, both in its choice of subject matter and also because of its survival. By focusing on calendar customs, among many other topics, these pioneers bequeathed an extraordinary legacy to future generations. Thanks to them, it is now possible to step back in time to witness the spectacle of these occasions, not only in context, but also as living events captured in motion as they actually happened a hundred years ago. Viewing the material in the Mitchell and Kenyon Collection today is the nearest we can get to being an eyewitness to each of the occasions from a wide variety of venues across the country.

The wealth and richness of this unique Collection may be illustrated by viewing and commenting on a representative sample of the available films. The Collection includes coverage of several calendar customs which took place between Easter and midsummer in Lancashire, north Wales, and Derbyshire. Following the course of these celebrations through this part of the year a century ago, provides a much fuller picture of how they were enacted at that time and reveals the changes and developments which have taken place since. The ten films selected were shot in seven localities: Preston, Llandudno, Bootle, Leyland, Manchester, Warrington and Buxton, between 1901 and 1907. Today, the viewer is immediately struck by several features which the events depicted have in common. These include: participation by large numbers of local people – typically hundreds, sometimes thousands; the orderliness and adherence to the established organisation of the events; the comparative uniformity of dress, both ceremonial for the occasion, and also delineating class differences, especially among male participants; the mixture of curiosity, humour and self-awareness in response to the camera – many people of all ages and classes, and especially boys and young men, smiling, waving, throwing their hats in the air and generally trying to get in on the act in good-natured reaction to the novelty of being filmed; the occasional response of some participants to the photographer or other person(s) in an official capacity who are attempting, usually off-camera, to guide or orchestrate certain scenes during filming, though rarely interfering with the actual established performance of the custom; the absence of other than horse-drawn vehicles, the horses being decorated in the traditional way; and the importance of brass bands at most of the events.

The customs depicted in these seven localities took place in the spring and early summer, from Easter until late June. Those in Lancashire and north Wales include Easter celebrations and a variety of traditional ceremonial processions in May and June. Those from Derbyshire focus on maypole dancing, and on well dressings, a custom still practised in towns and villages across the county today. The ten films allow us to view these various customs as they took place in each of the communities at the beginning of the twentieth century. We begin with the movable feast of Easter, one of the oldest and most enduring occasions for both ecclesiastical and secular celebrations, reaching back in time to pre-Christian rites welcoming springtime and the reawakening of the natural world after the dark days of winter. Among the most ancient customs associated with springtime and Easter are those involving eggs, which are obviously symbolic of fertility and continuity.[8] In many parts of Britain, it was customary for eggs to be rolled down hills on Easter Monday – a tradition widely practised in northern England, which continues today. Hard-boiled in water containing various natural dyes such as onion skins, to colour them, the eggs are often decorated in various ways and are given to children at Easter. The eggs were taken outdoors and rolled down any convenient slope. Egg-rolling on Easter Monday afternoon is a long-standing tradition at Avenham Park in Preston, Lancashire, in which hundreds of children still take part, although in recent times chocolate eggs and oranges often replace real hard-boiled eggs.[9] However, thanks to one of the films in the Collection, we now know that the celebrations in the early 1900s were somewhat different.[10]

The scene unfolding before us shows a huge crowd of adults and children – the children running down the grassy slope in pursuit of their rolling eggs. A newspaper report from 1903 estimates that, in spite of inclement weather, 'close upon 35,000 children were present'.[11] By any standards this was an astonishingly large number, indicating that the majority of the local population attended, whether as participants or spectators. The event is introduced by a showman, who doffs his top hat and bows towards the camera. The viewer is immediately aware of the full social context of the occasion. Almost everyone in view is looking at the camera, very keen to be in the picture. Nearly everyone present is wearing a hat – men and boys mostly in flat caps, a few wearing bowlers – many of the boys and younger men are waving their hats at the camera. In the foreground two women in full outdoor dress and bonnets are skipping, the rope being turned by two men, and other young women are seen skipping in the distance. We then have a close-up of three very young girls, all in their white Easter dresses, followed by a shot of a baby girl whose mother lifts her higher in her pram so she can be better seen by the cameraman. Later, the top-hatted showman takes eggs, presumably hard-boiled, from a bag and throws them into the surrounding crowd. All these vignettes bring the scene vividly to life, and demonstrate how everyone is thoroughly enjoying themselves. They draw the viewer into the event, making you feel you were actually there in that vast crowd.

After Easter, the next major occasion for traditional celebrations in the springtime calendar occurs on or around 1 May, May Day. Here the films really come into their own as documents of historical importance. Many May customs centre on or include a procession of some kind, usually ceremonial and fairly formal in its organisation, although sometimes more casual and informal. Despite their popularity and variety throughout England, both in the past and today, they have received surprisingly little attention from folklorists and social historians. Many of them have a long history, but most tend to remain localised, each enthusiastically participated in by the community concerned, having developed characteristic features which became an established part of the annual round of traditional events in a particular region, town or village. By their very nature, processions are not amenable to still photography, which explains why so few early images of them are found. At best, the still camera captures only a disconnected series of individual shots of selected sections of the parade, or of particular moments as it passes, or the photographer attempts a single panoramic view of the event as a whole, which is difficult to achieve if the procession is large and/or lengthy. The movie camera, on the other hand, is able to record the full spectacle of the occasion, both the procession itself and the actions and reactions of the onlookers.

Four films from the Collection graphically reveal what these Maytime celebrations were like in the north Wales town of Llandudno and in Bootle and Leyland in Lancashire, a century ago. The two films from Llandudno, both shot on 1 May 1907, brilliantly illustrate the spectacular, celebratory May Day procession.[12] Filmed on a breezy day against the backdrop of hills behind the town, the procession marches into view, led by a brass band and a man on horseback, followed by a cartload of hay and a series of elaborately decorated floats, drawn by horses also decorated for the occasion – a very rare sight nowadays. Horse-drawn vehicles dominate the parade; one with a Union Jack flag draped over the front bears the name of Howard Owen, undertaker, indicating that local tradespeople used the occasion to advertise their businesses. Several participants are dressed as clowns, both on horseback and in horse-drawn carriages, one top-hatted clown kneading dough on a table at the front of a chimney-sweep's cart. A black-faced minstrel then appears, waving a banjo, and is followed by a cart surmounted by a large noticeboard, headed 'Parisian Animated Picture Co.', advertising a 'Grand Reproduction of the Llandudno May Day Procession' at the Prince's Theatre on the following Friday and Saturday, 3 and 4 May and throughout the following week, at 'popular prices' of 2s, 1s and 6d, 'children half price'.

The rising popularity of film shows, especially of local events, is clearly demonstrated here and who could resist the tempting invitation at the bottom of the mobile advertisement: 'DON'T FAIL TO COME & SEE YOURSELF AS OTHER PEOPLE SEE YOU'? The cart carrying the advertisement is followed by a group wheeling decorated bicycles, which were a central feature of similar parades elsewhere,[13] even in the late twentieth century. Following them come horse-drawn charabancs crowded with passengers, and the camera then focuses on the cart with the advertisement which has come to a temporary halt. Two men wearing outsize masks stand on either side of it; the figure on the left of the picture carries a large wooden club, while the one on the right uses his sword to point to the information on the sign, before both finally remove their masks.

In the second film of the Llandudno procession some landau-style carriages pass by, followed by a group of men on horseback. Then we see the May Queen in a float festooned with masses of flowers, far more than would usually be seen in recent years. The parade pauses briefly for a close-up shot as she shyly smiles and waves from her throne amid all the flowers. In the late twentieth century the custom of choosing a May Queen from girls in schools and Sunday schools declined dramatically and a comprehensive study of the history of the May Queen customs is long overdue, although a few descriptions from specific localities are available.[14] A number of still photographs of the events are found in a variety of publications and in archives and other public repositories,[15] but many more no doubt languish in family photograph albums and collections, remaining largely inaccessible and vulnerable. On the other hand, local carnivals and similar events in many parts of England today still include a carnival queen, while the May Queen tradition continues to decline, except as part of a broader celebration such as that at Ickwell in Bedfordshire, which dates from the sixteenth century.[16]

The film not only shows that the May Queen was part of a major processional custom but also illustrates the characteristic content and variety of the pageant and the participation in the celebrations by a substantial proportion of the local population, features which today would be matched only by such major events as the Notting Hill Carnival. The Llandudno procession is seen to be fairly informal, with a strongly local flavour, utilising and/or adapting ordinary vehicles and making use of everyday materials. As the May Queen goes on her way, a wagon from the 'Llandudno Laundry' in Warehouse Street trundles past, followed by another horse-drawn vehicle with dark curtains like a hearse, with the name Brinsmead prominent on the front. Like many other aspects of the procession, and indeed of all the calendar customs in the ten films selected, these vehicles and the place of their owners in the community invite further investigation by researchers familiar with the local history. As for local tradesmen taking the opportunity to advertise, we of course find that hauliers and others, whose vehicles carry the elaborate floats in major public processions today, have their firm's name and contact details on the cab and/or body of the truck. The film demonstrates that the commercial element in calendar customs is not a new phenomenon.[17]

The May Queen figures even more prominently in the film of the Bootle May Day demonstration eighth annual carnival in 1903.[18] This five-day event culminated in the 'Grand Parade and Children's Flower Procession, Presentation of Prizes, Crowning the May Queen and the May Pole Dance'.[19] The section of the carnival shown in the film opens with a group of boys aged about ten, performing a standard northwest processional Morris dance. They are wearing dark trousers, white shirts and dark waistcoats. The film provides rare, if not unique, evidence that youngsters were being trained by local teachers and enthusiasts to perform at a time when there was considerable interest in documenting and reviving traditional dance. There appears to be no other available information on the existence of Morris dance teams in the Bootle area at that time. The performers have obviously been very well trained by schoolteachers or itinerant dance teachers.[20] We then see the May Queen and her attendants, all in white, with decorated white bonnets. The Queen carries a bouquet

M&K 391: *Bootle May Day Demonstration* (1903) forms part of a seven-film sequence, with this part showing the crowning of the May Queen surrounded by her attendants on 2 May 1903.

of flowers, and the procession halts for a few moments, so that the camera can get a good view of her and her attendants. As they move off, they are followed by another group of girls, walking two by two, all dressed in white, with simple, undecorated headdresses, and carrying staffs topped by ribbons. Behind them, we see a small group of boys, then a larger group of girls, many with decorated hats, and rosettes or pompoms dotted round the lower hems of their white dresses, and after them come more groups of mostly girls, plus a few boys, almost all the girls in white, all in a closely supervised, orderly procession, in strong contrast with their much more informal equivalents today.

A similar orderliness characterises the procession of adults and children filmed at the Leyland May festival in 1905.[21] The parade is led by a mounted policeman, followed by a brass band preceded by a top-hatted man carrying a staff. Then comes a team of Morris dancers wearing white shirts and trousers, and boater-style hats covered with flowers. They are carrying short sticks, or 'tiddlers', topped with ribbons (originally cotton waste bound together) and performing the dance as they move along in the procession, their leader walking ahead of them. They are clearly performing the Leyland Processional Dance,[22] in this case in the true sense of the term, i.e. as part of the larger public procession. Again, these must be the earliest moving images of the dance and are therefore of particular historical importance. The footage offers unparalleled opportunities for comparison with later performances of the dance. The dancers are followed by a group of boys wearing hats and white shirts similar to sailor suits, and by another uniformly dressed group carrying staves. Then come horse riders in formal costume, and behind them the May Queen in her carriage, accompanied by two uniformed footmen. A group of boys pushing bicycles brings up the rear.

Moving on to the period around Whitsuntide and early summer, the Manchester and Salford Harriers Procession, filmed on 22 June 1901, bursts into life and activity before our eyes. [23] Described as the Cyclists and Harriers Charity Parade in a contemporary press report, this is undoubtedly one of the most spectacular calendric events recorded by the Mitchell and Kenyon cameras.[24] A man in the full white costume of a clown, complete with conical white hat, cartwheels into view ahead of the procession. Then comes the figure of Lord 'Bobs' (Roberts), 'admirably portrayed by a little fellow mounted on a big horse',[25] followed by a band of musicians, including some from the Boys Brigade, and a group of youths, possibly cadets, and others in military uniform, soldiers wearing busbies, a helmeted group carrying staffs with small flags on the top and a motley group of men in a variety of military uniforms, some with the type of hat worn in the Boer Wars, the second of which was still being waged at the time. Compared with the processions discussed above, this parade begins in a strictly military style, but then becomes much less formal and regimented towards the rear where the people are walking along, with no apparent organisation. Of particular interest are several clowns and other participants, including one pushing an undecorated bicycle, who walk alongside the main procession, in a way reminiscent of the behaviour of supernumeraries in certain traditional calendric processions in continental Europe. Bystanders and other members of the public, many of them soldiers in uniform, also walk alongside and/or casually wander in and out of the parade.

As the procession continues, its central section becomes more and more disorganised. We see a second band of musicians, then a crowd including footballers, clowns, and more men in uniform. The parade then becomes more formal again as a party of sailors marches smartly along, together with two of their officers, one of whom carries his sword ceremonially over his right shoulder. Several of the sailors are wheeling bicycles, and most of them turn to look directly at the camera as they pass. They are followed by another group of soldiers, perhaps from an Indian regiment, and then towards the rear comes a crowd of happy participants, many in fancy dress, including a man in Cav-

M&K 429: *Manchester and Salford Harriers Procession* (1901), filmed on 22 June 1901 by the Thomas-Edison Animated Photo Co.

alier costume wheeling an elaborately decorated bicycle and more clowns pushing bicycles. A memorable vignette shows a young woman dressed as a clown and accompanied by a man who is presumably her husband or fiancé. As they walk along, another man in the procession comes up behind them and playfully pushes them close together so they can be caught by the camera. The film has an immediacy which conveys the exuberance, excitement and sheer enjoyment of the occasion. As is also true of the other processions described above, most of the participants are adults, whereas similar parades involving pushing decorated bicycles and dolls' prams in Bradford and other northern cities, usually on May Day, in the later twentieth century, mainly comprised children.

In marked contrast to the secular processions just described, the Warrington Walking Day, filmed on 27 June 1902, was a much more sedate and wholly religious occasion.[26] Similar to the Whit-walks which took place in many northern towns and cities, the Warrington event apparently began in 1832, as a 'procession of witness',[27] and, although the film is entitled 'Warrington Catholic Procession', children from other denominations also took part – no fewer than 22,000 of them in 1902.[28] This is an astonishingly high number compared with Whit-walks in more recent years. Once again, the essence of the occasion is evocatively captured by the camera. Groups of children from local schools, Sunday schools, and churches, mostly girls in white dresses and hats, walk towards us, the first groups carrying banners and garlands or posies of flowers, some of the more elaborate garlands being in the form of an arch carried by two older children, flanked by younger girls holding ribbons attached to the central garlands. Here, we see a merging of the secular springtime tradition of flowers and garlands, still noticeable in various parts of the country today, with the religious traditions of the various denominations. The groups are accompanied by adult supervisors. There is one group of boys in the parade, all wearing uniform, boater-style straw hats and with broad sashes over their left shoulders. Even in black and white, the film gives a lasting impression of this picturesque occasion which can be compared with recent accounts, and with colour photographs, such as those of the 1984 Walking Day in Warrington, in which some 6,000 people took part, including about 4,500 children.[29] The films of these various processional customs become increasingly important historically as many such events have declined substantially in recent years, including the Whit-walks, once especially popular in Lancashire and Yorkshire, but now largely abandoned.

The final three films in the selection depict an entirely different kind of custom: maypole dancing and the dressing of wells in Buxton, Derbyshire, in 1904.[30] Well dressing is largely confined to the county and, in contrast to the comparative rarity of still photographs of processional events, a substantial number of images of the custom have been preserved, along with newspaper reports and other accounts.[31] As the well dressings themselves are static, they are more amenable to still photography, but the film camera has a crucial role to play, not only in documenting them and the various other traditional events which take place at the same time, but also in providing the full social context of the celebrations, which are often still staged as

M&K 542: *Buxton Well Dressing* (1904), showing President George Kemp to the left of the elaborately dressed well, holding a young child towards the camera, June 1904.

part of a whole week of 'wakes' or carnival festivities throughout Derbyshire today. On this occasion, the prominent showman, President George Kemp,[32] not only promoted the events, but also arranged for some of them to be staged directly in front of his fairground show and commissioned Mitchell and Kenyon to record them on film. We therefore have clear evidence here of early financial and organisational support and sponsorship of these traditions and some of the performances are more obviously stage-managed than is the case with the processional customs discussed above.

The first of the three films shows a group of young girls, in white dresses and elaborately decorated white hats, performing a maypole dance on a platform immediately in front of Kemp's Bioscope show wagon, closely supervised by two men. Musical accompaniment is provided by a brass band standing on either side of the steps leading up to the platform. As the girls dance, a woman carries a baby across the front of the steps and puts it in George Kemp's arms. He then raises the child above his shoulders, moving her up and down in imitation of the dancers. At the end of the dance, a showman, perhaps one of Kemp's managers, takes off his top hat, waves it and bows to the crowd as if taking credit for the performance. The girls then walk down the steps in groups of four, holding hands, passing between the two rows of bandsmen. A crowd of other, mostly older, children then follows them in an orderly but informal procession. While the maypole is being taken down, all those standing round the wagon, including the bandsmen, file away, many of the men waving hats in salute to the camera, again emphasising the novelty of being filmed. Maypole dancing is still a feature of springtime customs in Derbyshire, such as the Ancient Garland Ceremony at Castleton.[33] The reintroduction of maypole dancing in the Victorian period quickly became popular. Early moving pictures are extremely rare, and this film allows us to study the dress of the performers, the actual event and the mode of performance as they were a century ago.

The second film opens with a posed shot of girls, older than those in the previous film, but similarly dressed, lined up in front of a maypole. On a signal, the girls turn immediately to face the maypole, which is fixed in a large X-shaped wooden base. The brass band stands behind the maypole, the bandsmen looking directly at the camera. This dance is more complex than that performed by the younger girls in front of Kemp's show wagon. Two girls dance to and from the pole while the rest dance in a slow-moving circle, figure-of-eight fashion. When the dance ends, the girls line up and face the camera, each holding out her arms in expectation of something. It turns out that they are all offering to hold George Kemp's now familiar baby which he carries over to them and puts in the arms of the girl in the middle of the group, so that the baby can be photographed with the dancers. He then encourages the dancers to look towards the camera and does so himself, tipping his hat in salute as he walks away.

While these two films reveal a great deal about events taking place in Buxton during the annual celebrations, the third focuses specifically on two well dressings. The theme of the first of these displays, the lilies of the field, is spelled out above the central panel of the triptych-style structure, the panel showing a typical natural scene with trees, flowers and birds. The two side panels, slanting diagonally outwards from the central one, are decorated with various traditional designs, many of which are still popular today, surmounted by the symbol of the cross. A triangular panel above the whole display states that this well dressing was established in 1844.[34] While a still photograph might well have recorded much of the display itself, the film camera again proves its worth here by recording the social context of the occasion. As we watch, George Kemp appears, carrying his small child, whom he holds so that she can put money in the collecting box in front of the well dressing. A man comes to speak to him, perhaps suggesting that he moves away so that the cameraman can get an uninterrupted view of the well dressing itself! The man with the collecting box walks up and down in front of the display, shaking the box to encourage donations. The camera then pans to the left, past a group of male spectators, to show a second, much less elaborate well dressing around a public fountain, to the side of which sits an old man with a collecting box. This simple display comprises narrow decorated panels on each side of the fountain, surmounted by an arched fleur-de-lys. Children come to get a drink from a cup at the fountain, followed by George Kemp, who also takes a drink, while the old man stands, doffs his hat to him and moves himself and his chair to the side to give the camera a clear view of the well dressing.

In conclusion, the brief resumés presented here can do no more than hint at the wealth of detailed information, depicted in motion as the events took place, in these and other films in the Mitchell and Kenyon Collection. These fleeting images contribute significantly to our knowledge of exactly how the events were conducted, rather than our having to read between the lines of extant written accounts. Such accounts are mostly very generalised and detached, whereas the films provide graphic details of the custom, its performance and its context, and give us a true-to-life record of the active involvement of local people in the celebrations.[35] The fact that the events were filmed, and the films have been preserved and are soon to be made accessible, opens a window onto the past; the films give us a fascinating picture of a bygone era, when leisure was a rare and precious commodity and when many of the wonders of modern science and technology we take for granted today were still in their infancy and aroused curiosity and amazement. The films of calendar customs reveal an overriding sense of community in each locality, despite class differences; people from different backgrounds joined in communal enjoyment on the few occasions in the year when the annual round of work paused briefly to allow everyone to relax and celebrate. In that slower, quieter, more orderly and innocent age of horse-drawn vehicles, far removed from the frenetic pace and pressures of modern life, the annual cycle of customs was an essential part of the solid, established framework in everyone's life – a traditional social structure which is much less evident today.

NOTES

1. For nineteenth-century accounts, see for example, George Lawrence Gomme, *The Gentleman's Magazine Library: Manners and Customs* (London: Elliot Stock, 1883); P. H. Ditchfield, *Old English Customs Extant at the Present Time. An Account of Local Observances, Festival Customs and Ancient Ceremonies Yet Surviving in Great Britain* (New York and London: New Amsterdam Book Company and George Redway, 1896); see also the journals of the Folklore Society: *Folk-Lore Record*, 1878–82, *Folk-Lore Journal*, 1883–9, and *Folk-Lore*, later *Folklore*, 1890–; and *Notes and Queries*, 1849–.

2. E.g. the County Folklore series published by the Folklore Society in the late nineteenth and early twentieth centuries.

3. See for example, T. F. Thiselton Dyer, *British Popular Customs* (London: Bell, 1876); Leopold Wagner, *Manners, Customs and Observances: Their Origin and Signification* (London: William Heinemann, 1894).

4. Early examples include the unique photographs of 'the old tup' custom in the Sheffield area, in S. O. Addy, 'Guising and Mumming in Derbyshire', *Journal of the Derbyshire Archaeological and Natural History Society*, no. 24 (1907), pp. 31–42; and in the numerous photographs in George Long, *The Folklore Calendar* (London: Philip Allan, 1930); the photograph of the Haxey Hood which is the frontispiece to Ethel H. Rudkin, *Lincolnshire Folklore* (Gainsborough: Beltons, 1936); and those in Christina Hole, *English Custom and Usage* (London: B. T. Batsford, 1941–2).

5. Among the foremost of these was Sir Benjamin Stone, whose work included a specific focus on English festivals, ceremonies and customs. See Sir Benjamin Stone, *Sir Benjamin Stone's Pictures: Records of National Life and History* (London: Cassell, 1906).

6. Fortunately, in recent years, writers on English customs have drawn on their own fieldwork and that of others to present updated information on contemporary events. See, among many others, Roy Christian, *Old English Customs* (London: Country Life, 1966); Christina Hole, *British Folk Customs* (London: Hutchinson, 1976); Homer Sykes, *Once a Year: Some Traditional British Customs* (London: Gordon Fraser, 1977); Brian Shuel, *The National Trust Guide to Traditional Customs of Britain* (Exeter: Webb and Bower, 1985); Roy Palmer, *Britain's Living Folklore* (Newton Abbot: David and Charles, 1991); Theresa Buckland and Juliette Wood (eds), *Aspects of British Calendar Customs* (Sheffield: Sheffield Academic Press, for the Folklore Society, 1993). For excellent modern overviews of the history of English customs, see Ronald Hutton, *The Stations of the Sun: A History of the Ritual Year in Britain* (Oxford: Oxford University Press, 1996) and Bob Bushaway, *By Rite: Custom, Ceremony and Community in England 1700–1880* (London: Junction Books, 1982).

7. See Vanessa Toulmin, 'The Cinematograph at the Goose Fair: 1896–1911', in Alan Burton and Laraine Porter (eds), *The Showman, the Spectacle and Two-Minute Silence* (Trowbridge: Flicks Books, 2001), pp. 76–87; Kevin Scrivens and Stephen Smith, *The Travelling Cinematograph Show* (Tweedale: New Era Publications, 1999); Vanessa Toulmin, 'Telling the Tale: The Story of the Fairground Bioscope Shows and the Showmen Who Travelled Them', *Film History*, vol. 6, no. 2, 1994, pp. 219–37.

8. For a full account of Easter customs, see Venetia Newall, *An Egg at Easter: A Folklore Study* (London: Routledge and Kegan Paul, 1971).

9. Shuel, *The National Trust Guide*, p. 24.

10. M&K 286: *Preston Egg Rolling* (c. 1901).

11. *Northern Daily Post*, 14 April 1903.

12. M&K 223–4: *Llandudno May Day* (1907).

13. Primary schoolchildren in Bradford, West Yorkshire, for instance, led a parade on the afternoon of May Day, or the nearest school day to May Day. A May Queen was chosen and boys wheeled their decorated bicycles in the procession, while girls wheeled their decorated dolls' prams. This custom continued until at least the late 1960s. I am grateful to Carolyn L. Widdowson for this information.

14. See for example, M. Swackhammer, 'May Processions at Roman Catholic Parochial Schools as Didactic Drama', *Lore and Language*, vol. 3, no. 3, July 1980, pp. 50–66 and Bernadette T. Hayter, 'Long Walk for Little Legs: The Relevance of Processions with Particular Reference to Roman Catholic Traditions', unpublished MA dissertation (Sheffield: Division of Continuing Education/Centre for English Cultural Tradition and Language, University of Sheffield, 1993).

15. Many of these are published locally and are often not widely known, e.g. the four photographs of the May Queen celebrations in Grenoside, Sheffield, three of which were taken in 1911, in Harold Wasteneys, *Grenoside Recollections*, Community Studies Series, no. 1 (Sheffield: Centre for English Cultural Tradition and Language and Division of Continuing Education, University of Sheffield, 1980), pp. 34–6. This publication also includes seven photographs of the hospital parade in Grenoside in 1908 (pp. 61–4) in which decorated bicycles, fancy dress and horse-drawn displays are reminiscent of the various processional customs discussed in this chapter.

16. Shuel, *National Trust Guide*, p. 33; see also pp. 26–40 for a concise and well-illustrated summary of May customs.

17. For an overview of this element, see J. D. A. Widdowson, 'Trends in the Commercialisation of English Calendar Customs: A Preliminary Survey', in Buckland and Wood, *Aspects of British Calendar Customs*, pp. 23–35.

18. M&K 389: *Bootle May Day Demonstration* (1903).

19. *Bootle Times*, 16 May 1903.

20. I am very grateful to Ivor Allsop, former Archivist of the Morris Ring, for this information, and for his expert advice on aspects of traditional dance in this film and in the film of the Leyland May Festival.

21. M&K 293: *Leyland May Festival* (1905).

22. Identified by Ivor Allsop.

23. M&K 429: *Manchester and Salford Harriers Procession* (1901).

24. *Manchester Courier*, 24 June 1901, p. 8, col. 2.

25. *Manchester Courier*, 24 June 1901, p. 8, col. 2.

26. M&K 375–80: *Warrington Walking Day* (1902).

27. Shuel, *The National Trust Guide*, pp. 58, 62–3.

28. *Warrington Guardian*, 1 November 1902.

29. Shuel, *The National Trust Guide*, p. 62.

30. M&K 540–2: *Buxton Well Dressing* (1904).

31. Probably the most substantial documentation of the custom of well dressing is in the Charlotte Norman Collection in the archives of the National Centre for English Cultural Tradition at the University of Sheffield. See also Crichton Porteous, *The Beauty and Mystery of Well-Dressing* (Derby: Pilgrim Press, 1949) and Crichton Porteous, *The Well-Dressing Guide* (Derby: Derbyshire Countryside, 1970).

32. For details of Kemp's life and work as a showman, see Scrivens and Smith, *The Travelling Cinematograph Show*, pp. 112–16).

33. See Brian Woodall, *A Peak District Calendar of Events* (Sheffield: Brian Woodall, 1976) and Geoff Lester, *Castleton Garland* (Sheffield: Centre for English Cultural Tradition and Language, University of Sheffield, 1977), which includes a 1918 photograph of girl dancers dressed in a similar way to those in the first of the three Mitchell and Kenyon Buxton films.

34. However, Charlotte Norman suggests that St Ann's Well in the town was first dressed in 1842, 'to thank the Duke of Devonshire for providing a water supply', the town's water supply having been instituted in 1840. She adds that three wells are dressed nowadays: St Ann's Well, Town Well in the market place and the Children's Well in Sylvan Park; see Charlotte A. Norman, 'Aspects of Calendric Customs in Derbyshire with Special Reference to Well Dressing: History and Geographical Diffusion with Analysis of Development in Context of Past and Present Calendar and Folk Customs in Derbyshire', unpublished PhD thesis (Sheffield: Department of English Language, University of Sheffield, 1988). An early photograph of a well dressing in Buxton market place is reproduced in Cyril Hargreaves, *Grandfather's Derbyshire* (Ilkeston: Moorley's Bible and Bookshop, 1977), p. 70.

35. As noted above, the films offer unparalleled opportunities for the detailed identification and interpretation of the scenes and events depicted, especially by historians and other experts familiar with the localities and occasions brought vividly to life in the Mitchell and Kenyon Collection.

14 'Startling, realistic, pathetic':[1]
The Mitchell and Kenyon 'Boer War' Films

Simon Popple

CONTEXT

The Anglo–Boer War of 1899–1902 is a fascinating period of imperial history in which the moving image lay at the heart of popular cultural activity. Cinema was crucial to the construction, dissemination and discussion of this bitter conflict, the last great imperial adventure of the nineteenth century and the first glimpse of the horrors of fully mechanised wars of attrition that would characterise the twentieth. Cinema, in combination with a host of other communications technologies, marked the Boer War out as the first fully mediated conflict in British imperial history.[2]

Despite the presence of film cameramen and journalists at the seat of war, the conflict was predominantly mediated through popular cultural forms manufactured on home soil. Journalists embellished dispatches from the front; war artists toiled in the drawing offices of Fleet Street; Mitchell and Kenyon staged 're-enactments' of Boer atrocities on the moors above Blackburn; and every major town and city was witness to regular theatrical, lantern and cinematic renderings of recent national and local events in relation to the conflict. Many of these forms of imperial representation were not new, and had evolved as a discernible tradition over the course of the nineteenth century. By the eve of the Anglo–Boer War, they had developed into a highly complex and reactive nexus of popular cultural forms that shared a number of dynamic relationships and articulated very specific aspects of current news issues, responded to popular sentiment and peddled a patriotic, if not jingoistic, imperial ethos. There was also a vein of criticism, impatience and satire running through such representations, mirrored in the range of films.

The films produced by Mitchell and Kenyon all originated on home soil, but offer readings of the conflict from a variety of perspectives. They operate on the basis of a spectrum of 'generic' forms, and this is how I intend to consider them. For the purposes of this essay, I have divided the films into four genres: Fakes and Re-enactments, Military Life, Celebrity, and Pageants and Festivals. These broad generic categorisations are imperfect and often overlap, but are a useful framework within which to differentiate specific qualities and themes such as patriotism, militarism, nationalism and deprecation of the enemy. Each section will focus on a representative film or short series drawn from the much larger war-related body of work represented by the Mitchell and Kenyon Collection at the *bfi* and the Cinema Museum material.

FAKES AND RE-ENACTMENTS

Mitchell and Kenyon's best known and perhaps most obviously Boer War films are those variously called 'sham', 'fake', 'staged' or 're-enactments'.[3] The exact status of these and similar films produced in Britain by R. W. Paul and in the US by James White for Thomas Edison is often complex and contradictory.[4] The films fall into four subcategories, ranging from straightforward re-enactments of combat, depictions of individual deeds of heroism and sacrifice, the comedic and satirical, to full-blown representations of enemy atrocities. Mitchell and Kenyon's staged films encompass all four types and were produced between 1900 and 1902, being described in their own advertising as 'Startling, realistic, pathetic'.[5]

Their subjects would have been familiar to contemporary audiences immersed in a broad range of narratives relating to the enemy's conduct of the war and to constant tales of heroism and bravery. Films with titles such as *White Flag Treachery* (1900), *Shelling the Red Cross* (1900), *A Sneaky Boer* (1900), *Washing Boer Prisoners (Washing a Boer Prisoner in Camp)* (1900*)* and *Poisoning the Well* (1901) clearly allude to atrocity stories circulating in the popular press and pick up what are constant themes throughout the course of the war such as hygiene and various abuses of the Geneva Convention.[6]

The film *Hands off the Flag* (1901) perhaps best exemplifies the content of these 'atrocity narrative' films. It depicts a group of nurses at a Red Cross station that has been captured by Boer soldiers. The Union Jack is torn down and the nurses are lined up, clutching the flag, about to be executed by firing squad. At the last minute, British troops arrive on the scene, rescuing the nurses and the flag, after having dispatched the Boers. The familiar stereotypes, drawn from a mass of popular cultural forms, are immediately mobilised by the film-makers and the narrative allows for a resolution in this case, perhaps because the two main subjects, the nurses and the flag, are unable to defend themselves. In other films of this series, such as *Tommy's Last Shot* (1901), the ordinary British troops do not fare so well. While these films might have played well with audiences, and reviews certainly suggest this, there was some general opposition to the production of this type of material as the following letter to the *Optical Magic Lantern Journal and Photographic Enlarger* clearly attests,

Boer Atrocities

Dear Sir, – I have recently received by post a circular from one of our leading makers of cinematographic films, containing details of what they call one of their latest films. It is headed 'Boer Atrocities', and it reads as follows:–

The opening of this picture shows a Transvaal mine with a sentinel on guard, and Boer commandant in the foreground. Three other Boers appear, bringing with them a captured British soldier, whom they search, and find concealed beneath his tunic a Union Jack, the sight of which drives them mad; the commandant seizes the flag, and covers it with abuse. The British soldier infuriated, attempts to recover it, but in the struggle is thrown to the ground and shot in cold blood … Perhaps some reader can inform me what good the issue of such films can do? In my opinion the issue of such has only a demoralising tendency, for it is false. It is a made-up scene, a playing to the gallery, and a means of instilling hatred in the heart of the young under the guise of patriotism. It is to be hoped that films of this character will not find a place in the Englishman's *repertoire.*

Yours. etc., FAIRPLAY AND HONESTY[7]

Representations of bravery and patriotism are strongly articulated in the other staged films, which deal with scenes of combat and activities in the field. The notion of 'realism' referred to in Mitchell and Kenyon's advertising seems to relate more to a sense of visual authenticity achieved than to any attempt to convince an audience that they were actually filmed *in situ*. While the combat scenes are by no means as grand or accomplished as those executed by James White in the US there is attention to detail in the use of uniforms, horses, small arms and even cannon. Audiences were well aware of the presence of faked films and of the propensity of certain exhibitors and film-makers to deceive audiences. One reviewer of a film show featuring Mitchell and Kenyon films at the fair at Stalybridge Wakes in July 1900 perfectly expressed his reservations,

When the war pictures were being exhibited one was naturally anxious to know how such portraits could be taken in close conflict, and we are reminded of a capital article upon this subject which appeared in a London contemporary not long ago. The writer in question spoke of the utter impossibility of portraits to be taken of a battle, and stigmatised the representations by the cinematograph as a fraud. He further explained that the pictures were taken at home, the 'soldiers' preparing themselves for the occasion.[8]

Just how audiences responded to and understood these films is a complex subject and one that will benefit from further contextual readings of these films. What is certain is that Mitchell and Kenyon presented their audiences with tableaux drawn from, and contributing to, a much broader popular-cultural representation of the war.

Among Mitchell and Kenyon's stereotypical and ideologised representation lies a single 'trick film': a critical comedy entitled *Chasing de Wet* (1901). Advertised as a 'new laughable trick film', it ridicules the British army's failure to capture the Boer commander, General de Wet. The film deploys the only example of stop-start substitution in this series as de Wet appears and disappears in a puff of smoke before the soldiers' eyes. This was again a popular satirical subject, the great *Punch* cartoonist, Edward Linley Sambourne contemporaneously depicted de Wet as Willow the Wisp.[9] This is the only slightly humanised and sympathetic representation of the enemy in this whole series of films, his cunning shown as something to be admired, if not appreciated. Representation of the enemy occurs elsewhere in Mitchell and Kenyon's non-staged films, but the dominant subject of these is the British military.

MILITARY LIFE

Although nearly all of the war films depict aspects of militarism there are a group that explicitly represent parades, exhibitions of military might and aspects of training. This was a common tradition within early film production and examples can be found in the catalogues of most early producers. R. W. Paul's catalogue for the season 1900–1, for example, contains a series of five films under the heading, 'Naval and Military'.[10] These cinematic representations were part of a much broader popular-cultural tradition, matched by live performances such as West's *Our Navy* and the touring troupe, 'Savage South Africa'.[11] The most striking of the Mitchell and Kenyon films celebrate the visit of eight torpedo boat destroyers of the Devenport Command to Trafford Wharf on 25 April 1901. The films show the progression of the boats up the Manchester Ship Canal, their arrival at Trafford Wharf and the subsequent civic reception of the sailors.[12] M&K 461: *Torpedo Flotilla Visit to Manchester* (1901), shows the boats passing through Barton Bridge aqueduct and is shot from the left bank and a promontory in the middle of the canal. The impressive structure of the destroyers is fully displayed and they make a bold and forceful impression. In the middle of this film, the second camera crew are clearly visible, using a handkerchief to signal.

CELEBRITY

At the heart of many of these films are representations of celebrities associated with the war. The cult of the war celebrity was an essential element of many popular-cultural forms and a key narrative component of the film and variety programme.[13] The centrality of the celebrity character within the performance is richly evidenced in reviews of the period. Audience reactions to cinematic and other representations of celebrities, such as Sir Redvers Buller, Lord 'Bobs' Roberts, General White and leader of the Boers, President Paul Kruger, are often carefully noted. They are also a good indication of the tenor of esteem or approbation in which individuals were held at various stages during the war and of regional affinities. Reviews of two A. D. Thomas shows from the *Manchester Evening*

News of November and December 1901, featuring films of Buller, possibly M&K 466–9: *General Buller's Visit to Manchester and the Thousands of Spectators* (1901) and M&K 420–2: *Lord Robert's Visit to Manchester* (1901), reveal overt audience partisanship.

The first review dates from 29 October 1901:

> The St James Hall Pictures. The capital entertainment at St James's Hall still finds abundant support … Last night the audience had an opportunity of giving expression to their feelings in regard to the Buller controversy. Some views of the General on the parade ground evoked great enthusiasm.[14]

The second is from 5 November 1901:

> Animated Pictures at the Regent. An entertainment similar to that which has drawn big audiences to St James's Hall was given last night at the Regent Theatre, and the experiment of devoting the whole evening to animated pictures seemed to be a substantial success. Few plays could have attracted such an audience as assembled at the theatre, and no 'striking situation' could have awakened more enthusiasms than did a picture of General Buller. The reception given to Lord Roberts when he appeared on screen was cold by comparison.[15]

Buller and Roberts were two of the most famous British military figures of the war and were bitter rivals.[16] Buller became commanding officer of the task force at the outbreak of the war in what at first seemed a simple anti-insurrectionist expedition that soon escalated. The British forces stationed in South Africa were besieged in three towns: Ladysmith, Mafeking and Kimberley, all cut off from their lines of supply. Buller's attempts at relieving them started disastrously with a series of heavy defeats inflicted by the Boers, most notably at Spion Kop. He was soon relieved of his command and replaced by Lord Roberts, or 'Bobs' to his troops. Buller returned to England to assume a command at Aldershot and was eventually sacked following a series of feuds with Lord Roberts in late 1901, sparking the aforementioned 'Buller controversy'. Both men visited Manchester that year and the events were filmed by Mitchell and Kenyon. Thomas, acutely aware of the topicality of the feud, combined a screening of the new film of Lord Roberts with earlier films of Buller. There is further evidence of this practice in a subsequent exhibition at the Court Theatre in Wigan the following month.[17] The 'controversy' was also exploited in almost pantomimic terms on the variety stage as a reviewer for the *Carlisle Journal* noted:

> In addition to the sword swallowing there are several equestrian items, a juggling performance, a clever troupe of performing dogs, some wonderful cyclists, and a quick change artist who rapidly made himself up as various well-known characters, including General Buller, as whom he was cheered, and as Lord Roberts, in which capacity he retired amid much hissing.[18]

M&K 466–9: *General Buller's Visit to Manchester and the Thousands of Spectators*, depicts the arrival of the general's entourage, the civic dignitaries and the large well-ordered crowds controlled by a phalanx of mounted police. M&K 422: *Lord Robert's Visit to Manchester*, is a far less ordered affair. The sequence opens with Lord Roberts addressing the crowd in front of the new statue of the late Queen Victoria. According to press reports, he spoke of the sadness and regret the war had occasioned for Victoria and of the bitterness of her last year, clouded by the death of her grandson. The subsequent shots reveal the unveiling of the statue, and an incident in the crowd as a woman is carried from the crush, attended by several police and soldiers.[19] There are several other shots of a surging and restless crowd that is barely being contained. The film also features several glimpses of rival cameramen jockeying for position, one of whom is Cecil Hepworth. These two films are characteristic of the depiction of the national celebrity in the regional context, as seen in a number of similar films, which depict major figures such as Lord Kitchener and are clear evidence of the potency of celebrity of the minor aristocracy and the officer class within British society.

The rise of photography, cheap literature and popular journals in the nineteenth century had helped establish the status of real celebrities and the culturally constructed national icons, John Bull and Tommy Atkins. They also allowed for the rise of the cult of the ordinary hero and new genres such as boys' adventure fiction, comics and popular biographies increasingly chronicled the lives and exploits of real and imagined heroes drawn from all strata of British society. The composite character of Tommy Atkins, the steadfast, ordinary, working-class British soldier featured heavily in a range of performance idioms, including Mitchell and Kenyon's *Tommy's Last Shot* (1901). This valorisation of the vulgar soldier was a new phenomenon. The ordinary soldier had traditionally been a somewhat despised cultural icon, and even within recent memory the Duke of Wellington had confessed to being more frightened by his own troops than the French. Yet the Tommy of the late Victorian and early Edwardian period was a figure of pride and imperial prowess, celebrated in many popular-cultural forms.[20] In this film, he and his comrades appear on the veldt amid the smoke of war. One Tommy appears badly wounded and is given water by a comrade to whom he

M&K 585: *Private Ward, V.C. Leeds Hero* (1901), featuring Private Charles Ward, V.C. seated at a table in what appears to be a backyard, being interviewed by Ralph Pringle in February 1902.

passes a letter. Attempting to escape and deliver the letter, he is shot and the film ends with a view of them all lying dead on the battlefield.

One of the most intriguing films in the Mitchell and Kenyon Collection draws on the persona of the ordinary Tommy. M&K 585: *Private Ward, V.C. Leeds Hero* (1901), is a film that features a silent interview with a popular embodiment of the 'plucky British Tommy' Private Charles Ward, V.C. Ward is pictured, seated at a table in what appears to be a backyard, being interviewed by showman Ralph Pringle. He is seen answering questions, gesticulating and illustrating the exploits that won him the Victoria Cross. Pringle is particularly animated, constantly touching the medal pinned to Ward's chest and frequently makes notes as Ward answers his questions. In an advertisement for the North American Animated Photo Company in the *Yorkshire Post*, Ward is described as a 'Leeds hero', and it is announced that a screening of this film will be attended on stage by local regiment, the Leeds Rifles.[21] Charles Ward (1877–1921) was a private in the Second Battalion Yorkshire Light Infantry and was decorated for conspicuous gallantry for actions at Lindley, South Africa on 26 June 1900. Ward's garrison was surrounded by over 500 Boer troops and his officers were all dead or wounded. He volunteered to take a message asking for reinforcements and twice crossed enemy lines facing withering fire to deliver messages. He was severely wounded on his return but the garrison was saved. He was also the last man to receive the Victoria Cross from Queen Victoria, and very much a 'local hero.' He served as a drill instructor in World War I and, on his retirement from military service, the people of Leeds presented him with a testimonial, £600 and a gold commemorative medal.

There is also a series of similar 'local' celebrity films including M&K 663–6: *Lieutenant Clive Wilson and the Tranby Croft Party* (1902), shot in Hull in April. These feature another decorated hero Clive Wilson D.S.O, although Wilson was of much higher social standing and an officer. These films are far more traditional in the sense that they mirror the arrival and civic reception model of the Roberts and Buller films.[22] The films were screened at a special event held at the Anlaby Circus under the patronage of the Wilson family:

> Many new pictures were introduced, but those which attracted the most attention were, of course, relating to the return of Lieutenant Clive Wilson from the war. The scenes at Hessle station, the central figure amongst which was Lieutenant Wilson, were faithfully reproduced and the Tranby house party also formed an interesting picture. During the proceedings the popularity of Lieutenant Clive was made manifest by the frequent applause of the audience.[23]

These Celebrity films show a constant tension between the desire to represent international events – often in the form of key national celebrities such as Buller, White, Roberts and Kitchener, and local events and personalities. They represent the war both on a macro and micro level, marrying notions of imperial, national and regional identity, and allowing local films to speak directly to local audiences.

PAGEANTS AND FESTIVALS

This final, and perhaps most intimate genre, explicitly cements such connectivity in a series of very personal films of community events, carnivals and wakes celebrations. These very localised films present us with some of the most carefree and joyous glimpses of these communities and their religious and leisure traditions. These films show how ordinary non-combatants reflected upon aspects of the war in their daily lives and how they externalised attitudes to the military, celebrity, patriotism and the enemy. We have already attempted to measure their responses as members of the cinema

M&K 424: *Manchester and Salford Harriers Procession* (1901), shot on the 22 June 1901, featuring a small child beautifully attired as Lord Roberts mounted on a horse and attended by representatives of various branches of the armed forces.

audience and as spectators at grand civic events, but more than any historical source, these films offer rich evidence of ordinary people responding to the war within their own contexts. They are pictured as the costumed embodiments of popular heroes and villains, dressed as soldiers, Boers, black Africans, Britannia, Kruger and Lord Roberts.

One film above all stands out, M&K 424: *Manchester and Salford Harriers Procession* (1901), shot on the 22 June 1901 featuring a charity cycle parade in aid of Manchester institutions by the Manchester and Salford Harriers.[24] The sense of locality was further enforced by the exhibitor A. D. Thomas whose rolling show was advertised under the title the 'War in Manchester, War in Manchester'.[25] The film shows a small child beautifully attired as Lord Roberts mounted on a horse and attended by representatives of various branches of the armed forces.[26]

POSTSCRIPT

These glimpses of the incidental minutiae of life: the fainting woman, the child on the horse and the fleeting celebrity of the ordinary soldier characterise a humanism common to all of Mitchell and Kenyon's films. They exist as testimony to an extraordinary period of history and the absolute potency of the moving image.

NOTES

1. Advert for Mitchell and Kenyon 'Boer War Films', *The Showman*, 6 September 1901, p. 11.

2. See Simon Popple, 'But the Khaki-Covered Camera Is the *Latest* Thing': The Boer War Cinema and Visual Culture in Britain', in Andrew Higson (ed.), *Young and Innocent? The Cinema in Britain 1896–1930* (Exeter: Exeter University Press, 2002), pp. 13–27.

3. Such was the sensitivity surrounding the status of these films that Charles Urban was moved to write to the *Optical Magic Lantern Journal and Photographic Enlarger* in December 1900 to express his concerns over the use of the terms, fake or trick films. The editor responded by saying that 'Mr Urban, the managing director of the Warwick Trading Company Limited, calls me to task for using the word 'fake' under the circumstances and explains that the style of picture we described should have been spoken of as a 'trick film'. This, he explains, differs from a 'fake' inasmuch as the general understanding of a 'fake' film is that of producing a film of a counterfeit representation of an actual event, such as has been practised extensively with South African war subjects, many of which were made in the suburbs of London, besides France and New Jersey, U.S.A. We may here say that no 'fake' subjects of the war have been issued by the Warwick Trading Company, all theirs being actual photographs taken at the occurrence of the various events in South Africa.' From *Optical Magic Lantern Journal and Photographic Enlarger*, vol. 2, no. 139, (December 1900), pp. 153–4.

4. Popple, 'But the Khaki-Covered Camera'.

5. *The Showman*, 6 September 1901, p. 11.

6. One of the key complaints was of the Boer misuse of the white flag.

7. *Optical Magic Lantern Journal and Photographic Enlarger*, vol. 12, no. 146, (November 1910), p. 96.

8. 'In the Fair', *The Reporter*, 28 July 1900.

9. 'De Wet O'De Wisp', *Punch*, 19 December 1901, p. 437.

10. Robert Paul Catalogue 1900–1, National Fairground Archive.

11. For a full account of 'Savage South Africa', see Ben Sheppard, *Kitty and the Prince* (London: Profile Books, 2003).

12. Seven reels of film survive – M&K 459–65: *Torpedo Flotilla Visit to Manchester* (1901).

13. Celebrity advertising was extremely common, for example Monkey Brand Soap frequently included war celebrities from both sides in their advertising campaigns.

14. *Manchester Evening News*, 29 October 1901, p. 1.

15. *Manchester Evening News*, 5 November 1901, p. 5.

16. For a full discussion, see Field Marshal Lord Carver, *The National Army Museum Book of the Boer War* (London: Pan Books, 2000).

17. 'Lord Roberts' visit to Manchester and the unveiling of the Queen's statue is shown, as also is General Buller's visit to the same city', *The Wigan Examiner*, 11 December 1901, review.

18. *Carlisle Journal*, 10 December 1901.

19. The event was marred by a fatal accident in which two women, Misses Norbury and Dewhirst were hit by falling masonry and Miss Dewhirst died. The event was also notable for crowd problems.

20. For example, the popular stage show, *The Tommy Atkins Review*.

21. *Yorkshire Post*, 7 February 1901, p. 1.

22. Jasper Redfern also filmed these events and is pictured in M&K 665.

23. *Hull Daily Mail*, 10 April 1902.

24. Two other films make up this sequence, M&K 428–9: *Manchester and Salford Harriers Procession* (1901).

25. *Manchester Evening News*, 25 June 1901, p. 1.

26. *Manchester Courier*, 24 June 1901, p. 8, col. 2. '… "Lord 'Bobs" was admirably portrayed by a little fellow mounted on a big horse'.

15 The Seaside and the Holiday Crowd

John K. Walton

The Mitchell and Kenyon films were produced at a time of transition in the British seaside holiday, especially in Lancashire. This area pioneered the development of the working-class seaside holiday, which was the preserve of a minority of occasional daytrippers and weekend visitors in the mid-nineteenth century. The market had been expanding rapidly since the 1870s in response to rising wages and family incomes, cheap transport, the opportunity to extend surviving traditional holidays (the 'wakes weeks' as such were a development of the 1890s) and the willingness of entrepreneurs in Blackpool and Morecambe to cater for working-class tastes and pockets.[1] In Blackpool's case, we can attach approximate numbers to this trend: there were up to 1.9 million visitors in 1893, three million in 1903 and approaching four million in 1913.[2] If these estimates carry any weight, Blackpool's visitors more than doubled from an already high original figure during these twenty years; and the extra visitors must have been overwhelmingly working class. But we cannot go beyond these overall totals, which are themselves approximate extrapolations from the statistics of incoming trains, to provide a convincing picture of the composition of the visitors, whether by class, gender or age, or by cultural preference, spending patterns or attitudes to fashion or personal display.

It seems likely that working-class visitors (especially those who stayed beyond a single day) would be drawn mainly from people at the crests of the 'poverty cycle': young people without children to support and older families where most or all of the children were contributing to the family income, and the financial benefits of female and 'half-time' child labour were being reaped, especially in the weaving towns of North Lancashire. But this is a matter of inference rather than direct evidence as is the assumption that the working-class presence would be dominated by the 'skilled' workers in regular employment, those who (for most purposes, most of the time) were, by the turn of the century, accepting some of the behavioural constraints of 'respectability', in contrast with an earlier generation, new to the seaside, that dressed loudly, scruffily or otherwise distinctively, smoked clay pipes, made a lot of noise, acted rowdily and annoyed their 'betters', whose vociferous complaints were prominent in the newspapers of the 1880s but have died away, in Lancashire at least, by the beginning of the twentieth century.[3] But it would be useful to have further evidence on this transition, which can be linked to interesting discussions of the seaside as liminal space and a venue for carnivalesque behaviour, and even with a particular working out of the 'civilising process'.[4]

Matters must be complicated in various ways. We know that the 'social tone' of Victorian seaside resorts in northwest England varied from place to place and within individual resorts, and changed according to the time of day, the day of the week and the time of year as well as over longer periods.[5] We know, for example, that Morecambe was viewed as catering more for foremen, white-collar workers and their families at the turn of the century, whereas Blackpool already had a more squarely working-class image.[6] We also know that Blackpool itself was never completely inundated by the tide of working-class visitors from the Lancashire cotton towns and (increasingly) beyond: it kept its own middle-class visiting public, which was less religious and more pleasure-loving than the Nonconformists who dominated at the rival resort of Southport and congregated especially at the northern and southern ends of the town. Here too, residential suburbs for the comfortably off were developing at the turn of the century, to supplement the homes of the local elite on Read's Estate at a safe distance inland from the central promenade, which was the great gathering point for the working-class visitors and their amusements.[7] Our evidence is qualitative rather than quantitative: it is drawn from the impressions of journalists, novelists and other social commentators as they tried to describe the Blackpool holiday crowds. But a more sophisticated analysis of the visiting public, to take account of its changing social composition in a convincing way, has remained out of reach. The Mitchell and Kenyon Collection provides important additional clues; but making sense of them will be a difficult and demanding matter, with limitations of its own.

We do have a template for at least a partial reading of the social composition of the crowds depicted in sources of this kind, in the form of an article by María Antonia Paz on depictions of the 'people of Madrid' in newsreel films between 1896 and 1936.[8] She divides her thirty-seven films into categories (such as culture, sport, politics, army, and including tourism and traditions) and divides those who appear into five age-based categories (0–14, 15–19, 20–40, 40–60, over 60), four social classes (upper, middle, lower and very low), and four 'races' (with a residual category for the unidentified and a separate category for gypsies). In order to make these judgments, she considers personal appearance and clothing: for example, how many women wear a hat, a pinafore, a shawl or a headscarf, and how many men wear a hat, a cap, overalls, a moustache? Here, as in Britain, the absence of headgear was an indicator of the kind of poverty that was unable to observe the most basic of dress codes. Shoes are also important social markers, when visible: in the case of Madrid, are the people in the films wearing shoes, boots or *alpargatas*, the light canvas footwear of the poor? Paz is also interested in whether alcohol and/or tobacco feature as items of consumption, although she makes no distinction between pipes, cigars and cigarettes.[9] She is well aware of the difficulty of assigning people accurately to age categories and of the perils of simply reading off articles of clothing as markers of social status. With such a small sample, it is also difficult to chart changes over time. But she offers us a potentially transferable methodology for analysing the Mitchell and Kenyon films, although it would have to be adapted to British circumstances and especially to the gradations between 'rough' and 'respectable' in British working-class society, which may have been more complex and subtle than in the case of Madrid.[10]

Any attempt to apply the Paz methodology systematically to the Mitchell and Kenyon Collection or to other visual sources depicting crowds in the past, would require a substantial research project (especially if the idea of attempted quantification were to be taken seriously). This would involve the detailed analysis of individual frames to look for markers of status and lifestyle and to estimate age, taking into account the swirling patterns of movement, the comportment and presentation of the self in motion and in relation to others, the sense of holidaymakers in action (whether joyful, rowdy, playful, relaxed, apathetic or resentful) that constitute the greatest and most demanding, original contribution of the Collection, in comparison with the still photographs that have survived in abundance but still need serious analysis in their own right.

A precise knowledge of the nuances of particular fashions and items of dress would be helpful here: what was last year's fashion, what was this year's, what looks impressive but was actually out of date or even possibly second-hand? We need a vocabulary to try to communicate, share and test out our perceptions of these multiple moving images and the meanings we may be able to attach to them. An additional problem when looking at holidaymakers is that by the early twentieth century most people were 'dressing up' while on holiday, showing off their best clothes to those who knew them, making a stab at being 'in the fashion' and hoping to impress new people by laying claim to higher status than at home, taking advantage of the element of anonymity that a holiday crowd of mixed geographical origins offered.[11] The women in shawls and clogs and the men in mufflers smoking short clay pipes, who feature in (for example) M&K 178–9: *Rochdale Tram Ride* (*c.* 1900), might have appeared at the seaside in this guise in the 1880s, but they now had Sunday and holiday clothes and were able to participate in the new democracy of dress.[12] But at the very least, by bringing out the varieties of individual experience, self-expression and demeanour within the overall grammar and discipline imposed by the 'civilisation of the crowd', this kind of approach undermines simplistic notions of 'mass tourism' and complicates contemporary ideas of the crowd as organism, even as it restores life and agency to the individuals within it.[13]

For the time being, an impressionistic assessment of what the films show us will have to suffice. We must remember that these were not representative holiday crowds: the holiday panorama was so kaleidoscopic and variegated that this could never have been possible, and we shall see that the crowds on view were capable of changing their composition and demeanour considerably within a few yards. They are the product of particular vantage points on particular days at particular times and it is important to be aware of what they exclude as well as what they include. Above all, they feature particularly 'respectable' parts of holiday Blackpool and Morecambe, at relatively 'respectable' points in the year: Easter and late June, before the start of the full-blown popular season, with only Whitsuntide representing a time of year when genuinely working-class crowds would be enjoying the first great traditional holiday of the early summer.

As to the locations, the North Pier was the first of Blackpool's three piers, and retained an air of social superiority: it offered an orchestra with some pretensions rather than a dance band, and eschewed the boisterous open-air dancing that soon became the hallmark of the South Jetty, later the Central Pier, which was opened specifically to cater for the 'trippers'. Its Easter Sunday church parade was an ostentatious and effectively exclusive occasion, with elaborately bound prayer books on display and at the turn of the century, it was probably the most socially elevated public space in Blackpool.[14] The South or Victoria Pier, which had opened only recently in 1893, was aimed at the 'respectable', middle-class visiting public that still dominated the southern end of the town, formally proscribing dancing to assuage local concerns, and although this upmarket atmosphere was soon to be compromised by the nearby development of what was to become the Pleasure Beach, the South Pier still had nearly as many social pretensions as the North at the turn of the century.[15] The Morecambe material is skewed towards the West End, which was also the 'best end', although we shall see that the crowd here looks rather more mixed and downmarket than in the Blackpool clips.[16] But we must emphasise the absence from the Collection of scenes on the beach, at the central places of entertainment such as the Blackpool Tower, Alhambra or Winter Gardens, at the emergent Pleasure Beach amusement park or (most significantly) on Blackpool's 'Golden Mile' between Central station and Central Pier, including the pier itself. The 'Golden Mile' was the great stronghold of the most populist end of the working-class holiday market, with stalls and waxworks featuring two-headed mermaids and similar delights, corn-cutters, phrenologists and palmists, while the pubs were thickest on the ground and probably at their liveliest in this oldest district of holiday Blackpool.[17] By omitting the central areas around the main railway stations and the August peak of the popular holiday season, this evidence privileges a relatively respectable face of the great Lancashire popular resorts.

There is also an interesting issue surrounding the presentation of these films. Who were they for? Where were they meant to be shown? By the time these films could be presented in Blackpool or Morecambe, many or even most of the visitors in the crowds would have returned home. What little evidence we have suggests that they were intended to represent the joys of the seaside in a generic way rather than showing people themselves and their friends on holiday. There is direct evidence that M&K 189, 195–9: *Lytham Trams and the Views along the Route* were shown at Blackpool's Alhambra and the Morecambe promenade and pier entrance pictures were shown at the local Winter Gardens throughout June and July and perhaps into August. The Blackpool Victoria Pier films may have been shown at the local Alhambra or Hippodrome. Blackpool and Morecambe films were shown as far away as Grimsby and Great Malvern, matching the widening spread of Blackpool's poster advertising campaign and the film of Morecambe between West and Central Piers was shown at Bradford, the heart of the resort's catchment area.[18] But the precise thinking behind the holiday crowd films remains opaque. We must also consider the possibility that the crowd scenes on Morecambe promenade at least, depicted locals rather than visitors: indirect support for this idea comes from the much more obvious evidence of intervention by the film-maker in encouraging action from the participants, who also reappear in ways that suggest a lack of spontaneity, in contrast with the Blackpool films. We need to remember that we are unable to tell, simply by looking at the film, who was a local resident and who a visitor: the amenities of the seaside were open to all and, outside the main holiday season, the presence of residents was all the more likely.

What then, do the films show us? I begin with the shot of the North Pier in M&K 205: *Blackpool North Pier* (1903), which presents us with a particularly elevated 'social tone'. The crowds here,

M&K 205: *Blackpool North Pier* (1903), holidaymakers on the North Pier, 1903. The North Pier was the first of Blackpool's three piers and as such, retained an air of social superiority.

on a cold day suggestive of the Easter holidays (people are well wrapped up, and there is nobody on the beach when the camera pans along the shoreline as far as the Tower and the gigantic wheel is not in motion), are impressively well dressed and decorous, even formal, in their demeanour. The subject matter is the huge throng of promenaders that fills the pier from side to side and end to end. The crowd is overwhelmingly adult, with a high representation of the middle aged and elderly, and more men than women, although there are several clusters of three or four women together. The small number of children includes a few boys wearing mortar-boards, presumably from one of the local boarding schools that also contributed their quota to the crowds. Most men wear top hats or bowlers with upturned brims and there are several older men with Victorian whiskers under top hats: the relationship between age, dress and facial hair (at least for men) is obviously important. Some younger men wear cricket-style caps and a few sport flat caps, perhaps the most proletarian headgear on view but not necessarily carrying those connotations. There are some very elaborate ladies' hats and nobody goes bare-headed. Formal neckwear is universal among the men but shoes are not visible. The few (male) smokers on view have wooden pipes with metal bindings, rather than the proletarian clay pipe: cigarettes are unusual in the seaside films.[19] The circulation of the crowd is also very formal and controlled, as it moves resolutely anti-clockwise round the pier, keeping to the right, with just a few eddies and cross-currents as people try to get into camera shot more than once: even this high-status gathering can accommodate a temptation to show off by breaking convention at the margins. This is the sort of privileged space that excludes those who cannot meet the governing sartorial and behavioural expectations and who would be made uncomfortable by prolonged exposure to it; and it is a reminder that such spaces existed even in late Victorian and Edwardian Blackpool.[20]

M&K 206–8: *Blackpool North Pier Steamboat* (1903), also from the turn of the century and taken on an obviously chilly day, seems less elevated in 'social tone'; but people going for a steamer trip would be less 'on display' than promenaders on the pier on what seems to be a special occasion (possibly Easter Sunday), and the apparent contrast should not be overstated. The limited display of big elaborate hats and veils among the women (though they are not absent) and the prevalence of mufflers rather than ties among the men, may simply be 'sensible' attire for the conditions. Plain skirts, simple blouses and overcoats were the order of the day on the *Deerhound*, *Belle* and *Clifton*, whose destinations are unclear: perhaps the Isle of Man, perhaps north Wales, perhaps Ulverston for the Lake District or possibly the much shorter trip to Southport. Caps and straw hats are much more in evidence than more formal headgear among the men and two men on the *Deerhound* combine bowler hats with mufflers. Among the patient and well-mannered queue boarding the *Greyhound* is a man with a basket under his arm who may be a shellfish vendor and this reinforces the impression that the steamer passengers are a less ostentatious, more downmarket branch of the North Pier's custom than the promenaders.

This alerts us to the multiple social identities of the North Pier; and what we are shown of the Victoria Pier is much more complicated, no doubt partly because some of it was shot during Whitsuntide. We have three distinct shots, one featuring high-class, summer promenaders; another showing a less formal Whitsuntide crowd on the pier; and a third presenting the audience at an open-air concert on the same day. This is the richest seaside material in the whole Collection. In M&K 203: *Blackpool Victoria Pier* (1904), we encounter a very similar middle-class scene to the North Pier promenade, except that this is a bright summer day, bringing out the parasols to remind us that fashionable milk-white skin still had to be protected from the sun and the vogue for the suntan was still almost a generation away.[21] Some women wore white or pastel shades but most dresses were dark, formal and heavily embroidered, and some very high-piled feathery and fruit-embellished hats were in evidence. As on the North Pier, this was an adult environment, weighted towards the older and visibly prosperous age groups. Children were few and far between: a boy in an Eton suit with a highly polished top hat stood out, as did a girl with a very large formal hat, making the point that this was an environment in which children were expected to behave with the restraint and control of honorary adults.

At first pass, the social tone of the Whitsuntide crowd on the Victoria Pier on 28 May, M&K 200: *Blackpool Victoria Pier* (1904), also looks overwhelmingly middle class; but a closer inspection reveals sharp differences in the visual impression conveyed by groups that are only a few yards apart. We begin with a display of good cloth and ornate dresses with a great deal of expensive-looking embroidery. The women wear big hats with flowers on the brim and floral dresses, while the men sport moustaches, cricket caps, starched shirts and ties. But as the camera pans to the left, towards the south, we move to an adjoining area where the women's garb becomes less ornamental, boaters replace floral hats and more of the men wear bowler hats. The overall impression is more dowdy and less expressive, but a lot of clean linen is still on show. As the camera pans further across the entrance kiosks of the pier, within a few yards the crowd becomes more downmarket again, more masculine, older and more whiskery, wearing no more elaborate headgear than a basic cap. Do these changes reflect microscopic zoning systems in which people know their place, as on the Alameda at Spain's San Sebastián at the same time, or (as seems much more likely) are they accidents of the moment, before the kaleidoscope of the crowd rearranges itself after the instantaneous gaze of the camera has moved on?[22] A few yards further on, near the kiosk, the crowd appears to move upmarket again. All this seems to suggest that the stories Edwardian Blackpool liked to tell about itself, that it was a socially mixed resort where the classes could enjoy themselves side by side in harmony, contained a strong element of truth. The *Blackpool Times* wrote in characteristically eloquent vein on this theme at this very time:

> A common meeting ground this (the Promenade) for all, for the merchant and the mechanic, the lady of fashion and the factory lass, for the plutocrat and the plebeian, the mightiest and the meanest. We all commingle on these spacious parades by the sea, for the time being having no castes, no precise distinctions of 'proper' and 'select' persons.[23]

But we need to keep in mind the difficulties inherent in trying to read social status from dress and demeanour in this environment, the aspiring lower middle classes being particularly difficult to place.[24] Female factory workers were often criticised, too, for spending surplus wages in their years of independence on fashionable dresses and 'cheap finery'.[25] The very limited proportion of children in the crowd (certainly less than ten per cent) also supports the idea that most working-class people could only afford seaside visits at the child-free crests of the 'poverty cycle', although this runs counter to representations of the 'wakes week' in contemporary dialect literature, which assumed that the children came too. Such dialect poetry was probably based on the transference of middle-class assumptions about the family holiday to depictions of the working class, although those who sought a cheap holiday with the children may have frequented parts of the town that offered cheaper pleasures than the piers, especially the beach itself, where sea and sand were free to all comers.[26] But such an argument also begs the question of where the children of the middle classes were. One memorably miserable face suggests that some of those who were present might have preferred to be elsewhere. Early photographs of the Pleasure Beach also show very small numbers of children, reinforcing the idea that this kind of seaside environment, unlike the beaches of family-centred, middle-class resorts, was more a playground for adults than children.[27] The coding of facial hair by age is also reinforced by these moving images: older men had beards and whiskers, younger men were clean-shaven or wore neat moustaches and the one relatively youthful, middle-aged man, with luxuriant Victorian whiskers, stood out spectacularly from those around him. These generational changes in the conventions of facial hair seem to have spanned class boundaries, prompting questions about how they came about, and what their implications may have been.

Best of all the shots perhaps, is the coverage of the open-air performance by the Hungarian Blue Band (apparently) and Flockton Foster's Entertainments in M&K 201: *Blackpool Victoria Pier* (1904), a mixed troupe in nautical costume who apparently specialised in Gilbert and Sullivan and had performed in the same place at the same time the previous year.[28] A feature of this film is an extended pan from the stage across the whole audience, which provides a wonderful opportunity for a detailed analysis on the lines suggested by Paz. We begin with views of the stage from behind the audience, some of whom are distracted from the band and pay more heed to the camera, with heads turned. This awareness of the camera's presence frequently affects behaviour, at the seaside as elsewhere. But then we get a slow, measured view of the whole audience from the stage.[29] It is an all-embracing mixture of age, gender and (apparently) class, with no suggestion that some parts of the audience are more 'respectable' than others in any systematic way, perhaps indicative of uniform pricing. Children are much more in evidence than in the other films and a range of hats worn by both sexes is on display, although there are fewer big floral hats and more straw boaters worn by women. The general

M&K 201:*Blackpool Victoria Pier* (1904) featuring Flockton Foster's Entertainments, end-of-pier entertainment and light opera company performing for the audience on the Victoria Pier in Blackpool.

impression of clothing styles is more restrained and low-key than the other pier films. There are little clusters of young women in particularly frivolous hats, however, suggesting parties of workmates from the same factory. There is also a little group of young girls in floppy sunbonnets. What really stands out, however, is that this is a more relaxed and unbuttoned crowd than the promenaders of the other Blackpool films. Smoking is much more in evidence among the audience here and some men are bare-headed, while a few toothless and rather rough-looking female faces stand out. It is also a responsive audience. There is a good deal of grinning, smiling and gesturing to the camera, and a teenage girl removes her hat to wave it exuberantly. There are, indeed, many reminders in this material of the scope for women to enjoy themselves without male company in this seaside setting, especially in friendly groups.[30] Here again, we see Blackpool as a social melting-pot with a widely shared mainstream enter-tainment culture, with no hint of this being in any way a segmented or niche audience and no distinct areas of the crowd dominated by particular types or characteristics. For some of this crowd perhaps, this would be a familiar experience and they might have seen these performers as they toured the inland towns in the off season; but for others it might be a one-off holiday treat, or even a temporary descent into popular entertainment, in the liminal territory of the seaside holiday, for normally more pretentious or strait-laced folk. Here we can only speculate.

The Morecambe sea front crowd material, from the landward end of the West End Pier in late June of 1901, is less convincing as a rendering of holiday crowds at play. The artifice of the pro-duction team is much more in evidence in M&K 247: *Parade on Morecambe West End Pier* (1901). Half a dozen men and women with linked arms surge forward and do a round dance, and a long line of people approach the camera, each with a hand on the shoulder of the person in front, per-forming a kind of conga. But this is not spontaneous gaiety: it has clearly been set up, although the participants seem happy to join in. As at Blackpool, the crowd seems socially mixed, with the women mainly wearing boaters with a few floral-trimmed hats and a few top hats alongside the bowler hats and yachting caps of the men. More teenagers and younger children are in evidence than at Blackpool, making their own contribution to the larking about that forms a feature of this film and the noticeable presence of young boys in caps may suggest that local lads had access to the Morecambe filming process in ways that Blackpool youngsters did not. This is altogether a more staged performance.

An interesting aspect of the Morecambe film is that the crowd here looks rather more down-market than that of Blackpool, challenging overall stereotypes about the two resorts. This is also true of the tram ride through Morecambe's West End, M&K 251: *Panoramic View of the Morecambe Sea Front* (1901), which fails to match the leafy suburban gentility (scattered family parties, gar-dens, parasols and cricket) of the equivalent journey from upmarket Lytham to Blackpool's South Shore. In neither Blackpool nor Morecambe, however, do we see the massed ranks of uniformly clad, cloth-capped, muffler-wearing working men who are supposed to be characteristic of the industrial working class from the late nineteenth to the mid-twentieth century, as presented by Eric Hobsbawm.[31] From this point of view, the seaside is a very different setting from the football ground and establishing the social status of individuals is not always a straightforward task. Some of the neatly attired young women were certainly factory workers, but others may have been domes-tic servants enjoying a free afternoon out of uniform in a leisure setting to which, unusually, women were readily admitted alongside men. This aspect of the gendering of leisure is one of the most important themes to be supported by the Mitchell and Kenyon evidence, alongside the confirma-tion it provides of the extent of social mixing across class boundaries in an increasingly 'respectable' atmosphere, at least in the areas where filming took place, and of the limited presence of children in these distinctive kinds of seaside environment. These were emphatically, in Harold Perkin's

M&K 247: *Parade on Morecambe West End Pier* (1901), taken on 26 June 1901 on the West End Pier, Morecambe, features the crowd staging a 'performance' for Thomas Edison's operators

phrase, 'structured crowds', but they also offered choice and agency to individuals, and the tempting phrase 'mass tourism' is certainly a misnomer.[32] What is also clear, is that there is ample scope for further research on the composition and behaviour of these playful seaside crowds, and that this wonderfully rich material is open to much deeper analysis than the introductory comments that have been provided here.

NOTES

1. J. K. Walton, 'The Demand for Working-class Seaside Holidays in Victorian England', *Economic History Review*, vol. 34, no. 3 (1981), pp. 249–65; J. K. Walton, *Blackpool* (Edinburgh: Edinburgh University Press, 1998), Chapter 4.

2. J. K. Walton, 'The Social Development of Blackpool, 1788–1914', PhD thesis, Lancaster University, 1974, p. 263, Table 5.2.

3. Walton, 'The Social Development of Blackpool', Chapter 8; J. K. Walton, *The English Seaside Resort: A Social History, 1750–1914* (Leicester: Leicester University Press, 1983), Chapter 8; J. K. Walton, 'Respectability Takes a Holiday: Disreputable Behaviour at the Victorian Seaside', in M. Hewitt (ed.), *Unrespectable Recreations* (Leeds: Leeds Centre for Victorian Studies, 2001), pp. 176–93.

4. Rob Shields, *Places on the Margin* (London: Routledge, 1991); Tony Bennett *et al.*, (eds), *Popular Culture and Social Relations* (Milton Keynes: Open University Press, 1986); and the extensive literature on the work of Norbert Elias.

5. H. J. Perkin, 'The "Social Tone" of Victorian Seaside Resorts in the North-West', *Northern History*, vol. 12 (1976), pp. 181–95. Simon Joyce, *Capital Offenses: Geographies of Class and Crime in Victorian London* (Charlottesville: University of Virginia Press, 2003), pp. 50–2, makes a similar point about the streets of early Victorian London.

6. J. Grass, 'Morecambe: The People's Pleasure, 1870–1902', MA dissertation, Lancaster University, 1972.

7. Walton, 'The Social Development of Blackpool', pp. 36–40, 51–6, 69–76.

8. María Antonia Paz, 'Cine para la historia urbana: Madrid, 1896–1936', *Historia Contemporánea*, vol. 20 no. 2 (2001), pp. 179–213.

9. See Matthew Hilton, *Smoking in British Popular Culture 1800–2000* (Manchester: Manchester University Press, 1999), for these and other distinctions.

10. The classic text here is still Peter Bailey, 'Will the Real Bill Banks Please Stand up?' (1979), reprinted as 'A Role Analysis of Working-class Respectability' in Bailey, *Popular Culture and Performance in the Victorian City* (Cambridge: Cambridge University Press, 1998).

11. For illustrations of this, see Walton, 'Respectability Takes a Holiday' and J. K. Walton, 'Scarborough', in Philip Waller (ed.), *The English Urban Landscape* (Oxford: Oxford University Press, 2000), p. 277.

12. For background to this, see J. K. Walton, *Lancashire: A Social History 1558–1939* (Manchester: Manchester University Press, 1987), Chapter 13; Patrick Joyce, *Visions of the People* (Cambridge: Cambridge University Press, 1991); and Trevor Griffiths, *The Lancashire Working Classes*, c. *1880–1930* (Oxford: Oxford University Press, 2001).

13. S. Wright, 'Sun, Sea, Sand and Self-expression: Mass Tourism as an Individual Experience', in H. Berghoff *et al.* (eds), *The Making of Modern Tourism: The Cultural History of the British Experience 1600–2000* (London: Palgrave, 2002), pp. 181–202; J. Golby and W. Purdue, *The Civilisation of the Crowd* (2nd edn, Stroud: Alan Sutton, 1999).

14. Walton, *Blackpool*, pp. 38–9; Walton, 'Social Development', pp. 307–8.

15. Walton, *Blackpool*, p. 92; Walton, 'Social Development', p. 323.

16. R. Bingham, *Lost Resort? The Flow and Ebb of Morecambe* (Carnforth: Cicerone, 1991).

17. See Gary Cross (ed.), *Worktowners at Blackpool* (London: Routledge, 1990), for this area in the 1930s.

18. *Blackpool Times*, 27 May 1904; *Blackpool Herald*, 12 June 1903; *Morecambe Visitor*, 5 June and 3 July 1901; *Bradford Evening Telegraph*, 30 July 1901.

19. For commentary on smoking styles, class and masculinity, see James Chapman and Matthew Hilton, 'From Sherlock Holmes to James Bond: Masculinity and National Identity in British Popular Fiction', in S. Caunce *et al.* (eds), *Relocating Britishness* (Manchester: Manchester University Press, forthcoming 2004).

20. See especially S. Gunn and R. J. Morris (eds), *Identities in Space* (Aldershot: Ashgate, 2001).

21. J. K. Walton, *The British Seaside: Holidays and Resorts in the Twentieth Century* (Manchester: Manchester University Press, 2000), pp. 99–101.

22. J. K. Walton, 'Policing the Alameda', in Gunn and Morris, *Identities in Space*, pp. 228–41.

23. *Blackpool Times*, 27 May 1904: an absolutely characteristic passage.

24. See for example, Arthur Laycock's Blackpool novel, *Warren of Manchester* (London: Simkin, Marshall & Co., 1904).

25. Allen Clarke, *The Effects of the Factory System* (Bolton, 1899, reprinted Littleborough, 1985).

26. A. H. Watkins, 'The Wakes Week', *Stockport Advertiser*, 21 August 1901. Thanks to Sue Barton for helpful suggestions.

27. Blackpool Pleasure Beach photographic archive, consulted by kind permission of the Pleasure Beach Company. Thanks to Ted Lightbown for help and advice, and to Gary Cross for having the idea in the first place.

28. Thanks to Timothy Neal for background research on this.

29. This begins at 10.07.09.00 on the film.

30. Catriona Parratt, *'More than Mere Amusement': Working-class Women's Leisure in England, 1750–1914* (Boston, MA: Northeastern University Press, 2001), provides some context for this.

31. E. J. Hobsbawm, *Worlds of Labour* (London: Weidenfeld, 1985).

32. H. J. Perkin, *The Structured Crowd* (Brighton: Harvester, 1981).

16 The Football Films

David Russell

The foundation of the Football Association in 1863 provides a convenient moment from which to date the origins of 'modern' football. Established by a small group of mainly ex-public and grammar schoolboys, the FA was to preside over a dramatic process of growth and downward social diffusion.[1] Originally a game for social elites, football rapidly became one of the central pastimes of the English (and British) working class with affiliations to the parent body growing from fifty to 10,000 between 1871 and 1905. Following the (controversial) legalisation of professionalism in 1885, the Football League was founded in 1888, attracting five million fans to the fixtures of its twenty-team First Division by 1905–6. This rich Collection of films therefore captures a game that was certainly well established within contemporary popular culture but was both still in a relatively early stage of its evolution and in the process of earning the cultural status and acceptance finally conferred by the visit of King George V to the 1914 FA Cup Final. There were many in the crowds that gazed into or waved at Mitchell and Kenyon's cameras who could easily remember life without this Saturday afternoon treat, this pleasurable ritual marking the passage from work to leisure. It is the capacity of these films to illuminate the game at this transitional point that adds to much of their interest. This chapter examines their value as sources for the study of Edwardian sporting and wider cultural history, although their role within contemporary sporting culture is also briefly considered.

The Mitchell and Kenyon football films are not the first of their type in Britain. Arthur Cheetham's shooting of the opening moments of the game between Blackburn Rovers and West Bromwich Albion in 1898 was probably the pioneering moment. William Walker filmed in Aberdeen later that year and Jasper Redfern of Sheffield followed in 1899.[2] Nevertheless, judging by the existing evidence, the company was comfortably ahead in terms of quantity, quality and ambition. The Collection contains fifty-five Association Football films made between 1901 and 1907, covering thirty-two separate games of which just under half can be clearly identified by the date played and the teams involved.[3] Most were Football League fixtures (often First Division) although at least one FA Cup tie was filmed, along with a representative match between the Football League and the Irish League at Hyde Road, Manchester in 1905 and an international between Wales and Ireland at Wrexham in January 1906, probably the first time that an international game had been recorded. Mitchell and Kenyon's base in Blackburn allowed the company close links with northern showmen and positioned them at the heart of the contemporary game. All the matches filmed, with the exception of the Welsh game, were played in northern England and the north Midlands. Lancashire provided the venue for about half of the locations identified.

Occasional reference will also be made to some of the eighteen rugby films (covering ten separate games) which have also survived from the period 1901–2. All are of matches played under the auspices of the Northern Union (from 1922 the Rugby League), a body that seceded from the Rugby Football Union in 1895 following the latter's opposition to the payment of players.[4] That fact

M&K 151: *Great Football Match, Leeds v Hunslet* (1901). Line up of the Hunslet team, taken 16 February 1901.

that there appear to be no Northern Union films made after 1902 may reflect the game's gradually diminishing status within the wider regional sporting culture in the early twentieth century.[5] Nevertheless, the rugby films contain much of value and are worthy of more than the minor comment they receive here.

Most matches appear to have been filmed with one and occasionally two cameras placed either somewhere near the halfway line, or close to or slightly behind one of the goals. The films followed a distinctive structure. The first reel focused on the emergence of the team and match officials from the dressing room, sometimes completed by a short action sequence. Given the commercial importance of capturing as many local faces as possible, the second consisted of extensive crowd shots, with substantial sweeps made along at least one side of the ground. The final reel was usually largely devoted to longer action sequences. Just one film, M&K 159: *Salford v Batley* (1901), appears to have pretensions to a more sophisticated narrative structure or documentary purpose. Beginning with a shot of washbasins in what were presumably the primitive changing rooms at Salford's The Willows stadium, it then cuts to a poster advertising the game next to which stand several well-dressed men, at least one of whom is clearly involved with the film company judging by his later work in directing players on to the pitch. The players then emerge in single file, although two of the Salford players seem to be arm in arm and one of the pair also appears to make a hand gesture to the camera. A slightly mystifying cut to a picture of one of the teams either arriving at or leaving the game on an open-top coach follows, before the film moves to the standard sequence of the players coming on to the pitch. Whether this represents a rare attempt at originality that failed to develop or just a one-off exercise is unknown but, along with its later action and crowd shots, it certainly showed an ambition way beyond the simple behind-the-goal shots of the kick-off and a little action that comprised Cheetham's first efforts just three years earlier.[6]

The films are perhaps best considered in terms of how they capture three broad topics: the development of the football stadium, the playing of the game and the social make-up and culture of football fandom.

Although early twentieth-century football grounds are the subjects of a substantial body of photographic evidence, the broad sweep of the film camera arguably allows the fullest picture of individual grounds currently available to historians. These films capture the elite game's venues at an interesting moment in their collective history. Enclosed grounds with entry gates, small grandstands and areas of banking made either from the dumping of earth, cinders and other waste, or as at Burnley's Turf Moor ground, by 'rearranging natural earthworks' had begun to appear in the 1880s.[7] The opening of Glasgow Ranger's Ibrox Park in 1887, Glasgow Celtic's Celtic Park and Everton's Goodison Park, both in 1892, ushered in the modern football stadium, with the topic's leading authority describing Goodison as 'the first major football ground in England'. With tall, covered stands on three sides and steep banking (partially covered in 1895) on the fourth, it attracted a crowd of 37,000 for the 1894 FA Cup Final and could undoubtedly have accommodated more. [8]

The films demonstrate the wide variety of grounds in the early twentieth century. Obviously, not all clubs could match Goodison Park. The films of Bradford City's inaugural Football League fixture in September 1903 at the Valley Parade ground they had inherited from Manningham Northern Union Rugby Club, shows only too clearly a ground virtually devoid of cover and with banking behind one goal only a few steps high. A number of fans can be seen perched astride the huge advertising hoarding that ran the length of the Midland Road side in search of the elevated view that was more readily available to patrons of bigger grounds.[9] Non-League Thornhill's Red House ground, filmed in 1902, appears unsurprisingly to have been even less sophisticated with fans standing only one deep along the touchline while others are grouped on a raised bank several yards behind.[10] There is, however, also evidence of what might be termed the second major phase of stadium development, which began about 1905 as clubs embarked on often ambitious programmes of expansion and refinement, testifying to the game's growing place within English sporting culture. Although none of the films viewed capture any of the often technically and aesthetically sophisticated structures designed by the key figure in contemporary stadium architecture and engineering, Scotsman Archibald Leitch (1866–1939), some important new grandstands can be seen. Blackburn Rovers' Nuttall Street Stand, for example, was filmed during a schoolboys's cup final just three months after its opening on New Year's Day, 1907.[11] Holding 13,500 supporters, with 4,000 seated, it was one of the key features of the £26,000 ground development of the club between 1905 and 1908.[12]

Not all new building was on the grand scale. A record of the more modest structures quite typical of many grounds is provided by the excellent shots of the recently opened Town End stand at Preston's Deepdale in 1904.[13] Built at the cost of £1,000 (part-funded by the proceeds of a bazaar), it held 6–7,000 people, with club officials confident that 'a few wet days would pay for it'. The little flurry of umbrellas that appears behind a goal during the course of a game at Bolton's Burnden Park, is a useful reminder of the potentially serious discomforts awaiting fans on the 'popular' sides.[14] The films also provide useful evidence of specific features that have long disappeared.[15] Footage of St James's Park, Newcastle, captured in 1901, offers what is probably the only visual evidence of a stand

M&K 109: *Newcastle United v Liverpool* (1901), filmed 23 November 1901 at St James's Park.

demolished as early as 1905, while films of Deepdale show the players emerging from the small, striped hut in the southwest corner of the ground that served as a changing room until 1906.[16] Its echoes of both mock Tudor and the bathing hut, capture well the spirit of slightly rustic playfulness visible in much sports ground architecture of the period which infused urban-industrial structures with lighter notes.[17] Again, a match at Burnden Park, probably filmed in 1904, clearly shows the cycle track that ringed the playing area from the stadium's opening in 1895 (a monkey cycled around it at the opening ceremony) until its removal in 1905.[18]

For this historian at least, the films deliver an unexpectedly stimulating route into the largely unexplored history of the links between advertising and sport. The late nineteenth century had seen a significant acceleration and enriching of advertising, as 'the minstrels of capitalism' found new guises and new languages with which to give expression to the emerging commodity culture.[19] Stadium advertising was often of a local nature with films showing adverts for a perambulator shop at Newcastle (no male escape from domestic obligations here), and perhaps more predictably, the Empire Variety Theatre at Bradford and 'Nuttall and Company's Lion Ales and Double Stout' at Blackburn.[20] The grandstand roof was clearly a favoured site even at this stage, with a particularly dense block of adverts visible at Sunderland's Roker Park.[21] There is, however, also clear evidence of the promotion of national brands including Bird's custard powder, Fry's chocolate and those two products whose supposed health-enhancing qualities were for so long promoted via association with football, Bovril and Oxo.[22] These national brands were usually featured on pitch-side hoardings, suggesting perhaps that, unlike the local products enshrined with sufficient effort on the grandstand roof to denote expectations of longevity, they may have been displayed for relatively short periods. In one unidentified game at Burnley's Turf Moor ground, at least three separate Oxo adverts were placed strategically around the ground raising at least the possibility that the presence of the film company had intensified the promotional activity.[23]

If the films can so usefully illuminate such an obviously static phenomenon as stadium architecture, it might be expected that their value in depicting activity on the field would be incalculable to the student usually reliant upon 'frozen' action photographs and hand-drawn sketches for their visual imagery. In reality, the films can at first disappoint. The modern viewer of the game between Newcastle and Liverpool in November 1901, would find it hard to endorse *Athletic News*'s view of it as 'one of the most memorable games that has ever been witnessed on the banks of the Tyne'.[24] Here as elsewhere, technical limitations reduce the action to a series of short and ill-connected sequences in which it is hard to follow clear patterns of play or deduce tactical niceties. The cameramen unsurprisingly often concentrated on those areas of the field or types of action that could be most easily captured with the result that we see a great deal of footage of goalkeepers, often dealing with events originating out of shot, and essentially static moments such as goal kicks and throw-ins in football and scrums in rugby. Moreover, camera position and/or the limitations of film stock meant that defining moments of play were often not captured. The 1906 Wales and Ireland game, for example, was a 4–4 draw but the resultant sections of the film that I saw appear not to have recorded a single goal.[25]

In one particular, the presence of the camera may have significantly altered events if not on the pitch, then at least on the way out to it. Virtually all the films show the players (usually the away team first) entering the field in single file, often being directed towards the camera by members of the film crew and with the aid of marker pegs sometimes visible in the ground.[26] Some players look relaxed – at least two appear to be throwing cigarettes away as they emerge – but most appear slightly selfconscious.[27] Beyond any camera shyness, this was perhaps because they were actually not used to emerging in this way. *Athletic News* certainly implied this when recording how the players of Everton and Liverpool 'filed on to the pitch one after another to please the cinematograph operator' in a 1902 Merseyside derby.[28] It is possible then, that in this albeit minor context, the film camera obscures rather than clarifies our view of the Edwardian game.

Any initial disappointments, however, soon evaporate. This partly results from the gradual realisation of just how good the films actually are, with their extreme clarity of image, their close-ups and the emotional (almost magical) sense that they are bringing the dead to life. Poor weather could sometimes impact on technical quality, with an intended showing of the 1904 Sunderland v. Newcastle fixture for Pringle's North American Animated Photo Company abandoned because 'owing to the unfavourable weather … it was found that it was no use'.[29] Overall, however, given the frequency with which press reports mention wet or dull weather in their coverage of games that were successfully filmed, it seems that the companies were highly skilled in their mastery of climatic vicissitudes. Moreover, these films were not significantly superseded for at least thirty years.

The *Daily Sketch Topical Budget* film of the 1923 FA Cup Final, for example (the first played at Wembley and thus a highly prestigious affair presumably demanding the best possible coverage), is not markedly different in its coverage of open play. A camera placed in an elevated position captures slightly longer sequences than is the case in the Edwardian films but it is only a matter of degree. A caption prepares viewers to see 'Bolton goalie's wonderful save' but in fact we only partially see Dick Pym's stop and we certainly don't see the initial shot by his West Ham opponent.[30]

British Movietone News's coverage of the 1938 FA Cup Final offers something of a technical leap forward with albeit very short sequences of play becoming discernible and the camera following the ball over distances for several seconds at a time. There is even a 'stop-motion' sequence where the action is frozen to allow a better view of one decisive moment.[31] However, there were still many limitations and it was not really until the 1940s and early 1950s that football films captured a level of detail that comes close to satisfying contemporary expectation.

There is too, a simple pleasure to be taken in what might be termed the exotic nature of what unfolds on screen. The heavy shirts and baggy shorts (exact dimensions varied according to club design) that so flavour the popular conception of the game at this time, along with goalkeeping strips identical to those of their teammates, can be savoured. Referees in their turn are invariably wearing jacket, shirt and tie (complete with heavy watch chains) and either trousers or plus fours, with the cap a fairly standard feature. It was not until the inter-war period that the more familiar black shirt (jackets were sometimes preferred) and shorts became standard dress. Although it must have often been impractically hot, the relative formality of the Edwardian referee's costume, half-reminiscent of gamekeeper or superior foreman, was arguably an asset in maintaining the necessary distance between players and officials.[32] The linesmen were generally similarly if slightly less elegantly attired and are notable for signalling with handkerchiefs rather than the flags familiar to later generations.[33]

Perhaps most important of all, however, is the fact that, while not providing any fundamental reconsideration of the game, the films reinforce and refine current knowledge in interesting ways and ones that open up possibilities for various longitudinal studies best rooted in cinematic evidence. In terms of action on the pitch, the films are valuable in highlighting several features that, although known to historians, are made far clearer and more powerful by the moving image. Perhaps the most striking is the goalkeeper's fear of the catch. Although by this stage goalkeepers had been afforded some limited protection from onrushing opponents, it was still a legitimate tactic to shoulder charge them; indeed, it remained so to a diminishing degree until the early 1960s in the British game. It is perhaps not surprising, therefore, that the films rarely show goalkeepers catching the ball. Instead it is punched, often with a swinging over arm action not unlike that of a bowler in cricket, kicked or trapped by keeping both legs together. In one typical sequence from a match between Bradford City and Gainsborough Trinity, Bagshaw, the Gainsborough goalkeeper, is shown punching the ball out and then knocking it down and immediately kicking it away when Bradford players speedily return it.[34] Only when there is no other player in camera shot do we see any footage of the ball being gathered. This was, of course, a necessary tactical ploy rather than a sign of fear and goalkeepers could certainly protect themselves very efficiently when needed. The Hull City goalkeeper, for example, is seen, ball on this occasion firmly in his grasp, shoulder charging his way through a ruck of players and even appearing to barge one of his own defenders out of the way.[35]

Given that it is difficult to discern some of the more subtle aspects of tactical development from football films until at least the 1940s, the Mitchell and Kenyon films are probably of their greatest value in illuminating broader cultural shifts visible through careful analysis of specific incidents. One of the most fertile areas here, already hinted at in the discussion of goalkeepers, concerns the cultural construction of masculinity. Although this topic has been increasingly fashionable in recent years, both within the wider academic field more generally and sports studies more specifically, football historians have paid surprisingly little attention to it.[36] Film presents a rich opportunity to scrutinise certain forms of behaviour that might illuminate changing notions of what constituted 'suitable' behaviour for a man. These include the degree and level of physical contact during play,

reaction on being injured, attitudes to referees and the nature of goal celebration. Although need-
ing to be used in conjunction with written records including press reports, FA disciplinary minutes
and players' autobiographies, film depicts actions that might often elude capture in other sources,
especially if they were seen as too trivial or habitual to require comment.

In the Mitchell and Kenyon films, there are a number of features that engage attention. The
relatively high level of physical contact has already been alluded to. Interestingly, players appear to
have taken the ensuing bodily punishment relatively uncomplainingly. In a game between Newcastle and Liverpool, a Liverpool player is shown receiving an extremely hard kick to the leg from an
opponent who immediately (and strategically perhaps) goes across to assess and apologise for any
damage caused. After some informal treatment from a colleague, the fouled player limps back into
action.[37] (Several rugby films show players hobbling back on to the field with clearly painful
injuries, testimony to the high levels of resilience always demanded within the game.)[38] A project
using cinematic evidence to plot changes over time to player response to heavy tackling and foul-
ing would at the very least record changes in footballing style and professional sporting culture and
ethics, but it might also shed useful light on notions of appropriate male behaviour within society.
Attention might also be paid to other similarly indicative forms of behaviour. The Edwardian films,
both of football and rugby, clearly show players appealing to referees in support of various claims
for goal kicks, corners, penalties or whatever, but there is very little sense of officials coming under
the sustained pressure so common in the modern game. Goal celebrations provide interest too.
Overall, the standard response seems to have been little more than a fairly short-lived display of
cheerful enthusiasm. Goal scorers tended to run a short distance, sometimes with arms upraised,
while backslapping and handshaking seems to have been the major form of congratulation offered
by colleagues.[39] There is certainly none of the hugging (and kissing) that worried commentators in
the 1950s or the gesturing, badge-kissing, shirt-waving and often highly orchestrated celebration
routines that feature in the modern game. This trajectory from the relatively controlled Edwardian
display to the hyper-theatricality of the modern game would reveal clues about far more than just
football and film is undoubtedly a crucial source for investigating them.[40]

Although both photographic and written records of the football crowd do exist, probably no
other extant source allows quite the level of visual detail and intimacy accorded by the long, sweep-
ing crowd shots so central to the makers' commercial purpose. In terms of social composition, evidence from the Collection generally confirms the picture of the crowd derived by the patient
research of football historians in the 1970s and 1980s.[41] This suggested that the majority of fans
were probably drawn from the upper working and, to a lesser degree, the lower middle classes. The
minimum admission price of 6d imposed in 1890, limited access (probably deliberately) for poorer
fans, although Mason has suggested that those from semi-skilled, working-class backgrounds probably began to attend in greater numbers after 1900.[42] A not insignificant minority of middle-class
fans, however, could be found at most grounds and usually in the status-demarcating confines of
the grandstand. The Mitchell and Kenyon films, interested primarily in the terrace dwellers who
might later make up the fairground and exhibition audiences, pay only little attention to the grandstands but those captured on the popular sides clearly fit the expected bill. Close attention to hat
codes, beyond the powers of the current writer, might reveal greater subtleties, but there is sufficient
evidence of cloth caps, mufflers and clay pipes to suggest a strongly working-class presence. Several
films capture miners in their pit dirt, their shifts presumably ending too late to allow a trip home
for a bath.[43]

While gauging ages accurately from photographic evidence is difficult, the film evidence shows
fans appear to be between fourteen and fifty. Certainly, virtually no young children are present and

the capturing of an elderly man with a stovepipe hat at one rugby match only serves to point up the lack of such faces in the other crowd shots.[44] Perhaps most interesting of all, is the almost complete lack of women fans in the films studied. Indeed, only two women have been identified among the hundreds of faces observable at the association football matches and just seven at the rugby games. Moreover, it is likely that most of these were connected with either the film companies or the show-men who had commissioned their work. Certainly, one of the two well-dressed women captured at some length at the Thornhill ground was the wife of showman Albert Wilkinson, also visible in top-hatted finery, and the other was probably a member of their party.[45] We can be less sure about the group of five similarly clothed women filmed in M&K 116: *Oldham v Swinton* (1901), a rugby match but the amount of time afforded to them is suggestive of their representing some special or 'novel' aspect.[46]

To the historian of association football this is slightly surprising. There is clear evidence of female attendance into the 1880s, with Preston North End famously withdrawing its previous right of free entrance in 1884 after an unexpectedly strong contingent undermined gate receipts at a match with Blackburn Rovers.[47] It is generally believed that the proportion of female fans fell after this point but both written and photographic sources record women, especially young ones, attend-ing in quite high numbers for certain games such as cup ties.[48] Largely because of this, it has been assumed that a small but significant body of women fans maintained some degree of regular

M&K 146: *Burnley Football* (*c.* 1902) shows the advertising boards strategically placed around the ground at Turf Moor.

attendance and the expectation of this writer at least, was that the far-ranging film camera would demonstrate a limited but definable female attendance at routine League fixtures. The Mitchell and Kenyon material confounds that view although its testimony is obviously not conclusive. As noted, the films showed little of the grandstands, where it possible that women gathered in the largest number. However, it is undoubtedly highly suggestive of a generally extremely low level of attendance, by women, and of the likelihood that any significant female presence did indeed only occur at cup ties where gender expectations were overturned in the carnivalesque culture of the 'special occasion'. It certainly underlines the need for a close and detailed historical ethnography of the football crowd drawing on the widest range of sources.

The culture and behaviour of football fans in this period remains relatively lightly studied. Potentially one of the most interesting questions relates to when fans began to develop a specific terrace style in terms of dress and forms of behaviour. In terms of the former, there is no obvious evidence on the films of fans wearing the club colours or favours that commentators were beginning to notice and photographers capture from the early 1900s, although the fact that so few films covered cup ties, where the festive element was at its most pronounced, might be a factor here.[49] Goal celebrations, in their turn, seem mainly to have involved clapping, cheering, with some waving of hats or newspapers above the head in a circular motion.[50] The one really contentious issue about crowds in this period concerns spectator disorder, with some historians stressing the ultimate orderly and restrained nature of crowds, and others arguing that 'spectator disorderliness was a problem of considerable proportions at association football matches'.[51] The highly selective nature of the film evidence makes it difficult to comment on this. If the cameras had visited St James's Park, Newcastle on Good Friday 1901, they would have recorded the serious fighting between rival Newcastle and Sunderland fans that forced the game's cancellation, rather than the apparently trouble-free scenes actually captured in a match against Liverpool a few months later.[52] However, even those emphasising the problems of crowd behaviour see the years 1901–7 as witnessing its lowest levels in the period to 1914 and the films tend to suggest a mood of cheerful orderliness. Footage of an unidentified game at Burnley does show a fan being led away from the terrace, presumably drunk but possibly a victim of the crush – surges caused by sheer weight of numbers can be glimpsed in the action sequences of this game – but there is no other evidence of misbehaviour.[53] One of the rugby matches, M&K 660: *Hull v Hull Kingston Rovers* (1902), ended with large numbers of fans, mostly but not exclusively young lads, running on to the pitch and generally playing to the camera by pulling faces and waving. Whether this is merely an extension of the 'acting up', much encouraged by the film companies and showmen whose representatives appear as cheerleaders on several films, or a regular part of sporting culture at this time is unclear. Swarming across the pitch was an end-of-game treat for many young boys at some English football grounds well into the 1950s and early 1960s and it is likely that the camera captured, albeit perhaps in exaggerated form, an early manifestation of this. If this, in this instance, clearly tolerated action also took place at football matches it would be suggestive of a fairly relaxed attitude toward crowd control born of a general belief that fans could be trusted.

The emphasis has been on the films as evidence but it is useful to end with brief comments on their wider significance within popular sporting culture. Clearly, the films enjoyed nothing like the contemporary importance exerted by the press or later by radio and television, and fans only saw their local clubs on film very infrequently. The overall impact of these films must not be exaggerated, therefore. They were, nevertheless, undoubtedly popular with football followers, providing some with a chance to relive the game and those unable to attend with a chance to enjoy glimpses of the action in a setting that captured something of the stadium atmosphere. A local paper noted

that pictures of the Bradford City v. Gainsborough Trinity match were 'so vivid and impressive …
that small boys in the audience are roused to enthusiasm and cry out "Now City" as though they
were again on the scene of play'.[54] More generally, these films connected football fully with two
central strands of commercial entertainment, the traditional one of the travelling show and the
emerging one of cinema.[55] The willingness, indeed, the need, for both forms to appropriate football was both a useful indication and reinforcement of its critical role within popular culture. Most
crucially, these films placed the fans in an absolutely central position, making them effectively collective co-stars in support of their sporting heroes and did so to an extent that has never really been
managed by any other medium (the radio phone-in is perhaps the closest). By making them so
much part of the spectacle, the films arguably gave spectators a further sense of their emotional
ownership of professional football, a sensibility that has always been willingly accepted as a substi-
tute for more tangible forms of economic or political control. If this is what is meant by football
being the 'people's game', then the local film had a part in making it such.

NOTES

1. For the early game, see T. Mason, *Association Football and English Society, 1863–1915* (Brighton: Harvester,
   1980); D. Russell, *Football and the English. A Social History of Association Football in England, 1863–1995*
   (Preston: Carnegie Publishing, 1997), pp. 5–75; J. Walvin, *The People's Game Revisited* (Edinburgh:
   Mainstream, 1994), pp. 11–95. Important recent contributions stressing the role of groups beyond public
   schoolboys and the FA include: A. Harvey, 'Football's Missing Link: The Real Story of the Creation of
   Modern Football', *European Sports History Review*, vol. 1 (1999), pp. 92–116 and J. Goulstone, 'The
   Working-class Origins of Modern Football', *International Journal of the History of Sport*, vol. 17, no. 1
   (2000), pp. 135–43.
2. Vanessa Toulmin, '"Local Films for Local People": Travelling Showmen and the Commissioning of Local
   Films in Great Britain, 1900–1902', *Film History*, vol. 13, no. 2 (2001), pp. 120–1, 130.
3. This chapter is based on analysis of a little over half of these films.
4. T. Collins, *Rugby's Great Split. Class, Culture and the Origins of Rugby League* (London: Frank Cass,
   1998).
5. D. Russell '"Sporadic and curious": The Emergence of Rugby and Soccer Zones in Yorkshire and
   Lancashire, c. 1860–1914, *International Journal of the History of Sport*, vol. 5, no. 2 (1988), pp. 185–205.
   There are also a small number of films relating to cycling, race walking (in this case the annual
   Manchester to Blackpool event), trotting and cricket.
6. Viewed at North West Film Archive, Manchester. Catalogued as film no. 649.
7. *Football Field*, September 1884, quoted in B. Tabner, *Through the Turnstiles* (Hatfield: Yore Publications,
   1994), p. 33.
8. Simon Inglis, *Football Grounds of Britain* (London: Willow, 3rd edn, 1997), pp. 155–6.
9. M&K 127: *Bradford City v Gainsborough Trinity* (1903). There are five films of this match M&K 124–8.
10. M&K 139 and 755: *Thornhill v Rotherham Town* (1902). Thornhill played in the Sheffield League. As
    Rotherham County the club joined the Football League in 1919, finally taking the name Rotherham
    United in 1925.
11. M&K 268: *Moss Street v St Phillips Football* (1907).
12. Inglis, *Football Grounds*, p. 50.
13. M&K 96–8: *Preston North End v Wolverhampton Wanderers* (1904).
14. David Hunt, *The History of Preston North End Football Club: The Power, the Politics, the People* (Preston:
    PNE Publications, 2000), p. 106; *Lancashire Daily Post*, 15 October 1904.
15. M&K 140: *Bolton v Burton United* (1904–5)

16. M&K 109–11 and 121: *Newcastle United v Liverpool* (1901). I am grateful to Alan Candlish for sharing his helpful research on St James's Park. M&K 96: *Preston North End v Wolverhampton Wanderers* (1904).

17. A number of Leitch's grandstands featured gables and other decorative features.

18. M&K 140: *Bolton v Burton United.* Inglis, *Football Grounds*, pp. 59–60.

19. Thomas Richards, *The Commodity Culture of Victorian England. Advertising and Spectacle, 1851–1914* (London: Verso, 1991), p. 3.

20. M&K 109: *Newcastle United v Liverpool* (1901), M&K 127: *Bradford City v Gainsborough Trinity* and M&K 135: *Blackburn Football* (1904).

21. M&K 118: *Sunderland v Leicester Fosse* (1907).

22. On Bovril's long relationship with sport, Peter Hadley, *The History of Bovril Advertising* (London: Bovril Ltd, 1970), pp. 89–91.

23. M&K 146: *Burnley Football* (nd).

24. *Athletic News*, 25 November 1901.

25. M&K 153–4: *Wales v Ireland at Wrexham* (1906). The full six-minute restored film does capture at least two of the goals in the match.

26. M&K 96: *Preston North End v Wolverhampton Wanderers*, M&K 118: *Sunderland v Leicester Fosse.*

27. M&K 96: *Preston North End v Wolverhampton Wanderers*, M&K 118: *Sunderland v Leicester Fosse.*

28. *Athletic News*, 29 September 1902.

29. *Sunderland Daily Echo*, 5 January 1904.

30. Viewed at North West Film Archive. Catalogued as film no. 636.

31. Viewed at North West Film Archive. Catalogued as film no. 419.

32. M&K 99: *Preston North End Football* (nd).

33. M&K 111: *Newcastle United v Liverpool.*

34. M&K 127: *Bradford City v Gainsborough Trinity.* See also M&K 113: *Hull Football* (nd) and M&K 121: *Newcastle United v Liverpool* (1901). M&K 139: *Rotherham Football* (nd) contains a very good example of the swinging over-arm punch.

35. M&K 113: *Hull Football.*

36. For a particularly suggestive piece, see C. Critcher, 'Putting on the Style: Aspects of Recent English Football', in J. Williams and S. Wagg (eds), *British Football and Social Change* (Leicester: Leicester University Press, 1991), pp. 67–84.

37. M&K 111: *Newcastle United v Liverpool.*

38. For example, M&K 149: *Hull Kingston Rovers v Wigan* (1902) and M&K 150: *Hull F.C. v Hull Kingston Rovers* (1902) and M&K 373: *Warrington Rugby* (nd), does show a player leaving the field for treatment.

39. M&K 119: *Sunderland v Leicester Fosse* (1907).

40. See *FA News*, October 1958, pp. 136–7. This is not to deny a considerable level of showmanship in terms of goal celebration, including the turning of cartwheels, in the Edwardian game. J. Woolridge, 'Mapping the Stars: Stardom in English Professional Football, 1890–1946', *Soccer and Society*, vol. 3, no. 2 (2002), p. 61.

41. See especially Mason, *Association Football*, pp. 138–60.

42. Mason, *Association Football*, pp. 150, 157.

43. Notably M&K 139: *Thornhill v Rotherham Town* (1902) shot at Thornhill, Rotherham.

44. M&K 141: *Salford v Batley* (1901).

45. M&K 139: *Rotherham Football.*

46. Two other women glimpsed further down the row may have been part of the regular clientele.

47. Mason, *Association Football*, pp. 152–3.

48. Russell, *Football and the English*, p. 57 for textual and J. Hutchison, *The Football Industry* (Glasgow: R. Drew, 1982), p. 55 for photographic evidence of women at cup matches.

49. S. Kelly, *You'll Never Walk Alone* (London: Macdonald, 1987), p. 22.

50. This was still visible in the 1950s, as evidenced by TV coverage of the 1953 FA Cup Final.

51. E. Dunning *et al.*, 'Football Hooliganism in Britain before the First World War', *International Review of the Sociology of Sport*, vol. 19 (1984), p. 225. For analyses placing less emphasis on disorder, seee Mason, *Association Football*, pp. 160–7; R. W. Lewis, 'Football Hooliganism in England before 1914: A Critique of the Dunning Thesis', *International Journal of the History of Sport*, vol. 13 (1996), pp. 310–39.

52. Inglis, *Football Grounds*, p. 259. Chronic overcrowding was the initial catalyst, forcing spectators onto the pitch where fighting broke out.

53. M&K 143, 146: *Burnley Football* (nd).

54. M&K 124–8: *Bradford City v Gainsborough Trinity*. *Bradford Daily Argus*, 8 September 1903. On this occasion, home supporters were happy to see a game in which their side lost. There is some evidence that films capturing games producing the 'wrong' result were never actually screened.

55. On football and popular culture more generally, A. Horrall, *Popular Culture in London* c. *1890–1918. The Transformation of Entertainment* (Manchester: Manchester University Press, 2001), pp. 149–85.

17 On the Move in the Streets: Transport Films and the Mitchell and Kenyon Collection

Ian Yearsley

Street traffic and transport are important elements in much of the Mitchell and Kenyon Collection. Their historical importance lies in the depiction of British daily life in a period of great change. The films are vital representations of current and evolving modes of transport and of the pattern and usage of the streets themselves. For centuries the horse had been the dominant motive power; motor-cars had been emancipated by legislation of 1896, but were still few in number.[1] Horse transport, at the height of its development, was still pre-eminent, but the first agent of change arrived in the shape of the electric tramcar. Pioneer electric lines had opened in Britain in 1883, but it was Frank Sprague in the United States who made a commercial success of it in 1888, and from 1891 onwards the electric tram spread to this country. Its success rested on proven American technology combined with local coach-building experience to produce the distinctive British double deck tramcar.

The real boom period of electric tramway growth in Britain, however, was from 1900 to 1903, although growth continued at a reduced pace throughout the period of Mitchell and Kenyon's activity. Not only did electric power replace horse traction on tramways, it also enabled them to offer competition to the steam-powered railways which had previously been unchallenged. Some railways had to electrify their own lines to meet this challenge and stem the loss of passengers. In 1898, trams were carrying fewer passengers a year than those travelling third class on the railways. By 1901, passenger journeys by tramcar exceeded those made in third class on rail, and by 1903, they had overtaken all railway classes. By 1912, tramway passenger numbers were double those in third class rail; even though numbers of railway passengers overall were still increasing, tram passenger numbers had grown by 150 per cent in ten years

Mitchell and Kenyon were therefore filming at a time of great change when both new developments and existing patterns of transport co-existed for a brief transitory period. These films offer the viewer glimpses of the horse tramways in their last years and an insight into the burgeoning technology of electric tramways. All this is presented against a background of street traffic that seemed essentially unaltered since the middle of the nineteenth century.

But the Mitchell and Kenyon films also demonstrate the way in which streets were used in the first decade of the twentieth century. Absent completely are many features taken for granted in the twenty-first century: traffic lights, road markings, lane discipline. M&K: *179 Rochdale Tram Ride* (*c.* 1902) demonstrates how horse-drawn traffic veered from side to side of the road, and the preponderance of horse droppings on the tram track in Spotland showed how horse drivers would select this better-paved part of the highway until they encountered, or were caught up by, the tramcar moving at an impressive twelve miles per hour. Legislation required tramway companies to maintain the road surface between the rails and for eighteen inches on each side; in later years, tramway managers complained that they were maintaining the road for their competitors to use. Goods vehicles often followed the tram tracks so that their wheels could ride on the smooth steel rails, as shown in M&K 186: *Jamaica Street, Glasgow* (1901). The disposal of horse manure was itself a considerable industry, much of it transported into the countryside for agricultural use, but some helping to create the fermentation under the garden hotbeds of which the Edwardians were so fond. Manure and ash, from the many household coal fires, represented a substantial body of freight to be carried through the streets.

Horse-drawn transport was labour-intensive: the animals needed to be fed, watered, housed and cared for at all times, whether they were working or not. Vehicles such as trams and buses, which were kept in continual service, needed fresh horses every few hours. Maintaining a two-horse tram-car in service for sixteen hours a day required at least ten horses, with one or two more to cover sickness and visits to the blacksmith for shoes. Stables were large and with piles of hay and straw around there was an ever-present risk of fire.[2] Large numbers of people worked in stables and associated businesses, providing harness, fodder, veterinary medicine and horseshoes. Signs announced livery stables which would provide a horse under contract, and bait stables which offered fodder and water for horses of a traveller or shopper. Not surprisingly, there was often far more capital tied up in horses than in the vehicles they pulled.

In *The Rise and Rise of Road Transport 1700–1990*, Barker and Gerhold comment that it was fortunate that road passenger and road freight transport were not mechanised simultaneously, otherwise there would have been widespread unemployment.[3] As it was, most of this mechanisation took

M&K 186: *Jamaica Street, Glasgow* (1901). The horse reigns supreme in Glasgow's Jamaica Street in 1901, yet within a year the last horse tram was to run. Electric trams had been running since 1898 and would soon operate

place after the bulk of Mitchell and Kenyon's filming was done, so that the films display horse street traffic close to its peak. Numbers of horses in use for road transport overall declined from an estimated 1,766,000 in 1901, but those in use for freight transport actually rose from 702,000 in 1901 to 832,000 in 1911.[4]

The films also show horse-drawn vehicles at the peak of their design development. With the limited power available from a horse the object was to design a vehicle as light and easy running as possible, often with minimal enclosure of passengers. Other than trams and buses, vehicles fell roughly into three classes: carriages with an elevated seat for a coachman in front; lighter vehicles, often two-wheeled, designed to be owner-driven; and goods vehicles in great variety ranging from simple carts to lorries for heavy loads to be hauled by a team of horses. Drivers seen on these films are almost exclusively male, although the two-wheeled governess car was specifically designed to be driven by a woman, seated near the back with children in front of her.

By 1913, motor taxis were commonplace. But in the Mitchell and Kenyon era, hackneys for hire were mainly four-wheeled enclosed carriages, officially known as clarences but more commonly as growlers, or else the faster, lighter hansom cabs, seating two passengers only with the driver perched on a high seat behind them. Very few hansoms appear in these films and it is not always possible to identify whether a closed four-wheeled carriage is a hackney or not. Taximeters were not fitted to horse-drawn hackneys until after this era, when they were already well on the way to being ousted by motor taxis, and there were no visible 'taxi' or 'for hire' signs. The hackney for hire was identified by dawdling along the street, if it was not waiting on a rank.

The films show how the drivers of passenger vehicles, especially coachmen on their box seats, towered head and shoulders above the pedestrian crowds, unlike the modern car driver who is at a lower level. Goods vehicles were often driven by the carter walking alongside his horses, or seated precariously on the front of his vehicle's load-space. Many of these vehicles had no space for the driver, and in some cases, such as milk floats and tipping carts for refuse, the driver stood up to drive, just as he did on the new electric trams.

There are also hand-propelled vehicles, ranging from coach-built perambulators and 'mailcarts', forerunners of the baby buggy, to carry babies and small children on the footpaths, to a whole variety of handcarts bringing deliveries of milk, groceries, cat's meat and other light goods, as well as the tools and stock-in-trade of jobbing gardeners and chimney sweeps. Bicycles are also represented in the form of the new 'safety' design with both wheels of similar size, rather than the fast-moving but precarious 'penny-farthing' of the late Victorian years. Even the latest bicycles often had only one brake, on the front wheel, with a metal spoon pressing on the tyre. Pedal cycles, which until the 1890s had been leisure vehicles for the better off, were now less costly and were rapidly becoming the most widespread form of private transport on the streets. Along with the electric tramcars, they helped to accustom the public to the idea of vehicles moving without the aid of horses and at greater speeds.

The often random movement of horse-drawn vehicles and pedal cycles is shown in many of the Mitchell and Kenyon films. It was matched by the behaviour of pedestrians, who were far less punctilious than present day road users in observing the distinction between the footpath and the roadway. People would meet and stop in the middle of the road to pass the time of day and hold conversations, and the slow speed of horse-drawn vehicles allowed people to weave their way between them at any point, without being in any way restricted to designated crossing places. One element which helped to swell the numbers of people on the streets was the messenger boy; many messages which today would go by phone, fax or email were then carried by teenage lads, either employed or working freelance.

The electric tram, with speed double that of the horse, began to change this random use and to impose some discipline. M&K: 177 *Tram Ride through the City of Sheffield* (1902) shows this on a journey filmed over the driver's shoulder. The film takes the viewer down the High Street, where the new generation of Sheffield supertrams now glide by, and turns left into the Haymarket, clearly showing the poles in the centre of the road used to support the overhead wires. Although the new electric cars stop at fixed stops, some men and women still board cars in motion. In horse tram days, able bodied men were expected to board and alight from cars in motion, to save the strain on the horses of frequent stopping and starting. Only for women, children or elderly men would the car be brought to a standstill and there were usually no fixed stopping places.

Even before electric trams arrived, steam power was tried, and there were several large steam tram networks particularly in the north and the Midlands, with about 800 locomotives pulling trailers, usually with a double deck. Wheels and moving parts were enclosed, so as not to frighten horses, and various devices were fitted to prevent the issue of smoke. M&K 527: *West Bromwich – Comic Pictures in High Street* (1902), gives a fleeting glimpse of a Wilkinson locomotive and double deck trailer of the South Staffordshire Tramway on the Dudley route, and M&K 175: *Living Wigan* (1902), shows crowds, probably specially gathered and encouraged by the exhibitor who appears in their midst, surrounding a Kitson locomotive and trailer in Wigan Market Place in 1902. The driver, no doubt primed to create a comic scene, clears a way with a hosepipe before setting off for Pemberton. In the background, there is a momentary glimpse of one of the new narrow gauge electric trams on the Markland Mill route. Steam was part of the search to find a more economic replacement for the horse; in the event it proved neither economic nor environmentally friendly; even in an age when buildings were encrusted externally with soot from coal fires, the steam locomotive in the streets was often looked upon, not always with justice, as dirty, noisy and smelly, while steam locomotives on railways were being extolled as achievements of modern technology.

The horse and steam era overlapped with that of the new electric tramcar and Mitchell and Kenyon recorded both, at street level, and from cars in motion. Horse trams, perhaps even more than the faster electric vehicles, provided an ideal platform for a cameraman to record a ride through the streets. M&K 246: *Panoramic View of the Morecambe Sea Front* (1901), shows this technique to advantage and offers splendid views of the landaus plying for hire by the visitors, although it shows little of the horse trams themselves, which survived to be the last of their kind in England in 1926. More remarkable is M&K 183: *Ride on Tramcar through Belfast* (1902). It shows a busy and complex horse tram system at its zenith, with cars displaying a whole variety of destinations, as the journey continues through the prosperous-looking streets of the city centre. Belfast tramways were electrified in 1905, and fifty of the 170 horse trams were rebuilt with electrical equipment to join 170 electric cars newly built by Brush at Loughborough.

Horse trams also figure in two films of Manchester taken in 1901, the year when the city's first electric route was inaugurated. M&K 172: *Manchester Street Scene* (1901), shows Market Street thronged with shoppers and office workers, with a seemingly endless procession of Manchester Carriage & Tramways Company horse cars of the Eades Patent Reversible type. These had the body mounted on a turntable, and by walking sideways, the horses could reverse the direction of the car at a terminus without having to be unhitched.

M&K 173: *Manchester Band of Hope* (1901), reveals a Manchester Band of Hope procession being passed by one of these horse trams; the car recedes into the distance with a steady but stately motion. In so doing, it demonstrates the sheer quality, both of the original production and of the recent film restoration and reproduction, which enables speeds and movements of people to be accurately reproduced without jerkiness so that the scenes become credible and immediate.

M&K 181: *Opening of Accrington Electric Tramways* (1907). The Mayoress of Accrington drives one of the trams in the inaugural procession to Oswardtwhistle on 2 August 1907. Passing on the left is a tramcar bearing dignitaries from Darwen: a similar party came in a brand new tramcar from Blackburn.

However, it was the electric tram that caught the imagination of people in the opening years of the new century. Never more so than when it was used as an illuminated set-piece to celebrate events of local or national significance. Trams had been decorated for such events since the 1860s; electricity made it possible to festoon a tram with coloured bulbs and turn it into a ship of light in the streets.

For the Coronation of King Edward VII, Liverpool took one of its early German-built trams and decorated it in fairground style, complete with 1,500 carbon-filament light bulbs and vast quantities of bunting. A rotary switch, driven directly from one of the axles, gave ever-changing patterns of coloured lights, while on the top deck a band played. First used in June and August 1902, it appears in M&K 417: *Visit of Earl Roberts and Viscount Kitchener to Receive the Freedom of the City* (1902), when these two heroes of the South African War were given the freedom of the city on 11 October 1902.

In their *Liverpool Transport Vol 2*, Horne and Maund say that in the flamboyant Edwardian era, the illuminated tram expressed colourful patriotism combined with municipal pride in the tramways and the achievements of electrical engineering.[5] It also brought crowds out to see it every time it appeared, so that extra fares accrued to the tramways. The Liverpool illuminated tram ran until the end of World War I, latterly disguised as a tank, and was then replaced in 1923 by an even more flamboyant set-piece tram which Liverpool also hired out to neighbouring tramway towns. With

M&K 417: *Visit of Earl Roberts and Viscount Kitchener to receive the Freedom of the City* (1902). When these two heroes of the South African War were given the freedom of the city on 11 October 1902 a specially decorated electric tram was part of the festivities.

yet more pronounced fairground styling, it had over 5,000 coloured lights in nineteen different patterns controlled by motor-driven switches, independent of the car's speed.

Tram tracks then linked Liverpool with most of South Lancashire, and the vehicle visited St Helens, Bolton, Wigan, Ashton-under-Lyne and Stockport. Its 1925 outing to Stockport for the town's Christmas shopping week involved a five-hour journey each way over the tracks of six tramways. Many others copied the two Liverpool illuminated trams; none matched their gaudy magnificence. But Liverpool was in so many aspects of tramways the pioneer that municipal delegations visited and then went home to copy the style, especially its early livery of dark red and white.

One of the electric tram ride films, M&K 194: *Port Soderic to Douglas Head* (1902), is of a pioneer electric line, filmed in 1902 although the line along the Douglas Head Marine Drive dated back to 1896. Its cars represent the period when British-built trams were equipped with electric motors and controllers manufactured in the United States, before the turn of the century when large American electrical manufacturers such as Westinghouse and Thomson-Houston established subsidiary companies in Britain and the British use of double decks dictated distinctive lines of development. One of the cars from the Douglas Head Marine Drive line, no. 1, survives in the National Tramway Museum, Crich, Derbyshire, and this car appears fleetingly during what is probably Mitchell and Kenyon's nearest approach to a white-knuckle ride. The line follows a tortuous course clinging to a cliff high above the sea and crossing ravines by bridges, one of which has a bend halfway.

During this period the top decks of electric cars were open to the elements and it was only in 1903, starting in Liverpool, that roofed top-covers began to appear, offering the promise of extra revenue when wet weather deterred riders from using open top decks. Horse trams, like all animal-drawn vehicles, had to be designed within strict weight limits and so if double decked they were always built with open tops. Steam cars, however, had no comparable limits and were often roofed, even if the top deck sides were left open. The purpose here was not so much to protect the passenger from the weather, but more from the smoke, smuts and cinders emerging from the locomotive chimney just ahead.

Top-covered steam tram trailers can be seen in M&K 167: *Electric Tram Rides from Forster Square to Park Gates, Bankfoot to Market Street* (1902), taken when the municipal electric cars were in the process of replacing the steam cars of the Bradford Tramways & Omnibus Company whose leases of corporation-built lines were shortly to expire. Steam tramway traction in the streets may well have seemed outmoded in the face of the new, clean and speedy electric cars. But steam trams can take the credit for being the first form of mechanical traction allowed some freedom, from 1879, on the streets, at a time when the law still decreed that other motor vehicles such as steam traction engines had to have a man walking in front carrying a red flag. Even so, traction engines were needed for the heaviest loads and there were more than 8,000 of them in England and Wales alone. M&K 622: *Bradford Coronation Procession* (1902) shows one in Bradford on 14 July without any registration number plate; these were to become compulsory for all motor vehicles except trams only on 1 January 1904. Accustomed to the short range and open style of horse vehicles, motorists asked why registration was needed, when surely the driver would be easily recognisable?

Another electric tram ride of this period is represented in M&K 164: *Tram Rides through Nottingham* (1902). Like M&K 177: *Tram Ride through the City of Sheffield*, this has special contemporary significance because part of this journey follows the route of the new Nottingham Express Transit tramway through the Market Place. Filmed from the driver's front platform, it takes the viewer along Listergate and Wheelergate into the Market Place, where one of the rarely photographed bogie tramcars is standing in the siding on the left, then turns right into Long Row and so into Queen Street. There are very few shots of double deck horse buses, as distinct from tramcars, in these films, but the one represented in this shot arrives and starts to unload its passengers. Contrary to popular opinion and many critical sources, it shows women as well as men travelling on the top deck.

At this point it should be noted that Mitchell and Kenyon filmed in Britain almost entirely north of a line drawn from Coventry to Lincoln, and consequently London is not represented. From 1870 onwards, tramways were largely excluded from the City and the West End and a very different pattern of transport developed there. London may have been the most photographed city of this period, yet as the Mitchell and Kenyon films effectively demonstrate, it was unrepresentative of towns and cities in the country as a whole.

In central London, the horse bus was developed to a vastly greater extent than elsewhere in Britain, and the London General Omnibus Company's horse bus fleet reached its maximum of 1,418 in December 1905. Operation was smoothed by the paving of many central London streets with wood blocks instead of the stone setts used elsewhere. This was done to reduce noise levels, but it aided not only the horse bus but also the emerging motorbus, which in London enjoyed a spectacular rise in numbers from 1911 onwards. This was not emulated in the tram-dominated provincial centres until twenty years later. Tramways in London, both horse and electric, formed a ring around the central area, their inward terminals meeting up with the area of wood block-paved streets.

Elsewhere however, the tramway was burgeoning and in M&K 189: *Lytham Tram Ride* (1903), we have a rare glimpse of a trainload of new tramcars being delivered. These are on low-loading well wagons of the Lancashire & Yorkshire Railway, en route from the British Electric Car Company of Trafford Park, Manchester, to the Blackpool, St Anne's & Lytham Tramways Company which had previously operated gas-powered trams. British Electric Car was a short-lived concern which tried to cash in on the boom in electric tramcar orders from 1900 to 1903 and the train provides one of the few railway shots to appear in the Mitchell and Kenyon Collection. Lytham at this time also operated Blackpool's Lytham Road tramway as far as the corner of Station Road, where the Blackpool Corporation tramway turned off towards the sea front. Passengers could transfer at this point. Film taken from the top deck of an electric tram on the first day, 28 May 1903, as it approaches this transfer point reveals a queue of Lytham-bound passengers waiting in the middle of the road, together with a man with a long, hooked, wooden pole ready to swing the trolley pole. Blackpool Corporation cars seen in this and in M&K 195: *Lytham Tram Ride* (1903) include several inherited from the pioneer 1885 conduit tramway, converted to the overhead system in 1899, and looking very old-fashioned when compared with the sleek new Lytham cars.[6] Alone among mainland electric tramways, Blackpool trams have survived into the present era of tramway revival, but the films show earlier routes which no longer operate.

Lytham trams were painted blue and white, while Blackpool at this time used a red livery. The orthochromatic film emulsions of the day rendered all reds as solid black and blues as light grey, so that for instance bright orange lettering on a dark blue background would appear black on light grey, so that the Blackpool cars appear dark and the Lytham ones light; at the time, both were bright colours.

Not only were passengers often on open vehicles or decks, but drivers were also exposed to the elements. Safety glass lay in the future, and there were doubts about the necessity or safety of having glass in front of a driver. Despite this, a few towns provided windscreens on tramcars, and examples appear in M&K 170: *A Tram Ride through Sunderland* (1904). During a ride through the main Fawcett Street, tramcars of several types are passed and two of them, a double deck and a single deck immediately behind it, have fully built-up vestibules with plate-glass windscreens. Blackburn's tram drivers were also protected from the weather in this way from an early date: M&K 180: *Captain Payne at Darwen* (1901), shows one of these approaching, still in as-delivered condition, with no headlamp and the 'decency board' to hide passengers' legs from the pedestrians fitted only at the sides and not yet across the front. This car and similar ones ran until 1949. Trolley poles of both Blackburn and Darwen cars at this time were mounted on one side instead of centrally; Darwen kept them this way till its last tram ran in 1946, and one of its original cars, delivered in 1900, is seen heading away from the camera.

Darwen plays a part in M&K 181: *Opening of Accrington Electric Tramways* (1907), for although the sequence of events matches the description in R. W. Rush's book *The Tramways of Accrington*, with the mayor driving the official first tram and the mayoress driving the second car, aided very firmly by a uniformed driver, neither the book nor contemporary press accounts mention the two trams bearing dignitaries from the neighbouring municipalities, Blackburn and Darwen.[7] The date is 2 August 1907 and both towns have sent their latest trams, delivered only a few months earlier. Darwen sent a small car, no. 17, designed to be operated by a driver alone, instead of a driver and conductor, and Blackburn's car is immediately identifiable by the curious destination 'Engaged Car' which was a local feature. But for the film, these municipal goodwill missions would never have come to light.

This quite long sequence provides a study of a celebration of municipal enterprise, with the mayor not only giving a speech from the front platform of the inaugural tram, but also demonstrating the scope of the undertaking by winding through all the destinations on the front indicator blind. It also, at the beginning, gives a rare glimpse of tramway construction with a horse-drawn reel wagon feeding the gleaming copper wire over the platform of a tower wagon behind it. And at the end of the film there is a long line of guests heading for the celebratory banquet at the town hall, finding their way through the stream of horse-drawn traffic.

The films record a time when people were increasing their mobility. The average person in 1891 was travelling no more than one and a quarter miles a day; by 1911, he would be travelling five miles a day; today he or she travels twenty-eight miles, of which nine are abroad by air. But the fourfold increase in travel came mostly in the Mitchell and Kenyon period, and much of it was made possible by the new electric tramcars.

Statistics like these are brought to life by these films. They enable us to contrast the teeming streets of the city centres and industrial districts with the tranquillity of the suburbs. They allow us to see how the streets, which one present-day commentator has described as 'sewers for traffic', were at that time places for meeting people and enjoying all kinds of passing entertainment, whether in the form of religious, political or philanthropic processions, or simply of a well-loaded tramcar, its open top deck passengers looking like a basket of flowers on the move, or yet again in the gaudy displays of advertisements, at that time unrestricted by legislation.[8]

They also enable us to see all sorts of skills being practised: driving vehicles in heavy horse-drawn traffic, riding a bicycle to avoid being caught in the tram tracks, driving an electric tram or a horse-drawn dray. They show us how a woman in a long skirt negotiated the steep stairs of a horse bus. It is not so clear how the men, so universally wearers of hats in the streets, managed to keep their headgear on in high winds. Besides the street scenes, there are glimpses of street traffic in films of sporting events and of people entering and leaving factories. The view of 20,000 employees going to work in M&K 35: *20,000 Employees Entering Lord Armstrong's Elswick Works* (1900), is frequently punctuated by Newcastle tramcars flashing across the screen; a similar car is still active at the North of England Open Air Museum at Beamish.

The Mitchell and Kenyon street sequences therefore turn myth into reality, statistics into experience, and the dry facts of history into the excitement of pageantry. They will form an animated illustrative benchmark against which future historians of street transport will be able to measure their own findings. They also offer a journey into streets of our family history; I found myself scanning the top deck passengers of Manchester horse trams to see if I could see my father and grandfather. They would have been on top because top deck fares were half those for travel inside the downstairs saloon; among the immediate benefits of electric trams were reduced fares for passengers, along with better pay and hours for drivers and conductors. The motor bus was no more than a cloud the size of a man's hand, and London County Council Tramways manager Aubrey Llewellyn Coventry Fell was in 1910 able to say with confidence: 'In ten years' time there will be not a motor bus outside a museum'.[9] Yet within one year of this statement, the motorbus had found its long-sought reliability in the London General B-type and within ten years it was challenging the supremacy of the electric tram itself. These films, however, do not look at the future; rather they preserve moments of animation and take us into the streets to witness them.

NOTES

1. The Highways and Locomotives Act of 1878 laid down that any mechanically propelled vehicle using the public highway should be preceded by a man on foot carrying a red flag and should not go faster than four miles per hour. This was repealed by an Act which came into force on 14 November 1896. For the story of the emancipation of motor vehicles, see William Plowden, *The Motor Car and Politics, 1896–1970* (London: Bodley Head, 1971). The annual London to Brighton run of early motor vehicles commemorates this event.

2. It was to meet this risk of fire in stables that automatic sprinkler systems were invented, along with ingenious devices for opening the doors of stalls automatically so horses could quickly be led to safety. The trade press in Britain concentrated on the new electric trams but there are numerous references in American periodicals such as *Street Railway Journal*.

3. Theo Barker and Dorian Gerhold, *The Rise and Rise of Road Transport 1700–1990* (Cambridge: Cambridge University Press for the Economic History Society, 1993). They point out that there were enough jobs left for those who preferred to work with horses and as late as 1924 there were as many horses in freight haulage as there had been in 1881.

4. Figures are taken from Barker and Gerhold, *The Rise and Rise of Road Transport*, p. 51 for numbers overall and p. 60 for horses in freight transport.

5. J. B Horne. and T. B Maund, *Liverpool Transport Vol. 2 1900–1930* (Glossop: Transport Publishing Company and Light Rail Transit Association, 1982), pp. 208–17.

6. Five films are titled *Lytham Tram Ride* in the Collection, M&K 189 and 195–9.

7. R. W. Rush, *The Tramways of Accrington* (London: Light Railway Transport League, 1961), p. 23. He refers to 'four gaily decorated single deck cars, driven by the Mayoress, the deputy Mayoress, Mrs A. S. Bury and Mrs Aitkin, all under the supervision of regular motormen'. Tram drivers were frequently called 'motormen' at this time. He makes no reference to the visiting trams from Darwen and Blackburn which are clearly visible in the film.

8. Barbara Schmucki, University of Darmstadt, Germany, in a contribution on 'Cities as Traffic Machines' to the Suburbanising the Masses conference at the National Railway Museum, York, 1997.

9. A. L. C Fell, quoted by Charles Klapper, in *The Golden Age of Tramways* (London: Routledge & Kegan Paul, 1961), p. 247.

18 Tram Rides and Other Virtual Landscapes

Patrick Keiller

1

Between the mid-1900s and the outbreak of World War I, the spaces and spatial experiences characteristic of industrialised economies underwent significant transformation. Many scholars have identified this: for example, in his afterword to the English translation of Henri Lefebvre's definitive *La Production de l'espace*, first published in 1974 (but in English only in 1991), the geographer David Harvey quoted from a passage in Lefebvre's opening chapter:

> The fact is that around 1910 a certain space was shattered. It was the space of common sense, of knowledge (*savoir*), of social practice, of political power, a space thitherto enshrined in everyday discourse, just as in abstract thought, as the environment of and channel for communications; the space, too, of classical perspective and geometry, developed from the Renaissance onwards on the basis of the Greek tradition (Euclid, logic) and bodied forth in Western art and philosophy, as in the form of the city and the town ... Euclidean and perspectivist space have disappeared as systems of reference, along with other former 'commonplaces' such as the town, history, paternity, the tonal system in music, traditional morality, and so forth. This was truly a crucial moment.[1]

Harvey had already quoted from this passage in his *The Condition of Postmodernity*, following mention of 'the incredible confusions and oppositions across a spectrum of possible reactions to the growing sense of crisis in the experience of time and space, that had been gathering since 1848 and seemed to come to a head just before the First World War' and 'that 1910–14 is roughly the period that many historians of modernism (beginning with Virginia Woolf and D. H. Lawrence) point to as crucial in the evolution of modernist thinking'.[2]

For Harvey, the crisis was one 'of technological innovation, of capitalist dynamics across space [and] cultural production'. He notes the slightly different emphasis of Stephen Kern who, in *The Culture of Time and Space 1880–1918*,[3] offered 'generalizations about the essential cultural developments of the period'. Other writers have dealt with these in detail: for John Berger, 'The Moment of Cubism' was the period between 1907 and 1914, and during the period 1900–14 'the developments which converged at the beginning of the twentieth century in Europe changed the meaning of time and space'.[4] Berger listed these as:

> An interlocking world system of imperialism; opposed to it, a socialist international; the founding of modern physics, physiology and sociology; the increasing use of electricity, the invention of radio and the cinema; the beginnings of mass production; the publishing of mass-circulation newspapers; the new structural possibilities offered by the availability of steel and aluminium; the rapid development of the chemical industries and the production of synthetic materials; the appearance of the motor car and the aeroplane.[5]

More recently, other writers (including Kern and Harvey) have stressed the role of telecommunications; others mention emigration (both within and away from Europe).[6] Some of these developments suggest comparisons with the present.

For Reyner Banham, in *Theory and Design in the First Machine Age*, 'a series of revolutionary gestures around 1910, largely connected with Cubist and Futurist movements, were the main point of departure for the development of Modern architecture'.[7] Banham's narrative is that of evolving concepts of space, specifically 'the change-over from the Lippsian idea of space, as felt volume … to the later concept of space as a three-dimensional continuum, capable of metrical subdivision, without sacrifice of its continuity'.[8] By 1929, Laszlo Moholy-Nagy was able to formulate the minimum definition: 'space is the relation between the position of bodies'[9] which for Banham confirmed 'the whole revolution in architectural theory that had been going on since 1908'.[10] One of Moholy-Nagy's earlier spatial expositions was his 1921–2 proposal for a film *Dynamic of the Metropolis*, which somewhat anticipates Vertov's 1929 *Man with a Movie Camera*. *Dynamic of the Metropolis* was never realised, but by 1929 Moholy-Nagy had made *Berliner Stilleben* (1926) and perhaps also *Marseille, Vieux-Port* (1929), so that the 'minimum definition' of modernist space was put forward by a theorist who was also an experienced film-maker.

In *The Condition of Postmodernity*, Harvey also quoted the famous passage from Walter Benjamin's 'The Work of Art in the Age of Mechanical Reproduction':

> Our taverns and our metropolitan streets, our offices and furnished rooms, our railroad stations and our factories appeared to have us locked up hopelessly. Then came the film and burst this prison-world asunder by the dynamite of the tenth of a second, so that now, in the midst of its far-flung ruins and debris, we calmly and adventurously go travelling.[11]

Benjamin's 'now' refers to film as it had evolved after the mid-1900s – his essay, published in 1936, mentions the films of Gance, Vertov and Ivens, but nothing earlier. However, it is less clear at what date 'came the film and burst this prison-world asunder'. The essay also famously stresses 'the incomparable significance of Atget, who, around 1900, took photographs of deserted Paris streets',[12] and it might seem to us (nearly seventy years later) that in many ways one can 'calmly and adventurously go travelling' (even) more easily in some of the films of the early 1900s than in those of Gance and Vertov.[13]

Whatever the date of the films that Benjamin had in mind, it is clear that something happened to the medium in the mid-1900s. There appears to have been a distinct lull in production in the middle of the decade, before which films tended to be one or two minutes long and to consist of one or very few relatively long takes, and after which longer films, with shorter shots, montage and narrative, often assisted by intertitles, are the usual form. During the lull, some of the pioneers ceased production, and others did so not long afterwards.

The earlier films are often actualities, and a significant proportion of actuality subjects were street scenes, railway and tram rides and other documents of everyday surroundings. Later films are far more numerous and much longer, but surprisingly few include as much imagery of ordinary landscapes. When they do, the shots are usually so short as to permit relatively little exploration even when examined frame by frame. The images of early film are also less likely to direct the viewer's attention to a single subject in the frame: one's eye can more easily wander in their spaces and because of this, they invite (or even require) repeated viewing. Even before the rediscovery of the Mitchell and Kenyon Collection it was easy to imagine that early film might offer a more extensive view of the landscapes of its period than the cinema of later decades, though any such judgment relied on a few particularly striking and important examples such as Dickson's *Panorama of Ealing from a Moving Tram* (1901).

With the rediscovery of twenty-eight hours of Mitchell and Kenyon negative, so much of it in unusually good condition, it appears that the virtual landscapes of the films of *c.* 1900 really are among the most extensive offered by the medium, at least in the United Kingdom. In this (as in many other respects) they are truly extraordinary, as it seems that the most extensive view of the landscape of another time is that offered at the moment of its transformation, a transformation brought about (at least in part) by the development of the very medium in which the opportunity to explore these long lost spaces was constructed.

If the development of cinema was a significant factor in the transformation of urban and other space during the 1900s, was this the development of cinema *per se*, or the development of cinema with editing, narrative and so on after the middle of the decade? Certainly, the references to Cubism, Futurism and so on, suggest that it was the construction of cinematic space through montage, close-up etc. that was the critical factor, in which case the early films, with their uninterrupted and lengthy spatio-temporal continuities (the tram rides especially) appear as a pre- or proto-modernist cinema, which was itself fragmented soon afterwards as part of a wider cultural transformation.

The distinction between these two kinds of cinema is very like that between the spatial concepts defined by Lipps and Moholy-Nagy. Banham saw these as sequential, but the idea of space as 'felt volume' only slightly pre-dated the subsequent, more abstract formulation – it appears that the word 'space' (raum) was not used in Lipps' (or any other architectural) sense before about 1900[14] – and Lipps' concept never really went away. With a revival of urbanism in architectural theory since the 1970s and comparable trends in art and cinema, we might see both Lippsian space and the spatial forms of early cinema as complementary to, rather than predecessors of, what came later.[15] In either case, we can explore the films in the hope that they reveal something of how urban space has changed in the century since they were photographed.

2

I have looked particularly at Mitchell and Kenyon's films of Nottingham and Halifax and visited some of their locations, and at their films of Bradford, Sheffield, Rochdale, Sunderland, Manchester, Glasgow and Belfast. The three rolls M&K 163–5: *Tram Rides through Nottingham* (1902), were photographed from the lower deck of a tram on a single journey through the city centre between its two main stations, so that together they offer a more or less unbroken spatial continuity over six minutes long. Among other tram films in the Collection, M&K 166–9: *Electric Tram Rides from Forster Square to Park Gates, Bankfoot to Market Street* (1902) together comprise an even longer ride of eight and a half minutes, starting from Forster Square in the city centre, along Manningham Lane to the gates of Lister Park and beyond, passing through what appears to have been one of the city's wealthier suburbs. These two series of films are, as far as I am aware, the most extensive, more-or-less continuous film documents of the UK's urban space of their period, perhaps the most extensive in all UK cinema.

Sheffield, Rochdale and Sunderland were also photographed from electric trams, and most of the Belfast film consists of two views from the top of a horse tram. The films of Manchester and Glasgow mostly comprise a number of static shots of pedestrian and horse-drawn traffic, those in the former from a slightly elevated viewpoint.

The single tram ride film of Halifax, M&K 614: *Tram Journey into Halifax* (1902) is one of several made in the town and consists of two views from a tram route along the road to Keighley (now the A629). In the first of these (forty seconds), the tram is travelling away from the town, with the

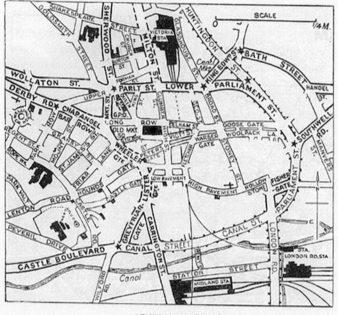

CENTRAL NOTTINGHAM.

Map of central Nottingham: M&K 163 (Station Street, Carrington Street);
M&K 164 (Carrington Street, Lister Gate, Wheeler Gate, Long Row);
M&K 165 (Queen Street, Upper Parliament Street, Milton Street).

camera looking diagonally forwards across a valley, passing a large mill.[16] In the second shot (1m 25s), the tram descends towards the town,[17] the camera looking back along the valley so that the mill in the first shot is seen.

Before the Mitchell and Kenyon rediscovery, the *bfi* National Film and Television Archive included five tram ride films from the early 1900s: Biograph's *Tram Journey through Southampton* (1900) and *Panorama of Ealing from a Moving Tram*; *Leeds – View from a Moving Tram* (*c*. 1903); Warwick Trading Company's *Norwich – Tramway Ride through Principal Streets* (1902) and Charles Goodwin Norton's *Horse-Drawn Traffic in Seven Sisters Road* (1898). These films are nearly all much shorter than the Mitchell and Kenyon tram ride films, and their total running time is under seven minutes, whereas the total of only those Mitchell and Kenyon tram ride films mentioned above (and there are many more) is over thirty minutes. The scale of this increase gives some idea how radically the rediscovery enlarges the virtual landscape of the early 1900s, and how much it moves it to the north.

3

On looking at the films, what struck me first (as someone who can just about remember north-ern towns and cities in the 1950s) was a contrast between their often familiar-looking landscapes and the unfamiliarity of the society glimpsed in them. The people in the films are visibly unlike us, and many of their attitudes – to sexuality, children, religion, the state, each other etc. – were unlike ours (though our knowledge of theirs is very partial). They might have looked forward to

M&K 163: *Tram Rides through Nottingham* (1902): Carrington Street. The perspective is now shortened by the Broadmarsh shopping centre (1975), which separates Carrington Street from Lister Gate.

M&K 164: *Tram Rides through Nottingham* (1902): Lister Gate.

M&K 165: *Tram Rides through Nottingham* (1902): Milton Street. Holy Trinity Church (left of film frame) gave way to a car park in 1958. The Mechanics' Institute (left of centre, where M&K films were exhibited) was replaced in 1964. The Victoria Centre (1965–72, right of photograph) was built on the site of Victoria Station, built in 1901.

material progress (electrification, for example) more confidently than we do, but they might also have been familiar (as we are) with predictions of future catastrophe (those of H. G. Wells, for instance), some of which were later confirmed. Most of them were much poorer than most people are today.

In the century since, the material and other circumstances of the UK's population have altered enormously,[18] but much of the urban fabric of the 1900s survives, often − like much of the rest of the built environment − in a surprisingly dilapidated condition. This might suggest (at least to some) that while we are far better off than our predecessors of 100 years ago (in terms of life expectancy, physical health, income, mobility etc.), other aspects of everyday life have been impoverished. In this sense, the films might be thought subversive, in that they echo questions about the ways in which present-day economies assess their wealth.[19]

Walking in the streets of Nottingham and Halifax today, while they are visibly both prosperous and relatively successful (more so than many UK towns and cities), one detects (or at least I think I detect) an absence. The built fabric of the centres of both Nottingham and Halifax has not been 'shattered' physically (as those of other towns and cities have) since the 1900s, but the decline of what Lefebvre described as 'the environment of and channel for communications … in the form of the city and the town' is easily recognised. With the increasing centralisation and seclusion of political and financial power, and the increasing shift of economic and other activity into virtual space, actual space often feels marginal, even in the centre of London. Also, despite suburban expansion and redevelopment during the twentieth century, many UK town and city centres still consist largely of ageing fragments of late nineteenth- and early twentieth-century landscapes, overlaid with a thin and often ephemeral layer of modernity. In this context, the survival of quite so much ageing urban fabric, often in a rather dilapidated condition, might be seen as part of a decline: the failure of the space to properly renew itself.[20]

However much one might qualify these observations, it is clear that the various modernist projects of rebuilding epitomised by the Futurists' assertion 'Things will endure less than us. Every generation must build its own city'[21] did not develop as anticipated. As Orwell wrote in *Nineteen Eighty-Four*: 'In the early twentieth century, the vision of a future society unbelievably rich, leisured, orderly and efficient − a glittering antiseptic world of glass and steel and snow-white concrete − was part of the consciousness of nearly every literate person'.[22] By the 1970s, it had become clear that this landscape was never likely to materialise. Building was never much mechanised or automated, so is now much more expensive than other kinds of production. In the older, advanced economies, cities now more often evolve in ways that begin with new perceptions of existing fabric, typically experienced in the UK as gentrification. Some of these perceptions involve art, literature and, occasionally, films; others follow developments in communications (rather than building) technology.

As it has become economically more difficult to renew the built environment, we have become culturally more anxious to retain it. The National Trust, for example, was founded in 1896. Conservation was no less a modernist phenomenon than cinema, and their coincidence hints at one of the effects that the rapid expansion of virtual space (of which cinema was a part) would have on actual everyday surroundings. The qualities visible in many of the Mitchell and Kenyon films are very like some of those that attract tourists to less advanced or (some) socialist economies − to places where artisanal production (or the past products of it) survive; where domesticity is still found in city centres, and where there are fewer cars, or at least less traffic engineering. In advanced economies, such environmental qualities are typically achieved or retained through socialist or social-democratic politics.

In this context, Lefebvre's shattered 'space of common sense' suggests both the spatial concepts of Lipps and the urban design of Camillo Sitte. In 1903 Lipps 'argued that our bodies unconsciously empathised with architectural form'[23] and Sitte, 'rooted in the craftworker tradition of late nineteenth-century Vienna … sought to construct spaces that would make the city's people "secure and happy" … He therefore set out to create interior spaces – plazas and squares – that would promote the preservation and even re-creation of a sense of community'.[24] These and similar ideas re-emerged in the postmodern urbanism of the 1970s, for which the Mitchell and Kenyon films might initially seem to offer some support, with their depiction of what to us appear 'traditional' urban spaces in which we might imagine we could be 'secure and happy'. We might also imagine, as present-day urban designers sometimes do, that such spaces 'would promote the preservation and even re-creation of a sense of community'. Sitte's polemic, however, was not in favour of the actually existing spaces of the 1900s – those that appear in the films – but against them, 'abhorring the narrow and technical functionalism that seemed to attach to the lust for commercial profit', and seeking 'to overcome fragmentation and provide a "community life-outlook"',[25] rather as we might today. Also, though Sitte is popular with present-day urban designers, his desire for spaces that he believed would promote 'community' was not unproblematic. As David Harvey writes: 'many of the Viennese artisans whom Sitte championed … were later to mass in the squares, piazzas and living spaces that Sitte wanted to create, in order to express their virulent opposition to internationalism, turning to anti-semitism … and the place-specific myths of Nazism.'[26]

The spaces of Nottingham and Halifax in the early 1900s might appear 'traditional' but they were subject to transformations at least as sudden as any we experience today. Perhaps the most visible of these was the introduction of electric trams, which became widespread during the late 1890s and early 1900s. These were not always the first powered vehicles to appear in city streets – steam trams already ran in some towns (one is very visible at the beginning of the Bradford series) – but the films photographed from electric trams, and those in which they appear, seem of a very different era to that seen in the films of Manchester, Glasgow and Belfast, in which all the vehicles are horse-drawn. Manchester, where hansom cabs and top hats are numerous, looks particularly old-fashioned (as London often does in films of the same period).

The electric tram offered an ideal platform for the camera (more stable than horse trams, which rocked) and the films publicised the trams, so that a kind of symbiosis developed between tramway operators and film production companies. Many people's first and possibly only encounter with a cine camera would have been with one mounted on a tram, so that we might see the tram ride films as both celebratory (electric trams were generally popular, and the people in the streets appear to have been happy to co-operate with the film-makers) and predatory, both instrument and document of a destruction. Halifax for instance, topographically unsuited to horse trams, had 'remained for the vast majority of its inhabitants an essentially pedestrian town until the end of the century, when an electric tramway system was finally inaugurated in 1898'.[27] By the time of the 1905 Ordnance Survey, Halifax had what might seem to us a utopian public transport system, with an extensive tramway network that ran up some of the steepest hills and was integrated with the railway.

The trams moved relatively slowly (they are often overtaken by bicycles) and do not appear to have diminished the tendency of people to walk and gather in the roadway. In most of the films, pedestrians generally keep to the pavements, but it was easy to cross the road, and as the trams ran in the offside lane, groups of people tended to form in the nearside lane at tram stops. In some of the films (in Halifax, in particular) people congregate in the roadway, though this may be partly a response to the unusual presence of the camera. In most of the films, the pavements are busy, but perhaps not more so than today.

In the films I have seen, all the streets appear to be paved with stone setts, as they probably had been for many years and would be for years to come. The trams do not seem to have required the replacement of the road surfaces, as was sometimes the case elsewhere. In central London, surfaces included rolled and rough macadam, granite squares, wood and asphalt, but in the north there was perhaps less variety. Asphalt, much of it a byproduct of oil refining, only became widespread with motor traffic, another change that dates from later in the decade.[28] Towards the end of the fourth Bradford tram ride film, tram lines are being laid outside the gates of Lister Park, and even at this distance from the centre of the city, the road appears to be paved with setts.

With the road surface hand-made with 'natural' materials, and pedestrians more likely to linger on it, the distinction between pavement and roadway was less marked than it is today, suggesting a space not unlike the 'urban room' so widely sought by postmodernist, urban designers, typically achieved now only by banishing or severely restricting vehicular traffic. This is perhaps one of the ways in which our perceptions of the space differ from those of people of the time, who probably found the streets extremely busy.[29]

The bicycle was another innovation of the 1890s. Some of the cyclists in the films look a little self-conscious, and this perhaps reflects cycling's associations with speed, mobility, independence, and even eroticism. Bicycles are more often seen in the suburbs, as in Rochdale and Bradford, but also in the centres of Belfast and Nottingham. The Raleigh company's enormous factory in Nottingham had opened in 1896 and was (according to the company today) the biggest bicycle factory in the world. Two of the cyclists seen in the Bradford films are women.

At a point in M&K 168: *Electric Tram Rides from Forster Square to Park Gates, Bankfoot to Market Street*, when the tram is stationary, one of the film-makers gets down and walks forward to exchange words with a group of four well-dressed young women, who appear in the next shot walking abreast on the road towards the tram, which is now moving. They all hold their skirts, as if to keep them from brushing the road, as do other similarly dressed women in this series. In the same sequence, a pair of fashionable-looking young men appear from time to time, walking quickly along the pavement to the right and slightly ahead of the tram, their long coats catching the breeze. Despite the restrictions of the women's clothing, these young people appear stylish and confident to a degree we might associate with later eras, and suggest that the society of the early 1900s, at least in Bradford, was not as deferential as people sometimes imagine. In this respect, and perhaps others (some of its architecture, for instance), Bradford looks almost American.

The hand-crafted appearance of the towns and cities of the Mitchell and Kenyon films might suggest that they were more socially and economically autonomous than they are today. Liverpool and Manchester had well-developed global connections, but in other places many of the largest employers, for example, were still locally owned. Family histories and census records suggest that it was not unusual to move about the country, but many people in individual towns and cities perhaps did not have much regular contact with other places. The train and the telephone were expensive, though business travel was increasing – the Nottingham chemist Boots, for example, had 250 branches by the turn of the century. Also, between 1881 and 1897, according to the Medical Officer of Health's annual reports, 775,272 emigrants arrived at Hull from Europe, most of them intending to go on to Liverpool, the major north European port of departure for emigrants to North America. Some emigrants settled between Hull and Liverpool, especially in Leeds and Bradford, and this influx must have been a cosmopolitan influence. At the beginning of the second Bradford film, for instance, the tram passes the well-established-looking shop of Albert Sachs, whose glass fascia carries the word 'Artist' and another beginning with 'P' which I suspect is 'Photographer'.

During the early 1900s, many large UK companies took advantage of the telephone to move their head offices to London, away from their factories but closer to each other and the City.[30] In Nottingham, two of the bigger employers – Boots and Raleigh – are still based in the city, and in Halifax, while the giant Akroyd and Crossley textile concerns do not survive, the headquarters of what is now Halifax plc (in 1900 'the largest building society in the world') is still based in the town, but none of these companies is still locally owned. Their directors are unlikely to exert influence locally in the manner of Edwardian industrialists, and their accountability is to distant shareholders and financial institutions. In M&K 611: *Mayor Entering his Carriage near the Town Hall, Halifax* (1902) in the street outside the town hall, one imagines at least a hint of real political and commercial power. When Halifax's textile industry began to decline in the 1890s, this was more than offset (for a decade or so) by the rapid growth of other industries,[31] and one wonders if a similar sized town would be able to weather decline so effectively today.

Since the 1970s, architects and others have tended to settle for a mixture of incremental change and conservation as a model for the evolution of town and city centres. This is very like the pattern that emerges from the films. Most of what is seen of the centre of Halifax had been rebuilt between the 1860s and the 1890s, and survives today. In the centre of Nottingham, while a large proportion of individual buildings appear to have been replaced, many in the 1920s and 1930s, the general form is little changed. The mainstream of urban development in the twentieth century was that associated with the car – low density suburbs and traffic engineering. Post-1970's urbanism has opposed the dominance of the car, attempting to revive the early modernist ('Lippsian') space of architects like Berlage (a space probably best experienced on foot) and promoting the bicycle and the tram (Nottingham's current tramway system began operation in 2003). We might see the spaces of the Mitchell and Kenyon films not as 'traditional' (and therefore lost), but – like their electric trams and bicycles (and the spatial quality of early cinema) – in terms of a modernity which was marginalised by later developments, but is partly recoverable.

The films might seem to offer a polemic for this – for streets without cars, for architecture, for public transport and for a less centralised, less dematerialised economy. At the same time we can assume that, as images, they bestow an illusory coherence on their subjects. The spaces of the films were dynamic, subject to tensions as unsettling as (and sometimes surprisingly similar to) those we experience today. Cities are increasingly seen as processes structured in time. In these remarkable films, we can explore some of the spaces of the past, in order to better anticipate the spaces of the future.

NOTES

1. Henri Lefebvre, *The Production of Space*, trans. Donald Nicholson-Smith (Oxford: Blackwell, 1991), p. 25.
2. David Harvey, *The Condition of Postmodernity* (Oxford: Blackwell, 1990), p. 266.
3. Stephen Kern, *The Culture of Time and Space 1880–1918* (Cambridge, MA: Harvard University Press, 1983).
4. John Berger, *The Moment of Cubism and Other Essays* (London: Weidenfeld and Nicholson, 1969), p. 6.
5. Berger, *The Moment of Cubism*, p. 5.
6. According to Kern, thirty million emigrants left Europe between 1890 and 1914: *The Culture of Time and Space*, p. 220.
7. Reyner Banham, *Theory and Design in the First Machine Age* (London: Architectural Press, 1960), p. 14.
8. Banham, *Theory and Design*, p. 67.
9. Banham, *Theory and Design*, p. 317.
10. Banham, *Theory and Design*, p. 311.

11. Walter Benjamin, 'The Work of Art in the Age of Mechanical Reproduction', in *Illuminations* (London: Fontana, 1973), p. 238.

12. Benjamin, 'The Work of Art', p. 228.

13. In this context, we might note the reappearance of some of the forms of early cinema in gallery film and international art cinema.

14. Banham, *Theory and Design*, p. 66.

15. See Tom Gunning, 'The Cinema of Attractions', *Wide Angle*, vol. 8, nos 3/4 (Fall 1986): 'The cinema of attractions does not disappear with the dominance of narrative, but rather goes underground, both into certain avant-garde practices and as a component of narrative films'.

16. Still standing, marked as 'Ladyship Mills (Worsted)' on the 1905 1:2500 Ordnance Survey.

17. Passing Old Lane Mill, still standing but vacant, then Lee Bank Mill and Old Lane Dye Works, both gone, ending at an interchange with the railway seen earlier in the shot, long since dismantled. Much of the valley has reverted to woodland.

18. Average income in employment increased about three times as much as indices of retail prices. The cost of housing has generally increased more than the average income.

19. See, for instance, T. Jackson, N. Marks, J. Ralls and S. Stymne, *Sustainable Economic Welfare in the UK 1950–1996* (London: New Economics Foundation, 1997), who report that the UK's Index of Sustainable Economic Welfare (ISEW) peaked in 1976, and has since dropped by twenty-five per cent to the level of the 1950s, increases in GDP per head etc. having been offset by environmental decline, increased inequality and other factors. Similar patterns have been found in other advanced economies, notably the US.

20. *Pace* Jane Jacobs, *The Death and Life of Great American Cities* (London: Penguin, 1964), p. 201: 'Old ideas can sometimes use new buildings. New ideas must use old buildings'.

21. See Kern, *The Culture of Time and Space*, p. 100.

22. George Orwell, *Nineteen Eighty-Four* (London: Penguin, 2000), p. 196.

23. See Kern, *The Culture of Time and Space*, p. 157.

24. See Harvey, *The Condition of Postmodernity*, p. 276 and Camillo Sitte, *City Planning According to Artistic Principles* (London: Phaidon, 1965), first published in Vienna in 1889.

25. Ibid.

26. Ibid., p. 277.

27. John A. Hargreaves, note on Halifax (North) 1905: Old Ordnance Survey Maps (Gateshead: Alan Godfrey Maps, *c.* 1994).

28. I have so far noted only one M&K film, M&K 405: *Liverpool Shops* (*c.* 1902), in which a car appears.

29. See for instance Georg Simmerl, 'The Metropolis and Mental Life', in *On Individuality and Social Forms* (Chicago, IL: University of Chicago Press, 1971), pp. 324–9. The essay was first published in 1903.

30. Kern, *The Culture of Time and Space*, p. 216.

31. See Hargreaves, note to Halifax (North) 1905 OS map.

Notes on Contributors

Dave Berry is the Research Officer at the Welsh Film Archive and has published widely on all aspects of Welsh cinema history.

Stephen Bottomore is an Associate Editor of *Film History*. He is especially interested in the social and cultural history of the first movies.

Richard Brown is an independent early film historian who has published widely on aspects of early cinema and exhibition history.

Leo Enticknap is a Senior Lecturer in Media Studies at the University of Teesside and a technical advisor to the Northern Region Film and Television Archive.

Tom Gunning is Edwin A. and Betty L. Bergman Distinguished Service Professor at the University of Chicago. He is the author of *The Films of Fritz Lang: Allegories of Vision and Modernity* (BFI Publishing).

Patrick Keiller is an architect and film-maker, currently an AHRB Research Fellow at the Royal College of Art, London.

Janet McBain has been Curator of the Scottish Screen Archive since 1976, presents screenings and writes articles on films in the collection.

Robert Monks, an authority on early Irish cinema has lectured, compiled a database of Irish films and is completing a history of Irish film-making 1896–1929.

Timothy Neal is Research Assistant to the Mitchell and Kenyon Project at the National Fairground Archive and has a particular interest in nineteenth-century animal performance history.

Simon Popple is Assistant Director of the School of Arts and Media at the University of Teesside and an early film historian.

Andrew Prescott was formerly Curator of Manuscripts at the British Library. In 2000, he was appointed Director of the Centre for Research into Freemasonry at the University of Sheffield, the first such university-based centre in Britain.

Patrick Russell is the Keeper of Non-fiction at the *bfi* and joint co-ordinator of the Mitchell and Kenyon Project.

David Russell is Reader in the History of Popular Culture at the University of Central Lancashire and has particular interest in sport, music and regional cultures.

Vanessa Toulmin is the Research Director of the National Fairground Archive at the University of Sheffield and joint co-ordinator of the Mitchell and Kenyon Project.

Rebecca Vick is Research Assistant to the Mitchell and Kenyon Project at the *bfi* and has worked on all the technical aspects of the Collection.

John K. Walton is Professor of Social History, University of Central Lancashire. He works on tourism, resorts and regional identity with special reference to Britain and Spain.

John Widdowson is Emeritus Professor, founder/former Director of the National Centre for English Cultural Tradition, University of Sheffield. His interests are linguistics, tradition studies and oral history.

David R. Williams is a retired Senior Lecturer in Film and Television at Bede College, Durham. He is a Fellow of the Royal Television Society, who has published widely on the history of film and television.

Ian Yearsley from the National Tramway Museum is a transport writer and historian.

Index